"No one is going to ask you in a hundred years if you are a game player, in the same way that no one asks you if you are a book reader or music listener or food eater. It's not going to be a question."

Robin Hunicke, *Us and the Game Industry*, 2013

DESIGNING GAMIFIED SYSTEMS

Designing Gamified Systems is a fundamental guide for building essential skills in game and interaction design to revitalize and reimagine real world systems – from cities and corporations to schools and the military. Author Sari Gilbert develops a set of core principles and tools for using game thinking and interactive design to build motivation, explain hard concepts, broaden audiences, deepen commitments and enhance human relationships.

Designing Gamified Systems includes:

- Topics such as gamified system design, behavioral psychology, marketing, business strategy, learning theory and instructional design
- Interviews with leaders and practitioners in this emerging field who explain how the job of the game designer is being redefined
- Exercises designed to both encourage big-picture thinking about gamified systems and help you experience and understand the challenges and nuances involved in designing them
- A companion website (www.gamifiedsystems.com) with additional materials to supplement learning and practice

Sari Gilbert is a professor in the Interactive and Game Design department at the Savannah College of Art and Design, where she teaches courses and workshops introducing students and professionals to the practice of gamified system design. Gilbert's twenty years of experience in interactive entertainment include designing and producing the top-selling JumpStart titles and serving as a Senior Producer at Disney Online. She has founded three companies devoted to innovation in the field of interactive entertainment. Gilbert also holds an MFA in Digital Media Design and an MA in Educational Technology.

DESIGNING GAMIFIED SYSTEMS

Meaningful Play in Interactive Entertainment, Marketing and Education

SARI GILBERT

Focal Press
Taylor & Francis Group

NEW YORK AND LONDON

First published 2016
by Focal Press
70 Blanchard Road, Suite 402, Burlington, MA 01803

and by Focal Press
2 Park Square, Milton Park, Abingdon, Oxon OX14 4RN

Focal Press is an imprint of the Taylor & Francis Group, an informa business

Library of Congress Cataloging in Publication Data
Gilbert, Sari.
Designing gamified systems: meanigful play in interactive entertainment,
marketing and education/Sari Gilbert.
    pages cm
    Includes index.
    1. Computer games–Design. 2. Computer games–Design–Psychological
    aspects. 3. Computer games--Design--Social aspects. 4. Play. I. Title.
    QA76.76.C672G54 2015
    794.8'1536–dc23   2014047834

ISBN: 978-0-415-72570-5 (pbk)
ISBN: 978-0-415-72571-2 (hbk)
ISBN: 978-1-315-85667-4 (ebk)

Typeset in Joanna and Dax
by Florence Production Ltd, Stoodleigh, Devon, UK

Contents

CONCLUSION 301

Acknowledgments

This book was an ambitious project, which could have not have been possible without the help, support and influence of so many people. This was definitely an effort that took a village, albeit a primarily virtual one.

I'd like to begin by thanking the many folks at Focal Press who helped make this book a reality. In particular, I'd like to recognize Sean Connelly and Caitlin Murphy for guiding me on my way and keeping me focused, and Karen Ehrmann for so adeptly helping me with image permissions as I tried to reach the finish line. I'd also like to thank Tony Nixon for his commitment to detail as a copy editor.

The individuals who contributed essential lessons and insights through interviews and writings to this book deserve substantial credit for adding value far beyond what I had initially imagined. I'd like to humbly thank Katie Salen, Nicole Lazzaro, Patrick Jagoda, Ken Eklund, Rajat Paharia, Sebastian Deterding, Josh Atkins, Eric Asche, Justin Mezzel, Harold Jones, Shawn Young, Lucien Vatell, Scott Eberle, Scott Nicholson, Brian Yoon and Kaitlin Feely for everything you brought to this book. I am so honored and grateful to have the participation of such brilliant and busy people.

Robert Nashak and Robert Batchelor both proved to be not only the best friends that I could have ever asked for, but also the best editors and reviewers that I could imagine. Robert and Robert, your relentless support and enthusiasm kept me motivated through the most challenging intersections of this work. I am so very lucky to have you each in my life.

I want to thank the Savannah College of Art and Design (SCAD) for supporting me with a fellowship during the writing of the book, allowing me to travel and collect valuable research material, without which the book and the website would not have been possible. I'd also like to acknowledge my colleagues at SCAD past and present, including: Ari Cookson, SuAnne Fu, Luis Cataldi, Tina O'Haily, Gregory Johnson, Anne Swartz, Jack Mamais, Charles Shami, Peter Weishar, Josephine Leong, Gustavo Delao and Brenda Romero. You are always inspiring me to find new things to love about teaching and exploring the worlds of interactive and game design.

I must recognize the merits and contributions of the designers and theorists whose work and vision laid the foundation for this field and my interests in it.

Ian Bogost, Jane McGonigal, Amy Jo Kim, Tracy Fullerton, Greg Costikyan, Raph Koster, Robin Hunicke, Jesse Schell, Eric Zimmerman, Henry Jenkins, Janet Murray and Donald Norman have each in their own way provided me with rich visions of what is and might one day be possible.

Thanks to Edward and Barbara Gilbert for a lifetime of support. Most importantly, I want to thank Nate and Sage Batchelor, who remind me each and every day about the critical importance and the absolute joy of play.

Introduction

Imagine a world in which every organization—corporations, schools, museums, government agencies—hired a game designer. In 2013, London's Victoria and Albert Museum (V&A), a century-and-a-half-old institution with a vast and diverse collection of 4.5 million treasures, did just that. Why? Because a museum that has everything from the original Winnie the Pooh drawings to the mechanical tiger of an Indian Sultan needs to figure out ways for visitors to navigate through vast amounts of information. The V&A didn't just need a game designer, it also needed someone who understood public space, education, marketing and business, and most importantly building relationships with and among people. So why did it choose a game designer?

For the past twenty years, engineers and designers like myself working in the computer industry have been creating games to solve real-world problems. In the past decade, a massive proliferation of mobile devices, social networking platforms and scalable and dynamic database technologies have made this challenge not only possible but also necessary. Now that most of us are networked, at all times and all places, companies from Coca-Cola to Oracle, and school systems from New York City to Los Angeles, are shifting towards play to accomplish critical objectives like increasing profits, building markets and teaching curriculum. Marketing departments, entertainment companies, schools, government agencies and museums will increasingly rely on designers with specialized skills to envision, innovate and construct these valuable play-based frameworks.

The emerging field of gamified system design (GS design) leverages game thinking and user-experience design to build motivation, explain difficult concepts, broaden audiences, deepen commitments and enhance human relationships. For game designers, exploring opportunities outside of the traditional game industry means developing a keen understanding of how games are merging with the real world and what skills need to be added to round out their practice. For those trained in interaction design, incorporating principles and practices from game design will significantly expand their domain of expertise to include the contributions games bring to the user experience, such as motivational and progressive feedback, dramatic elements and varied and unique social encounters. GS design combines game design and interaction design, while adding behavioral psychology, educational theory, instructional design, marketing and business strategy. It is growing rapidly and is here to stay.

The most exciting thing about GS design is that it offers ways of gaining leverage on complex and real systemic problems. Games allow us to play with structures that may have become too rigid or formal. They bring in new audiences. They make the repetitive or uninteresting enjoyable. Perhaps most importantly, they get people to interact with each other in new ways. With game-based approaches, play becomes a way of making change happen in the real world. Because GS design offers such a powerful toolbox, an interaction or game designer trained in the field can invent whole new approaches in a diverse array of fields to the way we play and interact in the world around us.

BEYOND GAMIFICATION

Early proponents within the field like Rajat Paharia, a contributor to this book, used the term "gamification" for this complex, emerging and varied field. Paharia founded Bunchball, a leader in the industry, whose clients include major corporations like USA Network, Coca-Cola, Wendy's and Urban Outfitters. Although his popular term "gamification" may continue to be used—especially for corporate marketing projects—it has become too limited a concept to encompass the whole of what is happening right now. For those in the game industry, it too often suggests easy solutions—let's create a points system with badges and rewards! For those outside the game industry, it suggests games-lite—ooh it could be like a game. . . .

But suppose the game was not something merely tacked on to a company's marketing system to build audience but was integral to the success of a task and could change the way people and objects interact. Programmers using Agile development (which will be covered in Chapter 5) play a version of poker (Planning Poker) to collectively estimate how large a feature (or user story) is and how long a programming task will take. The card game is a unique and effective approach for initiating conversations, revealing insights, exposing potential issues and solutions, redefining problems and eventually achieving consensus. Isn't this what an advertiser, educator or manager really wants to do? They want their system to work better.

This book uses the term "gamified systems" for the purpose of building critical analysis around frameworks employing game elements to accomplish goals outside of the context of games. Such structures as Planning Poker are "real world," so that the virtual play of the game when connected with non-play elements or components creates new ways of achieving tasks and solving problems. This is what GS design does.

WHY USE THE TERM SYSTEM?

A system is a framework of organized and related parts that in combination create a complex whole for the purposes of accomplishing a task or goal. These parts each have individual attributes and share relationships with the other parts, which then combine to create unique behaviors. Moreover, systems usually inhabit a specific environment that is defined within specific boundaries. The highway system (which will be revisited a bit later in this Introduction) is an excellent example. Cars are objects that share a relationship with each other, with other objects on or near the road (like painted lanes, signs and traffic lights), and with the many rules that dictate how these all need to behave in relationship to each other. The American highway system connects all sorts of road systems, and, in doing so, connects all sorts of people. But this necessary complexity also means that most of the important systems we rely on every day are also very hard to change.

This is where games come in. Games themselves can be described as systems. Rules, materials and procedures make up the interrelated objects and attributes that combine together in different variations to satisfy the goal of entertaining people. Although games succeed by entertaining, this book describes hybrid architectures which achieve goals that are external to any game context. In GS design, we link a game system to a non-game system. We thus use a newly designed, dynamic and engaging system to change a pre-existing, complex, real and necessary system. We can also use a gamified system as a kind of creative laboratory to design and test new real-world systems. Gamified systems rely on the objects, attributes and relationships found in game systems, combining these together with other non-game components to achieve goals beyond just pure entertainment.

Valve's *Portal 2* is one of a handful of popular game titles designed for entertainment that are being utilized to teach important and challenging concepts in the classroom. *Teach with Portals* modifies the popular game, providing educators with tools and lesson plans to develop game-based curriculums for teaching math, physics, visual thinking and game design. It includes the *Portal 2 Puzzle Maker*, a 3D design tool to create playable puzzles and levels that meets classroom curriculum goals by encouraging hands-on learning. *Puzzle Maker* is a good example of how to take a traditional game title and map it to goals outside of play, expanding the audience and the significance of the game in the process.

A more explicit example of a gamified system is the speed camera lottery conceived by designer Kevin Richardson for Volkswagen's 2010 Fun Theory Award, which was established to change the way people used the Swedish road system. It is well known that drivers resent speed cameras that send automated tickets, violating the terms of what rightly or not is seen as a kind of cat and mouse game. Used to committing minor infractions or errors when there is no visible police presence, people feel that an automated system is somehow inherently unfair. Richardson approached the challenge of changing people's behavior through fun, suggesting a lottery that would reward drivers for staying within the speed limit. In Stockholm, a radar and camera system tracked drivers staying within the speed limit and those exceeding the limit. Drivers going too fast were ticketed as usual according to the laws of Stockholm's road and highway system. Drivers following the rules had their information entered into a lottery, to be potentially rewarded with the money collected from the drivers who were breaking the law. Without the added possibility of reward for following rules, such a system would normally cause a generalized resentment. But, the game element made it successful. Average speeds went down by seven kilometers an hour. The *Speed Camera Lottery* worked because it took the objects, relationships, attributes and boundaries of the highway system and matched these to a motivational lottery-based game concept.

UNDERSTANDING MEANINGFUL PLAY

The topic of play and its role in the world is covered throughout this book, both in the chapter texts as well as in the interviews and content provided by many different practitioners building this field. In their book *Rules of Play*, Katie Salen and Eric Zimmerman describe meaningful play in games as serving two purposes. First, moment-by-moment system feedback related to player actions generates meaning for the player, in essence answering the question, "What does my particular behavior or activity mean in this environment?" Second, the summative evaluation of the total experience translates into a big-picture assessment of the system as a whole. It offers players perspective and the chance to reflect on whether the many components that make up the parts of a system work together to achieve its goals.

Salen and Zimmerman's definition applies to the field of entertainment-based games and it serves as a foundation for understanding meaningful play in gamified systems. However, gamified systems require a third component—the measurement of how a particular system is facilitating goals beyond the game environment. One of the most well-known examples of this idea is the celebrated game *Foldit*. Biologists and game designers at the University of Washington created a puzzle game where players fold protein structures in order to help scientists innovate biological solutions for eradicating diseases. By combining play with crowd sourcing, *Foldit* produced significant contributions to the field. Whereas scientists had spent fifteen years trying to configure the structure of the enzyme of the AIDS-related virus (M-PMV), players of the game were able to generate an accurate 3D model in just ten days. *Foldit* proves that the most interesting gamified systems make players agents of real change and demonstrates that meaningful choices can translate into substantial contributions.

ABOUT THIS BOOK

The goal of this book is to expand what has up to this point been called "gamification" in two ways. The first is by articulating, illustrating and in some cases proposing frameworks, methodologies and principles to encourage a common vocabulary and to grow the field for analysis and implementation. The second goal is to help designers gain knowledge and practice creating gamified systems for organizations and institutions outside of the traditional entertainment-based game industry. Although the book emphasizes design in the expanding fields of interactive entertainment, marketing and education, the concepts and practices introduced can satisfy a much wider range of GS design projects.

Road signs

Within the book's text you will see the repeating symbols pictured right. These icons are meant as road signs providing digestible and memorable moments of reflection about (1) knowledge, (2) principles and (3) guidelines. You may note that principles appear only in Part I of the book. This is an intentional design choice as these four chapters deal primarily with the study and analysis of gamified systems, and principles are meant to enhance this particular part of the learning process.

References to players, users and participants

As you begin reading you will notice that the individual interacting with the system being described is sometimes referred to as a player, but in other cases is called a user or participant. These terms vary based upon the structure of the system being described. Although some of these present themselves as playable game structures, others do not, and are not played like a game is. In Chapter 2, the spectrum of gamified systems is described, which details these differences and should support the range of labels.

How this book is organized

This book is divided into three parts. The first two chapters provide a foundation for understanding the field of gamified system design, including its surprisingly long history and a framework for conducting analysis. Chapters 3 and 4 explore the positive effects of gamified systems and meaningful play on human behavior and learning. Chapters 5, 6 and 7 provide a toolkit for the practice of GS design, covering the discipline as a whole and the application of principles from game design and interaction design. The last part of the book introduces readers to individuals and organizations in the fields of education, marketing and entertainment, all of whom are utilizing game principles and thinking for their initiatives. These concluding chapters emphasize the challenges and particularities that the gamified system designer needs to know in order to be an effective partner in developing applications, frameworks, events, businesses and organizations.

I. The foundation

Chapter 1: "Introducing gamified systems." Introduces gamified systems and their history, with the goal of enriching the discussion about the expanding relationship between games and the real world.

Chapter 2: "Building the spectrum." Covers frameworks and characteristics for analysis. The commonalities and distinctions between games and gamified systems are explored for the purpose of clarifying their key characteristics and defining a spectrum of gamified systems.

Chapter 3: "Positive performance." Looks at the field of psychology to understand the ways that play and game-based structures promote happiness and motivation.

Chapter 4: "Fun is learning." Explores the connection between fun and learning by providing an overview of the most established educational theories related to the field.

II. The toolbox

Chapter 5: "What is gamified system design?" Articulates the practice of GS design, demonstrating the skills and processes required to perform the task most effectively.

Chapter 6: "Applying game concepts." Provides frameworks for understanding game structures, using patterns from specific game genres to encourage more avenues of design exploration.

Chapter 7: "Visualizing interaction and information." Demonstrates how to employ principles of user experience design, information visualization and interface design for play experiences, management tools and data dashboards.

III. In the field

Chapter 8: "Designing gamified systems for education." Introduces the reader to people working in and projects related to games and learning. This includes a study of the methodologies, processes and roles to effectively create systems for engagement, instruction and analysis to meet a variety of audiences in a range of settings including schools, corporations, the military and the consumer marketplace.

Chapter 9: "Gamified system design for marketing and entertainment." Shows how the fields of marketing and entertainment leverage GS design to satisfy a wide range of business initiatives, including brand building, corporate strategy, product sales and high- and low-level promotion and audience building.

Exercises and companion website supplements

Throughout this book you will find a variety of exercises designed both to encourage big-picture thinking about gamified systems and to help you experience and understand the challenges and nuances involved in designing them. The interviews and insights from practitioners in the field give a picture of the opportunities that lie ahead as well as some of the key conceptual landmarks of the field as it has emerged. The companion website (www.gamifiedsystems.com) includes additional materials to supplement your learning and practice as you work through the book. By the end, you should gain a solid theoretical framework that matches a valuable set of practical skills. So, if you are ready to enter this new and exciting field, it is time to get started.

NOTES

Bogost, Ian. "Gamification is Bullshit." *The Atlantic*, August 9, 2011, http://www.theatlantic.com/technology/archive/2011/08/gamification-is-bullshit/243338/.

Coren, Michael J. "Foldit Gamers Solve Riddle of HIV Enzyme Within 3 Weeks." *Scientific American*, September 20, 2011, www.scientificamerican.com/article/foldit-gamers-solve-riddle/.

Deterding, Sebastian. "Pawned. Gamification and Its Discontents." Presentation at Playful 2010, London, September 24, 2010.

Edery, David and Ethan Mollick. *Changing the Game: How Video Games are Transforming the Future of Business*. Upper Saddle River: FT Press, 2009.

McGonigal, Jane. *Reality is Broken: Why Games Make Us Better and How They Can Change the World*. New York: Penguin Press, 2011.

Paharia, Rajat. *Loyalty 3.0: How Big Data and Gamification are Revolutionizing Customer and Employee Engagement*. New York: McGraw Hill, 2013.

Ray, Justin. "London's Victoria and Albert Museum Hires Video Game Designer in Residence." *Complex*, June 11, 2013, www.complex.com/style/2013/06/londons-victoria-and-albert- museum-hires-video-game-designer-in-residence.

Robertson, Margaret. "Can't Play, Won't Play." *Hide&Seek*, October 10, 2010, http://hideandseek.net/2010/10/06/cant-play-wont-play/.

Salen, Katie and Eric Zimmerman. *Rules of Play: Game Design Fundamentals*. Cambridge: MIT Press, 2004.

Schell, Jesse. "When Games Invade Real Life." Presentation at DICE 2010. Las Vegas, February 19, 2010.

Schultz, Jonathan. "Speed Camera Lottery Wins VW Fun Theory Contest." *New York Times*, November 30, 2010, http://wheels.blogs.nytimes.com/2010/11/30/speed-camera-lottery-wins-vw- fun-theory-contest/.

Tassi, Paul. "Valve Wants GLaDOS to Teach Kids Physics, Math and Chemistry in School." *Forbes*, June 21, 2012, www.forbes.com/sites/insertcoin/2012/06/21/valve-wants-glados-to- teach-kids-physics-math-and-chemistry-in-school/.

I THE FOUNDATION

1   INTRODUCING GAMIFIED SYSTEMS

CHAPTER QUESTIONS

At the end of this chapter, you should be able to answer these questions:

*   What is a gamified system?
*   What are the core ideas behind these frameworks?
*   How do play-based frameworks encourage exploration?
*   How do they create relationships between organizations and individuals?
*   Can you describe three early examples of systems that used games and play to accomplish specific goals?

INTRODUCTION

The line between what is game and what is life is quickly receding. Logging on to our social media feeds and tools for personal and professional exchanges, we are at the same time cajoled with gifts, rewards and the promise of enhancing our social networks by others who promote these dreams. Game-play has become for many of us a routine part of our online experience. The "game layer," that mental and physical space of play we almost effortlessly engage in throughout the day, seems like a natural outgrowth of our networked existence.

If the move towards a more gamified world seems inevitable, the shift also offers the potential for creating novel, meaningful and life-changing experiences that add maximum value on multiple levels. This chapter introduces the fundamental concepts behind gamified systems and examples of them in history. It broadens the discussion about the growing interplay between games and reality, providing conceptual tools to open up the emerging field of gamified system (GS) design.

IS THIS A GAME?

Petrified Forest National Park, Arizona: It is July, and I am watching four children aged eight to eleven from two families wrapping their arms around large stumps of petrified wood. After the tree hugging, they feel the texture of the wood and identify its many colors. They then play a game of bingo, filling the boxes by looking for insects, birds and animals on a nearby path. Finally, they walk slowly through the entire museum, where they study documents and artifacts, and read about the history of the park and its many different inhabitants. If you remember being a child, or if you work with or have children of your own, you know that such exhibition of enthusiasm on any day, let alone one that is blistering hot during summer vacation, is absolutely not characteristic. And yet, these kids are entranced. They are driven to learn and prove their knowledge so that they can be recognized as Petrified Forest Junior Rangers. Books in hand, they approach a park ranger, who solemnly reviews and certifies their work. For most kids, this kind of program is their first real engagement with a federal official, and this particular ceremony has these kids entranced. He asks them to raise their right hand and recite the Junior Ranger oath to protect, learn and explore. After the oaths are completed, the children each receive a Petrified Forest Badge, and the ranger tells them that they only have 399 parks left to go. The game is on, and the kids are ready and planning to collect Junior Ranger Badges from every park in the country.

Figure 1.1 The Junior Ranger Program is available at 400 national parks

"Do you think the Junior Ranger Program is a game?" I ask the children, some of whom had already been acquiring badges throughout the summer. "Well, it does get me to explore like a game," responds one boy. "Because I know I'm getting a badge, it makes me more interested in learning about the place," his sister chimes in. The Parks Service does not call the Junior Ranger Program a game. Nor do the children treat it as mere entertainment when they are taking their ranger pledges, which they do with the utmost respect and sincerity.

Although the Junior Ranger Program may not be a game in a traditional sense, there is something about it that is game-like, gamish, or **gameful**. That last term comes from the game designer Jane McGonigal, referring to events or processes that employ aspects commonly associated with games. In fact, the Junior Ranger Program illustrates many of the core ideas that make gamified systems so powerful. Good gamified systems promote exploration by connecting game elements like badges or points to the process of discovery in the real world. In the case of Junior Rangers, this exploration includes the investigation of a place, its artifacts, inhabitants and history, all of which might very well be passed over, ignored or dismissed by visitors both young and old if it were not for the program.

Figure 1.2 A park ranger checks the children's books and then engages them in the Junior Ranger oath. The children are then given badges.

Gameful

A concept proposed by game designer Jane McGonigal referring to experiences that feel like a game, inspiring the feeling of play.

Figure 1.3 Hats are used to display badges from across the nation.

Exploration experienced in gamified systems is nurtured and sustained by the cooperative and competitive instincts of individuals sharing the experience. As Junior Rangers work to complete their tasks, their parents, grandparents, camp counselors or teachers take on the fundamental roles of guides and mentors, providing direction for meaningful knowledge discovery. This kind of **social expansion** occurs when people who are not officially playing nevertheless contribute intentionally to a game. They participate along with the player but experience the game from an entirely different perspective. The Ranger Program allows adults to act as mentors, using its playful structure to guide children towards deeper engagement with the national parks. Once children are in this exploratory mindset, adults may use the opportunity to facilitate additional moments of learning extending beyond the program itself.

Social expansion

Social expansion brings participants who are not considered "players" into the play experience.

Exploration promotes relationships to people and places, and to organizations trying to facilitate this engagement. Giving individuals tools to explore on their own terms is a powerful way to grow a relationship with the institution that enables this sense of agency. In the case of Junior Rangers, the freedom to go at their own pace, on their own path, stopping along the way for photographs, snacks, story-telling and unexpected surprises, creates unique and memorable narratives empowered by the beauty and history of the place, and the mission of its caretakers. At each park, visitors uncover stories of the people, animals and objects that came before them. These historic narratives combined with their own experiences enable optimal moments for reflection.

Directed guidance combines with individual freedom to create the potential for personalization, identification and recollection. This encourages the process of emergence. **Emergence** can be understood as the unplanned-for or unintended experiences, behaviors or dynamics that occur through the use of a system. These tend to be unique to each individual experience. Exploration and social bonding are ways that the Junior Ranger Program facilitates personal and collective stories about a park and the experiences shared there. With approximately 400 parks rewarding kids with individual badges, it builds a strong sense of emergence across the entire park system. Collecting these 400 badges also provides a motivation to travel with parents and family members across the country, visiting and discovering its parks and monuments. Given the freedom to assign their own meaning of value to badges, children can create personal narratives about each achievement and the interactions they associate with it.

Emergence

The unplanned or unpredictable patterns and outcomes that occur through interaction of smaller units (like rules or object) within a system.

Junior Rangers tells us something else as well—small, well-designed systems can generate bigger games and bigger forms of engagement. Although the Junior Ranger Program may fall low on the spectrum of gamified experiences as I define them in Chapter 2, the children who participate in it from around the world use the collection of badges to create a meta-game. **Meta-games** emerge beyond or outside of a specific system. What is important for the game-aspect is not the badges or what they individually represent but the totality of the potential collection and the expanding sets of relationships and accomplishments. In the case of Junior Rangers, through the pursuit of the total collection, participants lead themselves and their families through a process of discovery and appreciation of individual parks and the national park system. It has the potential to be a very long meta-game, which could span across years of travel throughout the entire country.

Meta-game

A meta-game is a bigger game or concept that emerges through play, transcending the written or implied game structure.

GS design principle #1—bigger meaning

Small systems can generate bigger engagements. With the right design choices, individual elements can lead to bigger meanings. Collecting badges or rewards can mean significantly more if they are part of a larger system.

TOWARDS A GAMIFIED WORLD

> Play must serve something which is not play.
> —Johan Huizinga, Homo Ludens: A Study
> of the Play-Element in Culture

Games in fact have a tendency to leap the fence, and the best games take us places mentally and physically where we have never gone before. Play has helped cultures over many centuries to cope with, understand and master the complex and confusing world in which we live. Johan Huizinga in his seminal 1938 book *Homo Ludens: A Study of the Play-Element in Culture* described how playing out scenarios and exploring imaginary spaces and narratives has been fundamental to the development of human civilization. This interplay between life and games is the place where gamified systems can make truly significant contributions. Gamified systems combine opportunities for structured play with the generation of real-world data, enabling individuals and communities to have the ability to explore and attend to the world around them. Through such amplification comes a greater possibility of understanding and negotiating the various complexities that constitute reality.

GS design principle #2—guided exploration

Gamified systems combine opportunities for structured play with real-world data, enabling individuals and communities to have the ability to explore and attend to the world around them.

Our contemporary world moves at a pace where the opportunity to find time to stop, explore and experience the world (digital and physical) around us often seems unavailable. Media modify and re-contextualize our experience, often flattening and de-prioritizing the things that we might have once spent time tending to. Gamified systems offer the opportunity to re-frame reality. The careful and playful direction of attention and focus can create whole new meanings and attitudes about the world.

GS design principle #3—directed focus

Gamified systems can re-frame reality, directing attention and focus to create new meanings and attitudes about the world.

WHY MAKE IT VOLUNTARY?

The best games are voluntary and should always be considered an opportunity rather than a requirement. Indeed for Huizinga the most important characteristic of play is "that it is free, [it] is in fact freedom." He believed that play should be entirely outside our "ordinary" life, and should serve the purpose of providing a place for relaxation, and for the "interludes in our daily lives." The voluntary nature of play has been to this point a critical definition of games. Players must choose to play, and that play needs to be separate from the consequences of their real lives.

Keep it voluntary

The play of any gamified system should be voluntary.

Until recently, a relatively clear boundary existed between spaces of play and other contexts where a person's actions have material effects and consequences. The playground or the playroom were places where you were not likely either to hurt yourself or to break something. At the same time, spaces of play were spaces of freedom. Huizinga defined this boundary as the sacred spot or **magic circle** where players were free to play outside the rules of the real world. But as the boundary of this circle blurs, challenges about appropriate contexts and motivations for play arise. Encouraging voluntary participation means paying attention not only to people's desires but also to their belief systems and their fears. As schools, institutions and companies focus their efforts on creating gamified systems for their constituents, they must understand the ethical choices that they need to make when pursuing such efforts. Gamified projects that intersect with our real lives should provide a measure of personal security separate from the game environment, guaranteeing to the player that the repercussions of his in-game actions will not carry over into his real life. Ultimately, gamified system designers need to have a sense of what is and is not an appropriate use of this powerful concept.

Magic circle

For Huizinga the magic circle is the space where a game takes place and is bounded and free from the rules of the outside world.

Assure the player's safety

Playing a gamified system should not pose a threat to a player's personal, physical or material world outside of the game context.

GAMIFIED SYSTEMS: WHAT ARE THEY?

The term "gamified system" takes an architectural approach to negotiate the shifting boundaries between play and not play. A game is by itself a system that provides for the mechanics and dynamics of play. A gamified system must provide a structure for game components to function as catalysts for their non-game counterparts. Consequently, a gamified system should achieve two interrelated purposes:

1. *Facilitate an enjoyable and engaging experience.*
2. *Achieve and measure goals external to the system.*

Engagement means the level of participation that a user has with a system and consequently the organization or brand associated with it. A gamified system can provide a way to build awareness and sustain and reward loyalty. Through data analytics, engagement can be measured quantitatively by looking at the amount of time a person interacts with a system and its community. For example, tracking the number of times a user logged in weekly to a website is one vector used in the measurement of engagement. Engagement can also be measured more qualitatively, looking at the types of engagement that a user has with a system and a community. A person who invites a friend through Facebook to play with or against her demonstrates a higher degree of loyalty and engagement than a first-time user. As a metric, engagement measures sustained involvement and diversity of interaction with a gamified system.

Engagement

The participation of a user or player with a system is referred to as engagement. It can be measured both quantitatively and qualitatively.

Monitoring engagement and assessing the success of a gamified system requires clearly articulated goals that exist outside of the game context. Goals may be driven entirely by measuring engagement, and certainly this has been true of games designed purely for entertainment. Other goals might focus on driving specific user behavior. For instance, a health and fitness app might have a target behavior goal for a user to input the number of miles he walked each day. Some gamified systems might be focused entirely on instruction or learning. Others might prioritize the collection of data, money or online signatures. Whatever the goals are, they are fundamental for driving the many decisions made for design and implementation.

Gamified systems must create engagement through opportunities for varied and long-term interaction. Moreover, goals external to the system must determine what these opportunities look like. Both criteria emphasize measurement and analysis, and this helps in crafting a definition:

> **Gamified system:** A system that incorporates game methodologies to generate data by utilizing inputs and outputs related to a non-game context.

This definition prioritizes the non-game data that is going into and coming out of the structure. In successful gamified systems, this data is collected, measured and analyzed, and the information is used to reward players, create engagement and refine goals.

Considered a blueprint for gamified systems *Foursquare* put users in competition to link their virtual identities with real-world spaces. The original application enabled a player to become a "mayor" of a local business (like a café or bar) by frequenting it and "checking in." Although the mobile application has moved

Figure 1.4 *Foursquare* signs let users know where they can check in. © 2014 Foursquare Labs, Inc. All of the *Foursquare®* logos and trademarks displayed in the screenshots are the property of Foursquare Labs, Inc.

away from its play-centric design, the original application is still considered a seminal example of linking the real with the virtual through a game. Providing unique badges and special status for a wide range of activities, and physical rewards and special discounts for its users, *Foursquare* motivated thousands and eventually millions of people to check-in to locations around the world. Functions like real-time status and location updates created strong mechanisms for social networking with friends. The title of mayor used competition and status to strengthen the sense of community in a geographic area like a downtown of a city or town. Identifying common loyalties, the feature connected strangers while building interest in a contested location.

> We are capturing this amazing signal about what millions of people are doing in the real world at every moment of the day in cities all around the globe. We have seen that when we aggregate check-in patterns across many individuals, we can measure features of cities at a higher resolution than was ever possible before. I think this data can act almost like a "microscope for cities."
>
> —Blake Shaw, *Foursquare*'s data scientist

Anonymized real-time streams of every check-in enabled companies to analyze and compare large amounts of time-sensitive data about customers without

Figure 1.5 *Foursquare*'s data dashboard for partner locations. © 2014 Foursquare Labs, Inc. All of the Foursquare® logos and trademarks displayed in the screenshots are the property of Foursquare Labs, Inc.

worrying about privacy issues. These businesses were able to use this information to reward loyal customers, increase profits, and test out pricing models and marketing plans in different locations. The gamified system allowed for the building of a user base of 50 million as well as a client base of partner companies, and it also provided a series of directions for the company's evolution. Once essential for building an active audience and client base, game elements like badges and points have fallen by the wayside. The company is now leveraging the massive and dynamic data set it has collected over the years to turn *Foursquare* into a customized and localized recommendation tool meant to compete with Yelp. Though many former players are not happy with this change, the company plans on generating nearly twenty times the revenue that it had been making two years before the change. Game elements were once appropriate for growing an audience, but are no longer considered the key to the new business priority— making money.

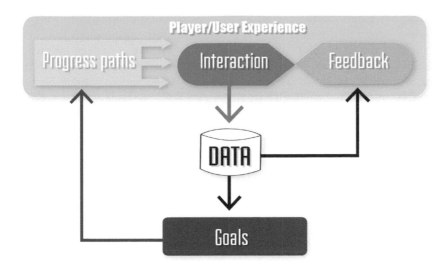

Figure 1.6 The gamified system architecture is a unique structure that feeds goals and tasks beyond the player or user experience.

Junior Rangers and the original *Foursquare* are both models of gamified systems. They create environments for reflection and engagement through the confluence of external goals, data and game elements. Just like games, gamified systems succeed by providing a series of meaningful choices in environments that includes chance, uncertainty and conflict. Although there may not always be a clear end or win-condition, gamified systems provide structure and feedback to drive users to accomplish both short-term and long-term goals. As Figure 1.6 illustrates, paths of progression like story arcs, badge collection, obstacles and quests provide clearly defined objectives. These in turn drive interactions supported by on-going feedback, including rewards, support from friends and community members, and guides and cues at the interface level. Interactions initiate the generation of data, like GPS locations or number of check-ins, which can then be utilized in a variety of ways to meet target goals or tasks external to the user or play experience. This structure—paths, interactions, feedback, data and goals—in many ways defines gamified systems, applying to digital and non-digital experiences alike. Historically, the most successful gamified systems have kept all of these aspects in mind.

GS DESIGN IN HISTORY

Employing games and game concepts to educate, motivate, persuade and problem-solve is not a new activity. In fact, many forms of gamified systems have been used to influence people to participate and engage in unfamiliar environments and processes throughout history. Not surprisingly, some of the earliest gamified systems involved the military. Since the Prussian Army began playing wargames during the Napoleonic Wars and perhaps earlier with the Chinese variant of chess played with generals, military organizations have been at the forefront of this process. Scenario planning, training in strategy and tactics, recognizing the effects of the introduction of new technologies, understanding causes of and solutions for defeat, and recruiting driven and knowledgeable new members into the military itself have all been goals for wargames at various times.

More recently, the game *America's Army* was developed by the US military for the purposes of marketing and recruitment. A multiplayer tactical shooter originally created in 2002, the game was and continues to be phenomenally successful. In fact, over a third of all visitors to the game site clicked through to the Army's recruitment page. Downloaded over 40 million times, the US military realized it had a powerful platform, and decided to put it to work. It now uses modifications of the original game to simulate fighting in different locations and prepare soldiers for the field. Some wargames have even been designed to deal with the unthinkable consequences of the job. HUTSPIEL, developed in 1955 at Johns Hopkins University, was a strategy game that let players simulate the experience of using nuclear weapons on human populations. Gamified systems are powerful instructional tools that have the potential to let individuals test out serious and indeed deadly situations, which in some cases, as HUTSPIEL intended, might lead to critical decisions about the fate of the human race.

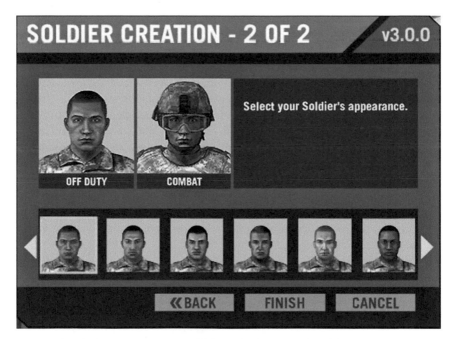

Figure 1.7 *America's Army* character creation and customization screenshot from *America's Army: Proving Grounds 2013* (US Army) © America's Army 2014, All Rights Reserved.

Figure 1.8 H.G. Wells playing his hobby wargame *Little Wars*.

Wargames help the military succeed. But, they have also been used as tools for avoiding wars. H.G. Wells, the acclaimed science fiction writer (*The War of the Worlds, The Time Machine*) created the game *Little Wars* in 1913 to influence players to question the merits of the impending war. In what is now considered the first hobby wargame, players would enact battles, using projectiles that fired matchsticks at figures, representing their death. Wells said about the game, "You only have to play at *Little Wars* three or four times to realize just what a blundering thing Great War must be." However, in the case of Wells, the ostensible goal failed even though the game continued to survive as a hobby that engaged many of the deeper goals of the wargame tradition.

But game systems predate the military and have historically been used to shape cultural life and social norms. The Olympic Games did this, pulling together the competing city-states of ancient Greece. Dating back to the 9th century, the *Chinese Promotion Game* was designed as a way for thinking about the nature of bureaucracy. It is based upon the older Indian game *Snakes and Ladders*, which was originally created to teach children about the punishments and rewards associated with moral and immoral behavior, but evolved into an aristocratic decision-making game. Using the same type of tiled board, the Chinese game adds job titles associated with the Chinese government bureaucracy. Players roll dice to either move up positions or be demoted from positions, with the winner being the player who reaches the highest rank up the promotional ladder. It is believed that in the 17th century young men waiting to take their examination for government placement would play this game together for the purposes of mentally and emotionally preparing themselves to take the test. By playing through the procedures of this particular game, which was so largely based on chance, players had the opportunity to consciously recognize the arbitrary nature of placement in the Chinese bureaucratic system, relieving some of the psychological stress on aspiring students.

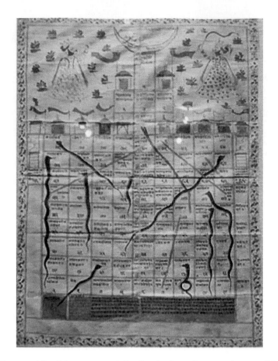

Figure 1.9 *Snakes and Ladders* was originally designed to teach moral lessons to children in India.

Although most historical examples of gamified systems are structured as pure games, having goals external to the system (I explore this category of "Alternate Purpose Games" in more detail in Chapter 2), there are also historical precedents of games with a more porous structure, blending the real world with game elements. Improvisational-theater games are an example of such a phenomenon. More recently associated with well-known comedy troupes like Second City in Chicago, these games actually date back to the 1930s when Viola Spolin invented theater games while working as a drama supervisor in Chicago's settlement houses. Her goal was to provide a means for immigrant and inner-city youth to communicate and problem-solve despite their economic and racial barriers. Each game she designed was a simple system for teaching individual techniques and concepts related to theater performance and human communication. One example, "the gibberish game," involved three performers on a stage. Two of them would make up a language and speak it while a third would translate for an audience. Spolin's practice derives from the idea that games can liberate humans from their self-conscious driven behavior to make them more open and receptive to the world. Relying on only rules and players, improvisational theater play is affordable, portable and has proven effective at bridging social and linguistic barriers between its players. Gamified systems like this provide effective and accessible mechanisms for building and strengthening human relationships.

GS design principle #4—permission to experiment socially

Gamified systems like improvisational theater games can provide a bridge for racial, economic and language barriers outside of the game context.

Getting people from different cultures to communicate is one way of facilitating relationships; promoting opportunities for romance is another. On the lighter side of improvisational game play are games that focus on matchmaking, a classically modern problem reflecting the breakdown of older family and kinship networks that traditionally arranged these pair-ups. Before reality television dating shows like *The Bachelor*, there was *The Dating Game*. The ABC game show usually featured a young woman known as "the bachelorette." Sitting behind a wall that separated her from three men known as "the bachelors," the bachelorette would try to determine which man would make the best date. At each round she would read a pre-scripted question and ask the different bachelors in the order of her choosing to answer it. Bachelors had to improvise their answers, while trying to make themselves seem appealing and their competitors less so. The rules of the game forbade questions or answers related to a bachelor's name, age, occupation or income. At the end of the game, the bachelorette would choose one of these bachelors before they met face-to-face. Although the show was created for entertainment purposes, for the bachelor and bachelorette it was a legitimate way to find a mate. After the show the new couple were sent on a date paid for

Figure 1.10 *The Dating Game* was a popular show in the 1970s, where the winner won a date with the judge. Reprinted with the permission of the artist, Alex Waskelo.

by the television network. Although a chaperone from the show usually came along to pay bills and fares, the date (often a weekend at a hotel) took place entirely outside of the televised game-context.

While some are looking for love, others are simply looking to make their job more fun. Though applying games to work may not always seem like an entirely beneficial pursuit, experiments have shown some appropriate applications. Dennis Chao, a systems administrator at the University of New Mexico, developed psDoom to provide System Administrators with a more enjoyable interface for managing computer networks. Using the Doom source code released in 1997 by ID Software, Chao developed a modification (commonly referred to as a MOD) of the game. The MOD, which was further developed by David Koppenhofer, allowed players to kill or re-prioritize system processes by shooting different monsters. Each monster represented a distinct process running at that time. Rather than using UNIX-based tools and inputting text commands, system administrators could accomplish the same tasks through play. Chao's goal was to take a game that his colleagues enjoyed playing and enable them to play it as a vehicle for doing their work.

Marrying real-life with game thinking, gamified systems have earned an important place in the long and substantial history of games. The emphasis on achieving goals external to the experience of play distinguishes these early

Figure 1.11 *psDoom* lets system administrators manage their systems by playing a version of the first-person shooter *Doom*. Reprinted with permission from Dennis Chao and David Koppenhofer.

efforts. They also open a window onto the future. The history of games goes back thousands of years but it is only now that technologies and networks have matured to the point that gamified systems can come into their own.

KEY TAKEAWAYS

- A gamified system can be defined as: *a system that incorporates game methodologies to generate data by utilizing inputs and outputs related to a non-game context.*
- Like games, gamified systems should be voluntary, take place in a safe environment and include elements of chance and uncertainty. They should also include one or more players or users, provide conflict, include rules, and outcomes or goals for the user to pursue.
- GS design should achieve two interrelated purposes:
  1. *The manifestation of an enjoyable and engaging experience.*
  2. *The achievement (and measurement) of articulated goals external to the system.*
- The unique architecture of a gamified system includes progress paths and interactions, which generate feedback and data. These are all meant to accomplish an external goal or task.
- Using GS design to teach, persuade and motivate people is not a new practice. Game systems have been used for centuries to instruct players about making choices in their real lives.

EXERCISES

1.1 The meta-game

Study a game or gamified system that includes badges or rewards. How do you think the collections of these create a bigger meaning for individuals playing or using the system?

1.2 Exploration

Investigate location and exploration. Evaluate a location-based game or gamified system and identify the ways that it encourages exploration in the real world. Are there elements or features that you think could be added or modified to expand this exploration?

1.3 Voluntary vs. involuntary

Should gamified systems always be voluntary? Make an argument about if and when it is ever appropriate to make the use of a gamified system mandatory. Describe which scenarios may be fitting for such an implementation. Consider different examples of systems used on the job or at school.

RECOMMENDED READINGS AND RESOURCES

* *Homo Ludens: A Study of the Play-Element in Culture,* by Johan Huizinga, 1971 (reprint).
  A seminal historic text for designers interested in deciphering the important role that play has in our lives.

* *Reality is Broken,* by Jane McGonigal, 2011.
  Jane McGonigal's call to action is an impassioned and convincing argument about the power of games to improve our world.

* www.Gamification.co.
  A regularly updated and growing web resource that contains a large database and archive of articles and reviews about gamified systems.

INSIDER INSIGHT

NICOLE LAZZARO LEADS THE WAY

Interview granted with permission by Nicole Lazzaro.

> I answer the question "WTF? Where's the fun?"
> —Nicole Lazzaro

Nicole Lazzaro is the founder and President of XEODesign, an award-winning firm that helps organizations increase engagement with play. Widely recognized as one of the top women working in video, social and mobile games, she is also recognized as one of the pioneers and leaders in the field of gamified system design. Lazarro has spent the past twenty years crafting expertise in Player Experience Design (PXD) for companies that include: EA, Ubisoft, DICE, LucasArts, Disney, PlayFirst, the Cartoon Network and Nickelodeon, and titles including *Diner Dash, Myst* and *The Sims.* Lazarro is a world-renowned speaker who shares

Figure 1.12 Nicole Lazzaro.

her valuable ideas about play and her "4 Keys 2 Fun" methodology for creating optimal play experiences through emotions. She has spoken at the US State Department, and has been widely cited by global news media services including Wired, Fast Company, ABC News, CNN and CNET.

Tell me about your company, XEODesign.

We create engagement to unlock human potential and improve the quality of life through play. XEODesign has spent the past twenty-two years working on player experience for a variety of clients including game companies, software corporations, educational and governmental institutions to figure out what makes things fun. We coined the term "player experience," which is an extension of the idea of the user experience.

In terms of gamified systems, we help these clients learn to create game engagement outside of the game industry. In fact, we have worked with both Cisco Systems and Oracle to create gamified systems for database design. We use methodologies we have developed based on "The Four Keys of Design," a framework for play that I built over the past ten years. Part of this is based on thousands of studies we have conducted independently watching players play. We leverage this information to help companies use games to support their goals and help game designers optimize their games. Our company also offers design and development services to create a game all the way through execution.

Can you talk about some of the work you have done outside of the game industry?

One of the most enjoyable workshops we have done was for the government of Singapore, working with their employees responsible for designing trains and the train systems. Together we created a whole series of games, sort of in a game jam context. Using paper, pencils and dice we made prototypes for game ideas including one for teaching procurement policies to encourage recycling at the food court.

Our Playshop is a whole day of play, which is about creative acclimation. We just conducted a Playshop for a social network. We use play activities to put people in the right play space so that they can be more productive together and achieve certain goals. We have had fantastic results. We worked together to conceptualize elements of games to connect, collaborate and accomplish the goals of the site. The idea behind this is that play puts users in a unique state, which helps them accomplish certain tasks.

Can you describe your process?

We start by doing research, watching people play, which is an essential part of play design. We collect three types of data: video recordings of what players said and did, players' questionnaire responses, and verbal and non-verbal emotional cues recorded by capturing player faces and measuring micro-expressions during play. We then identify the core activity loops, what specific activities they are participating in and then group these into four styles of play: easy fun, hard fun, social fun and serious fun. Easy fun is about wonder, fun, and exploration. It is what I refer to as the bubble wrap of game design. It is the interactivity that gets you interested. It is the headspace that allows for idea generation and creativity. Hard fun is about frustration, and the need to have a personal triumph over diversity, like fighting the boss monster. This is where difficulty, skill and mastery come into the picture. Social fun is about people, because collaboration is the key to fun. Social fun provides a huge swath of interactions, including cooperation and communication. It opens emotional

Figures 1.13a and 1.13b Rapid game prototyping at XEODesign's *Playshop* workshop.

connections between players that can help create social bonding. Serious fun closes the loop, providing ongoing sense of accomplishment and feedback through replication and rhythm.

What does the future of gamified system design look like?

This is the next generation, and is the future where interaction design is going. Games are leading interaction. We can learn from games to create much richer experiences. Tools that people need to use are not currently designed to put people in the right headspace. We can use the language of games to get people into the right frame of mind to accomplish their tasks. That is where we can take inspiration and ideas from the art of game design.

I am passionate about a future where we can use games to influence positive change in traditional institutions, like schools and corporations. There are significant opportunities to join together to apply techniques from game design to rethink the way traditional services and organizations accomplish their goals. There are opportunities in every industry. The Information Age has unlocked so many capacities to collaborate and create new structures and patterns. It is the time to take our skills and re-architect the way traditional systems are designed and developed. We have the capacity to get people into a play state, and make them more curious and open to challenges. Doing this means that we can accelerate learning, performance and research. The great thing about play is that it is a no-cost obligation. We can try out our future without any downside.

What advice can you give to aspiring or working GS designers?

Your job as designers is to create experiences that fit us better as human beings. In your next project consider how you can make the person feel. How can you build curiosity, wonder and surprise? What goals and challenges are you giving players to master? Are you finding new opportunities to create social fun and get people to interact together? Finally, think about how you create a sense of progression over time. By leveraging the language of games you can take real tasks, simplify and clarify the goals and the world, and then amplify the feedback.

PATRICK JAGODA ON THE VALUE OF GAMIFIED SYSTEMS

Interview granted with permission by Patrick Jagoda.

Patrick Jagoda is the co-founder of the Game Changer Chicago Design Lab where he leads design projects primarily related to social justice. As an Assistant Professor of English and an affiliate of Cinema and Media Studies at the University of Chicago, Jagoda specializes in new media studies, 20th-century American literature, and digital game theory and design.

Figure 1.14 Patrick Jagoda.

What is it about gamified systems that make them relevant?

In approaching gamified systems, it is important to think about the significance of games in our historical moment. Games have become a prominent metaphor and material reality of everyday work and play in the early 21st century. American culture, in particular, is saturated in game metaphors and structures. We need only think of television dramas such as The Wire, which uses "the game" as a metaphor of the drug trade and survival in postindustrial America. Similarly, novels and films such as The Hunger Games and Ender's Game remind us how central games of competition and chance are to contemporary society. Then we have the ubiquitous reality TV shows that entangle everyday participants with game rules and objectives. The prominence of game metaphors, across media and lived realities, is perhaps not surprising if we think about the popularity of videogames among Millennials who have been playing these games for much of their lives—and are now coming of age. Regardless, given the cultural centrality of games, it is essential to think about the critical potential of gamified systems.

What are some of the unique opportunities presented by gamified systems?

In my practice, I have isolated four unique ways that games and gamified systems can encourage players to engage the rules, protocols and goals that constitute our world in a critical fashion. First, unlike earlier linear art forms, games can invite concrete activity and participation. Second, digital game systems, in particular, offer real-time data processing and respond to emergent player actions that promise, in some cases, to alter behaviors. Third, games can use their formal systems to help players experiment with large-scale social, political and economic systems. Finally, gamified systems enable flexible and player-centric design that encourages players to explore social values and ideologies.

So, what makes these systems different than other forms of media? What are they better at achieving?

Games stand in contrast to ethically or politically oriented art forms, such as novels, in so far as they can encourage critical engagement through mechanical metaphors and can empower players through action-oriented simulations. Gamified systems require consistent action from a player who wants to explore the non-linear system or traverse its challenges. Let me give you an example. Richard Preston's non-fiction thriller *The Hot Zone* or Steven Soderbergh's film *Contagion* are both cultural works that have much to teach a reader or viewer about the spread of viruses across global networks. Neither work, however, depends on the kind of activity that we see in a serious game such as *Killer Flu* by Persuasive Games. In this game, the user plays as an avian flu pandemic that must mutate and infect the human population. The game-play consists of clicking on non-player characters, transforming a flu strain in order to infect them, and directing those same characters across the game grid to highly populated areas. Through the difficulty of winning, especially at the highest level, the game underscores that panic and terror are not ideal responses to a pandemic. Instead of spreading fear, this game promotes information sharing and the expansion of epidemiological services. *Killer Flu* suggests how serious games and gamified systems might offer unique ways to teach and motivate through participatory play.

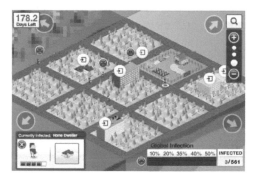

Figure 1.15 *Killer Flu* lets players explore how the flu develops, spreads and mutates.

How can gamified systems learn from videogames?

A key mechanism that gamified systems carry over from videogames, in particular, is the capacity to motivate players through data and feedback. Many games have hypermediated interfaces that may include health bars, progress markers, map positions, time displays, messaging options and other information. These data systems make players aware of their success or failure, and they also enable real-time game-play adjustments. For example, the game *Re-Mission* by HopeLab focuses on behavioral and psychological data that correlates with successful cancer treatments. This game, which targets teens and young adults, has been shown to motivate healthy behavior among patients, including consistent use of medications. The game offers both information and game-play feedback through twenty levels that unfold inside a patient's body. In this case, Re-Mission's two-way data stream informs, engages and involves players.

How can gamified systems facilitate new ways of thinking?

These implementations help players engage with large-scale structures or networks, such as global pandemics, economic systems or the phenomenon of climate change that may otherwise seem unthinkable or inaccessible. Game designers often discuss games as formal systems made up of rules and goals. Games are also able to model or simulate complex social systems—and to invite players to play with and learn about them. For example, Jane McGonigal's Superstruct, which she calls a massively multiplayer forecasting game, encouraged players to brainstorm solutions to global issues such as viral outbreaks, food shortages, energy crises, the proliferation of global refugees and threats to civil rights. This gamified system, which extended to both virtual and physical spaces, encouraged the creation of innovative ecologies such as the "Appleseed ecology" that promoted information sharing among farmers as well as urban farming strategies. A number of other Alternate Reality Games, such as Evoke, Traces of Hope and Speculation (the last of which I co-designed), have also grappled with massive global systems through game-play.

What do you think is the future of gamified system design and the study of it?

In the 21st century, gamified systems have insinuated themselves into everyday life in a world where more aspects of life unfold via digital and networked technologies. The critical potential of gamified systems is something that requires ongoing discussion and debate. In any case, the field of gamified system design demonstrates the fact that no game or game-based system is neutral. All such systems include a broad range of built-in assumptions, biases, ideologies and values. When designers seek to create any gamified system, they should therefore use play-testing and analysis to interrogate its effectiveness in achieving specific educational, artistic, psychological or consumerist outcomes. Designers should also actively explore the range of values or ideologies that their system may, intentionally or unintentionally, advocate.

NOTES

Bogost, Ian. Persuasive Games: The Expressive Power of Video Games. Boston: MIT Press, 2007.

Bogost, Ian. How to do Things with Video Games (Electronic Mediations). Boston: MIT Press, 2011.

Chao, Dennis. "Doom as an Interface for Process Management." Presentation at SIGCHI '01, Seattle, Washington, April, 2001.

Deterding, Sebastian, Dan Dixon, Rilla Khaled and Lennart E. Nacke. "From Game Design Elements to Gamefulness. Defining 'Gamification.'" Paper presented at MindTrek '11, Tampere, September 28–30, 2011.

Djaouti, Damien, Julian Alvarez, Jean-Pierre Jessel and Olivier Rampoux. "Origins of Serious Games." *Serious Games and Edutainment Applications*. Edited by Minhua Ma: 25–43. London: Springer-Verlag, 2011.

Huizinga, Johan. *Homo Ludens: A Study of the Play-Element in Culture*. Boston: Beacon Press, 1971. [Note: The original version of this book was published in 1939 and translated to English in 1955.]

Jagoda, Patrick. "Gamification and Other Forms of Play." *Boundary 2*, 40:2 (2013): 114–144.

Jinny, Gudmundsen. "Movement aims to get serious about games." *USA Today*, May 19, 2006, http://www.usatoday.com/tech/gaming/2006-05-19-serious-games_x.htm.

Kim, Amy Jo. "MetaGame Design: Reward Systems that Drive Engagement." Presented at the Game Developers Conference, San Francisco, CA, March 9, 2010, http://www.slideshare.net/amyjokim/metagame-design-3383058.

McGonigal, Jane. "Gaming Can Make a Better World." Presentation at TED, Monterey, CA, February, 2010.

McGonigal, Jane. *Reality is Broken: Why Games Make Us Better and How They Can Change the World*. New York: Penguin Press, 2011.

Montola, Markus, Jaakko Stenros and Annika Waern. *Pervasive Games: Theory and Design*. London: Taylor & Francis, 2009.

O'Brien, Heather L. and Elaine G. Toms. "What is User Engagement? A Conceptual Framework for Defining User Engagement with Technology." *Journal of the American Society for Information Science and Technology*, 59:6 (April 2008): 938–955.

Palmer, Doug, Steve Lunceford and Aaron J. Patton. "The Engagement Economy: How Gamification is Reshaping Businesses." *Deloitte Review*, 11 (2012): 55–57, http://www.deloitte.com/view/en_US/us/Insights/Browse-by-Content-Type/deloitte-review/c7cee86d96498310VgnVCM1000001956f00aRCRD.htm.

Perella, Steve. "Full Coverage of Anonymized Foursquare Check-in Data Now Available Exclusively from Gnip." *Gnip*, May 23, 2013, http://blog.gnip.com/gnip-foursquare-partnership/.

Seth Priebatsch. "The Game Layer on Top of the World." Presentation at TEDxBoston, Boston, MA, July, 2010.

Salen, Katie and Eric Zimmerman. *Rules of Play: Game Design Fundamentals*. Cambridge: MIT Press, 2004.

Spolin, Viola. *Improvisation for the Theater: A Handbook of Teaching and Directing Techniques: Third Edition*. Evanston: Northwestern University Press, 1999. [Note: The original version of this book was published in 1963.]

Trevor, Timpson. "Little Wars: How HG Wells Created Hobby Wargaming." *BBC News*, August 2, 2013, http://www.bbc.com/news/magazine-22777029.

Walsh, Mark. "Foursquare Killing Check-in to Save Itself." *Mediapost*, May 2, 2014, http://www.mediapost.com/publications/article/225016/foursquare-killing-check-in-to-save-itself.html.

2 BUILDING THE SPECTRUM

CHAPTER QUESTIONS

At the end of this chapter, you should be able to answer these questions:

- What are some of the similarities and differences between games and gamified systems?
- How would Caillois characterize the differences between formal and informal play?
- What are the three defining characteristics of gamified system (GS) design?
- What are two poles of the gamified system spectrum?
- What is the difference between the game layer, a system that is game-like and an Alternate Purpose Game?

INTRODUCTION

As games and reality continue to intersect, new forms of GS designs will inevitably emerge. The momentum for such innovation requires the combined knowledge and skill of game designers and interaction designers. A conceptual framework of gamified systems facilitates this process, providing designers with a common vocabulary leading to practical methods for analysis and design.

Developing this framework should begin by identifying the commonalities and the differences between games and gamified systems. Once these distinctions are made, we can identify the primary characteristics of gamified systems. These steps will inevitably lead us towards a spectrum of gamified systems.

GAMES VS. GAMIFIED SYSTEMS

Although games and gamified systems share many similarities, including goals, rules and game materials (as characterized in Figure 2.1), the distinctions are what make this new field both compelling and contentious. By occurring in the context of daily life, a gamified system has the potential to strengthen the connections an individual has to people, places, ideas and tasks in her daily life. This may occur as a part of a feedback loop that is integrated into the same

Characteristics	Games	Gamified Systems
Has a goal or set of goals	●	●
Includes some aspect of chance	●	●
Requires one or more players	●	●
Includes rules	●	●
Play is voluntary	●	●
Play takes place outside of daily life	●	
Generates data	●	●
Data generated serves goals beyond play		●
Driven by goals beyond entertainment		●

The voluntary requirement for games is much more of an ethical issue when applied to gamified systems. It is important to remember that enjoyment or engagement can be at odds with obligatory tasks.

Figure 2.1 Games and gamified systems share many common characteristics, but are distinguished by their differences. Although play in a gamified system should be voluntary, it is not a requirement. Gamified systems take place within daily life, not outside of it as games do. Although games and gamified systems both generate data, gamified systems use data collected to serve goals outside of the game context.

interactive system where an individual is performing an activity. Let's take an example of an employee participating in a quality assurance system and competing against others based upon the number of quality bugs reported. In this scenario, the framework is responsible for the conversation between the task (bug testing) and the game-related concepts associated with the values generated by that work. Examples of such game elements might include levels, points or rewards. In another situation, this translation may occur in parallel with a person's actions. This might happen when a person exercises and then reports the information about time and activity after the fact in a fitness program. Because gamified systems have goals that extend beyond the game context they must rely on the collection and analysis of data (in one form or another) to measure effectiveness. These metrics can provide rapid feedback, letting designers craft and refine the overall experience on an on-going basis.

THE OLD RULES OF PLAY

Approaches to game design have traditionally been structured around the opposition between play and games. Although this opposition may seem to have deep cultural roots, the distinction was not that important until 1959 when in his work *Man, Play and Games* the French philosopher Roger Caillois expanded Huizinga's concept of play by introducing characteristics essential to its ultimate structured form—games. Caillois distinguishes two types of play. The first, *paida*, also known as informal play, is unscripted and improvisational, not bound by any rules. The second type of play, *ludus*, or formal play, follows rules or even a script and corresponds to what we commonly call games. By making the distinction between play and games, Caillois could then fit different kinds of activities on a spectrum between the two. Activities that are less planned or structured sit towards play, whereas those with reproducible fixed rules sit towards games.

Caillois also noted that both forms shared certain attributes. In particular, he described four categories of play: *agôn*, *alea*, *mimicry* and *ilinx*. *Agôn*, the Greek word for contest or competition, allows players to showcase their abilities and prove their knowledge. *Alea*, which means dice in Latin, refers to aspects of chance. As "a surrender to destiny," chance creates variability in game-play. It keeps players on their toes, a process Caillois calls "negation of the will," because chance elements force the rethinking of well-laid plans and strategies. Rather than simple randomness, this periodic renewal of the game creates a more even playing field for players who are less skilled or experienced than others. *Mimicry* corresponds to simulation and role-playing, and allows players to engage in behaviors and experiences that are not possible, encouraged or condoned in the real world. Finally, *ilinx*, refers to the opportunity for risk-taking and vertigo. Primarily used to create instability for a player, *ilinx* changes the player's mental and even physical experience of the world in some way.

Paida (Play) ———————————▶		*Ludus* (Game)
Informal and unscripted		Formalized, reproducible, rule based
Unregulated physical play like wrestling for fun	**Agôn** (Competition)	Head-to-head games with clear win-conditions like Chess or a console based fighting game
Improvisational word-play like rhyming	**Alea** (Chance)	Dice based competitions, lotteries and sweepstakes
Playing dress-up or house	**Mimicry** (Role-playing)	Playing a character whose actions are pre-defined by statistics
Spinning in place	**Ilinx** (Physical risk)	Playing a sport with physical consequences like boxing

Figure 2.2 Examples of activities based on Caillois's taxonomy (adapted from Caillois's original taxonomy).

DEFINING A GAMIFIED SYSTEM SPECTRUM

The introduction of computers, consoles, handheld devices and the Internet has meant that our experience of games has changed radically since 1959. The distinction between games and reality is increasingly blurred. Perhaps it is time for a new spectrum for gamified systems. Although GS design is an emerging field, there are enough examples to begin to identify some of the common characteristics or attributes in the manner of Caillois. In the case of gamified systems, however, the key distinction is not between play and games but along a continuum that ranges between experiences that are not games at all and those that are games for pure entertainment.

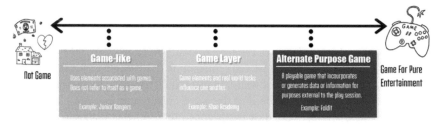

Figure 2.3 The gamified system spectrum places gamified systems along a continuum between games for pure entertainment and the world of material consequences.

On one side of the spectrum we can imagine an area that exists outside of any game or play context—beyond Huizinga's magic circle. It is a space where we have little to no control over external circumstances, such as the weather or global financial markets. It is also a place where we experience the material effects of our actions and the actions of others in a context that in its current form allows for little or no play. For instance, working more hours at your job might translate into more money into your paycheck. This may be voluntary but only in the sense that it is driven by goals radically distinct from the workplace itself. On the flip side, having your hours cut by your manager is likely to earn you less and can be something that you have little or no strategic control over, even if you follow the workplace "rules." There are also non-game aspects of games. The most notorious example is "goldfarming" in massively multiplayer games (MMOs), where workers in China play a particularly tedious and repetitive aspect of the game to amass gold that can be sold to players who do not want to spend time building up a character.

On the opposite side of non-game experiences are game systems where the only agenda other than generating revenue is player entertainment. These systems are primarily focused on creating an enjoyable self-contained player experience, although, with the exception of some console games and non-electronic board games, it is increasingly rare to find games not connected to some kind of system for amassing data on users. The category of pure entertainment is questionable for other reasons as well. Game designers consciously or unconsciously embed their own cultural perspectives in their designs and mechanics, and for this reason most games put forward a certain kind of ideological or moral agenda not unlike traditional media such as film and television. For instance, many games imply that characters' motives are good or bad by crafting behaviors or characteristics that can be read as being devious, criminal, heroic or virtuous. The 2001 game Black & White, where players' actions as either a kind or angry god, directly influences change in the characters and the environment embodies this idea. Games like SimCity and Civilization have particular theories of social conventions, urban planning and history that they put forward through gameplay. But although these devices may affirm or influence the player's own opinions about these ideas, these intentions are rarely articulated as the goals of the game developer and are almost never monitored as a measure of success or failure of the system, which is why such games should be considered "pure."

Sitting between the two poles of "not-games" and "games for pure entertainment" are the three forms of gamified systems, organized according to how much or how little the structure resembles a game. Sitting in the center of the spectrum are systems that fit in the game layer category. **Game layer** systems represent the majority of gamified systems. They are recognized through their patterns, which marry real-world tasks to game elements. **Game-like** systems sit closest to the "not games" area of the spectrum. Although they may promote a sense or experience of play, game-like systems do not depend on actual game components. The third category, **Alternate Purpose Games** (APGs) are games in which a particular set of external goals has been substituted for the more generic "entertainment." Consequently, they are closest on the spectrum to "games for pure entertainment."

Game-like systems

> I made losing weight another fantasy sports league, calculating points® values, thinking about the stats behind it and making it work.
> —Devon, 29, about the Weight Watchers dieting system

Sitting closest to a non-game experience are systems that could be referred to as game-like. Although they may utilize an element or elements associated with games, these systems are not necessarily experienced like a game. Neither are they communicated as being playable or gamified to the end-user. Yet, users may leverage these elements to create a game-like experience for themselves. The points system found in the Weight Watchers weight loss program is an example of this type of structure. Logging in to a personal profile to view their statistics, like their weight and the amount of points they have consumed, it can be played like a game. Like an RPG, users can view and manage their statistics, which in this case are weight and points used. They can also develop and plan strategies and scenarios around maximizing the points they have left to use that day and week. Losing weight can be experienced like a leveling system. As dieters succeed at their goals, they increase their abilities, becoming healthier, fitter members of the Weight Watchers community.

While Weight Watchers is one example, there are many systems that are game-like. For instance, Quest to Learn, a school created by Katie Salen, a contributor to this book, considers itself a game-like school. These frameworks may use points, badges or rewards to keep individuals motivated to continue participating within the structure. Or, they may use concepts derived from computer and table-top gaming like quests, guilds or missions. Although those who are the most engaged and interested might turn it into a playable experience, not everyone will see it as a game. This absence of explicit playable intentions is the defining mark of a game-like system.

Game-like

Game-like systems do not pretend to be games. Instead, there is some aspect of the framework that can be experienced as playable by an individual. Examples: National Parks' Junior Ranger Program, Quest to Learn.

The game layer

The term game layer is attributed to Scavengr founder Seth Priebatsch, who introduced the concept as a speaker at Boston's 2010 TEDx. In his presentation, Priebatsch set the groundwork for this idea by describing the prior decade (2000–2010) as that of the social layer, which made it possible for the current decade (2010–2020) to usher in the game layer. This insight suggests that, once the infrastructure for social networking had been built and adopted by hundreds of millions of Internet users, the next obvious step would be the creation of play-systems to leverage that architecture. Taking real-time statistics of football players each game so that *Fantasy Football* players can compete in their leagues is a perfect example of this. What makes the game layer so compelling is that it stresses the re-negotiation of the magic circle, emphasizing the permeable state that now exists between what is game and what is not game.

The majority of gamified systems fall into the game layer category. The thrust being the tie between the set of tasks the user is performing and their corresponding connection to game elements. Although some rely on points or badges, and more use these in combination with leaderboards, there is a significant amount of room for expanding this combination and experimenting with many more game elements and concepts. Depending upon the structural choices of their designs, game layer systems may be considered to be more or less in the direction of a purely entertainment-based game. For example, the use of narrative elements like characters, back-story or a fiction that is revealed over time are likely to enable greater opportunities for emergent play. The use of clear win-conditions and

> **Game layer**
>
> Game layer systems connect tasks in the real world to game elements. Examples: The original *Foursquare*, *Khan Academy*, *Fantasy Football*.

mechanics that facilitate collective or collaborative play are a few more methods that could push game layer systems towards the game side of the spectrum.

Alternate Purpose Games

Alternate Purpose Games (APGs) can be understood as playable game systems that leverage game procedures and game content to satisfy goals outside of the game context. *The Landlord's Game*, created in 1902, is an early example of an APG. Its creator Elizabeth Magie wanted to teach and persuade players to embrace an obscure concept, Henry George's "single tax theory." He believed that people should be taxed once, and the amount should be based upon the income generated through property ownership. The game has of course fared better than the theory. In part this was because the game was at a broader level meant to remind players of the unfair distribution of wealth that existed between landlords and renters. Ironically, however, even this aspect disappeared in the 1930s as the game was later modified to become the popular game about land-based capitalism we now know as *Monopoly*. A game like *The Landlord's Game* might be referred to today as an educational game or even "edutainment," a term commonly used during the growth of the computer game era in the last decade of the 20th century. Games like these are driven by educational or instructional objectives, yet are designed to be entertaining. As time goes on, because APGs are only partially gamified systems, they tend to move closer and closer towards pure entertainment.

The political agenda behind *The Landlord's Game* makes the original *Monopoly* more than an educational game. Like H.G. Wells's war game, and the much earlier *Snakes and Ladders*, these types of games also fall into the category of persuasive games. Game theorist and designer Ian Bogost describes these as games that influence behavior through the use of procedural rhetoric. Essentially, players are encouraged to believe an argument by playing out the rules and procedures provided through a game system. Games that are educational, instructional or utilize procedural rhetoric for the purpose of persuasion have also been referred to as "serious games." These have been defined as *games that do not have entertainment, enjoyment or fun as their primary purpose*. This is a somewhat debated and debatable category, but should nevertheless be covered as part of the growing canon of systems that fit under the APG umbrella.

Aside from instruction and persuasion, APGs can fulfill a variety of objectives. For instance, advergames are developed entirely for the purposes of driving particular marketing and/or sales of products, brands or services. An example of

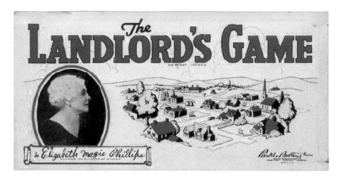

Figure 2.4 Elizabeth Magie's *The Landlord's Game*, which was later modified into the popular game *Monopoly*.

this was DaimlerChrysler's *Jeep 4x4: Trail of Life*, which was developed to promote sales of the Wrangler Rubicon in 2001. The game provided players with a simulated experience of driving the car through the Mayan jungle. It was downloaded nearly 400,000 times. What's more, 14 percent of the first car orders came from individuals who downloaded the game. From cars to cereal, adver-games have come to be an essential part of the marketing mix of any consumer-driven company. However, like any APG, their value tends to diminish over time, and unlike *Monopoly*, where persistence was one of the goals in designing the game itself, they rarely outlast a product cycle.

Over the past few years, some APGs have also gone in the other direction, towards more sophisticated engagement with gamified systems. In these cases, the act of playing in turn produces valuable data that can be stored, collected and utilized for purposes outside of the game context. The game *Foldit*, which was discussed in the introduction of this book, is perhaps the best-known example of this. Players fold proteins and amino acid chains as a part of a puzzle-based game. The scores and permutations are then stored and shared with participating scientists. *Foldit* has been immensely successful at achieving its goals. As the *Foldit* community grows, scientists continue to look to its player base to help solve new challenges. New puzzles are added regularly to the game, and the game-play becomes an important aspect of the research process. The games are supplemented with valuable content like podcast interviews with *Foldit* scientists explaining their research with the hopes of developing a stronger public science dimension and

Alternate Purpose Games

Alternate Purpose Games (APGs) are playable games that are driven by goals external to the game context. This umbrella category includes serious games, persuasive games and advergames. Examples: *Foldit*, *Superflu* and *Snakes and Ladders*.

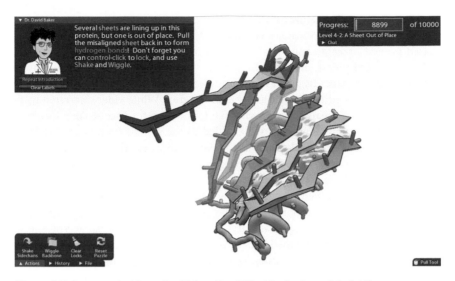

Figure 2.5 A screenshot from the University of Washington's protein folding game *Foldit*. Courtesy of the University of Washington.

a wider audience for the game itself. Storing, sharing and analyzing user data, and using crowd sourcing to do this, have injected the APG with measurably innovative dimensions.

The spectrum of gamified systems provides a common language to guide the choices made in a project. Used as a method for continually assessing direction and goals, it clarifies the methods and processes associated with design and implementation, benefitting all the stages of development.

CHARACTERIZING GAMIFIED SYSTEMS

Now that we have spectrum defined, we can begin to get more granular. There are five characteristics of gamified systems that can be clearly identified. These are:

1. Non-game goals.
2. Game concepts and components.
3. The role of data.
4. Emergent opportunities.
5. Pervasiveness.

Let's examine each of these in more detail.

Non-game goals

A gamified system is driven inherently by goals external to its game elements. Non-game goals articulate the purpose of the project. Gamified system goals vary depending upon the nature of the project and organization that is pursuing it. Knowledge or skill acquisition is commonly considered the goal of learning-based systems. *Khan Academy*, the online learning resource, hosts approximately 10 million unique students each month. On its website, the not-for-profit organization describes its goal as "changing education for the better by providing a free world-class education for anyone anywhere." While videos narrated by its friendly founder Salman Khan provide the foundation for *Khan Academy*'s success, it is the game components that were added to the system starting in 2010 that provide valuable feedback and assessment. Both of these (feedback and assessment) are cornerstones of the organization's product roadmap. Without game concepts, these goals could neither be measured nor met. However, these goals had to be identified first before the game layer was added.

Quickly, the game components became essential for evaluating and responding to an individual performing an activity. *Khan Academy* members can accrue energy points and earn galactic-themed badges as they participate in the courses, viewing video lessons and answering questions about subjects ranging from biology to art history. Students receive numerous visual cues that track their activity and indicate their progress towards short-term and long-term learning goals. In the same way that a role-playing game (RPG) details character progress with an RPG skill tree, *Khan Academy* provides a visual map to users that highlights the set of skills required to master subjects, and the progress that the user is making towards

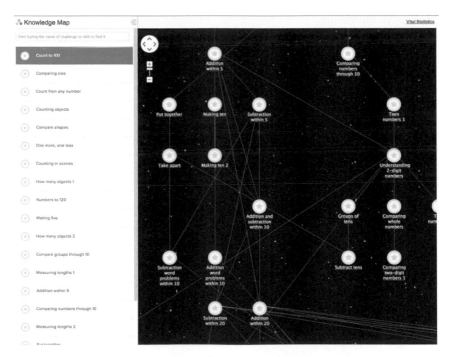

Figure 2.6 *Khan Academy* provides a visual map, highlighting progress towards the mastery of skills on a learning path. Courtesy of Khan Academy.

this mastery. This provides the student with a quick picture about the areas that she is succeeding in and those where she needs more support.

Khan Academy is designed for long-term engagement, creating and extending a knowledge path. A user may start the program studying fractions in fifth grade and stay through to learn calculus in high school. He may at the same time contribute the knowledge he has gained to help others who are learning the skills he has already mastered. Providing a rich, measureable and on-going system of rewards and incentives for users, and a comprehensive picture of their learning progress, enables a long-term relationship with the student with deep and varied engagement. In this sense, the game elements also support another objective of the organization, which is to grow activity and sustain engagement within the community. By growing this devoted community Khan Academy was able to break from an advertising revenue model in 2010 and fully embrace not-for-profit status.

GS design principle #5—long-term engagement

By providing a rich, measureable and on-going system of rewards and incentives for users, and a comprehensive picture of their progress, GS design enables long-term relationships promoting deep and varied engagement.

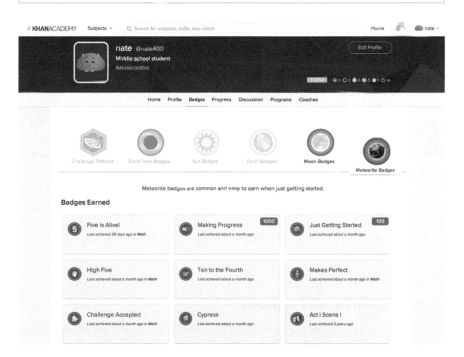

Figure 2.7 *Khan Academy* rewards users with points as they watch videos. Profiles display avatars, badges and real-time statistics. Courtesy of Khan Academy.

The important measurements here are **key performance indicators** (KPI). Defined in tandem with goals, KPIs always relate to measureable behavior of an audience, and are used to determine success relative to goals. For example, an organization might set a goal for the number of times a week a user will interact with the system. Targeted behaviors and attitudes should also be defined. Through its gamified elements, Khan Academy collects a huge amount of data about its user base. As a result, it can not only measure the frequency of usage of the areas within the site but also far more subtly measure the effectiveness of its entire curriculum for particular individual users and aggregate categories.

Key Performance Indicators

Key Performance Indicators (KPIs) measure behavior of an audience to evaluate the success of a particular program or initiative. Some examples of KPIs include:

* The number of **Daily Active Users** (DAU).
* **Monthly Active Users** (MAU).
* **Average Revenue Per User** (ARPU). This metric takes the total revenue generated for the month and divides it by the number of monthly active users (monthly revenue/MAU).
* **Stickiness** (DAU/MAU). This measurement looks at how often people are returning to the site by dividing the number of daily active users by the number of monthly active users.

The goals articulated at the beginning of a project and then later refined over time will ultimately drive and define the direction and development of a gamified system. These goals, external to the game itself, shape all the choices made about the structure, components and technical implementation of the entire project. At the same time, they cannot be effectively measured with such granularity or met with such sustained usage without the inclusion of game elements.

GS design principle #6—external goals drive design

GS designs distinguish themselves by being driven and shaped by non-game goals.

Game concepts and components

Encouraging the spirit of play, gamified systems are at some level simply games. Designers need to pay particular attention to classic aspects of game design, the rules of play defined by Caillois and others. Game concepts add much more to a system than fun, surprise and challenge. They provide structure, direction and timely feedback, and they encourage and reward behaviors that correspond to external goals. Ultimately, game concepts provide the essential bridge to the real world.

A good example of this is a game that is strongly tied with traditional Dungeons and Dragons-like (D&D) RPGs. *HabitRPG* is a game, which although visually inspired by RPGs is actually a tracking application for motivating users to practice desirable habits on a daily basis. Users go through the typical D&D starting motions of creating a custom character and at the same time creating a set of habits and to-do lists that they would like to accomplish. They can also define personal rewards that they can grant to themselves when they have reached a particular goal.

As *HabitRPG* users complete tasks, they check these off, immediately gaining experience points. Elements like points quickly reward users and provide real-time feedback about progression, facilitating what is known as onboarding. **Onboarding** is a concept derived from human resource professionals, which emphasizes the quick acclimation of a new employee to a work environment. The same idea applies to users or players of interactive and game-based systems. Khan Academy uses energy points in a similar manner. These are granted the moment a member begins watching a video. This proven and fundamental mechanism brings in a layer of play during the pursuit of serious objectives. Other methods for welcoming new users include invitations, rewards, gifts and showing initial progress on a progress bar.

Onboarding

Onboarding is an idea that comes from human resources professionals. It relates to the process of acclimating a new employee to the practices, ideologies and people in the work environment. The idea is considered applicable to the process of easing new players into game or interactive systems.

Once a person is initiated in to a game either through an elaborate process like character building or even a very simple process like choosing a token or color, a gamified system should offer moments for the user to develop an emergent personal experience from this basis. Recognizing and rewarding progression is an excellent means to accomplish this. By regularly logging in to the system, and checking off completed goals, *HabitRPG* users can level up their character, and increase their strength and defense. Leveling systems, like those found in massively multiplayer online role-playing games (MMORPGs) provide players with public recognition, and a growing and more powerful set of abilities as well as virtual objects like weapons and armor. They can also gain silver and gold, which generates an economy for purchasing items. Particular items like weapons can then increase the rate of experience points granted to the user, generating complex layers of motivations and strategies. By returning to log in and create and record positive behavior, a member is not only encouraged to continue with the system and her good habits, but also to do so over time knowing that there will be more surprises, rewards and indeed new strategies for success to come.

This emergence of shifting strategies over time is essential. As a user becomes more committed to a system, he is likely to develop a personal narrative about and connection with the challenges he has overcome and the different ways in which this was achieved. In the case of *HabitRPG*, this process might lead to a deeper relationship to his character and the new habits he has mastered through its development. With this particular instance, such a narrative of difference is precisely the opposite of the repetition usually associated with habit. In other words, the system makes habits fun. As the user continues to engage he must have opportunities to not only prove his mastery but also to have a sense of ownership and status, demonstrating his commitment to the community. This too changes the negative associations of the word habit, which can often seem private, repetitive and asocial, in other words boring. Providing forums, taverns and parties members in the *HabitRPG* community can encourage each other and play together. By actively participating in the community a user can retain and enhance his level of interaction.

Although most gamified systems today use points, badges and leaderboards (PBLs), there is actually a large toolset for designers to choose from. Mechanisms for ranking are just a small handful of the potential game components that are available to the GS designer. Pick-ups, side quests and missions are just a few of the numerous design patterns available for consideration. Exploring the expanding space of possibilities for growing this practice is covered in Chapter 6 of this book. These ideas should be considered when looking for the most appropriate and inspiring game elements to match your project goals.

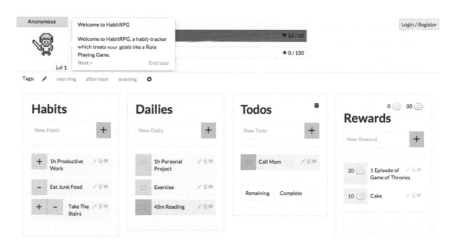

Figure 2.8 *HabitRPG* lets users track habits and daily activities, and rewards them like a game. Courtesy of HabitRPG.

> GS design principle #7—game components as a point of translation
>
>
>
> Game elements can create a conversation between the real world and the game world. Game elements should encourage targeted behavior, integrating and generating data to support project goals.

The role of data

> If I had all the data and all of that stuff back when I played football, the 1500 catches that I had, over 20,000 yards, 208 touchdowns, I think I probably would have just doubled everything.
>
> —Jerry Rice, NFL Hall of Famer on *Fantasy Football*

Data is information. It can be collected, compared and combined in numerous ways and then used for analysis and learning. Goals help determine how a gamified system incorporates and processes data. These decisions in turn influence the subsequent development of that system. One of the best examples of this process is the game of *Fantasy Football*. *Fantasy Football* was first developed in 1962 as a way for a limited partner in the Oakland Raiders, a public relations manager, a barkeeper and a reporter to play around with ideas about how good football teams come together. Bill Winkenbach had already created similar games for golf and baseball, but the goals of *Fantasy Football* or the Greater Oakland Professional Pigskin Prognosticators League (GOPPPL) were much more precise and as the name suggests had to do with data. The charter explicitly wanted "to increase closer coverage of daily happenings in professional football." Baseball already had a long-standing and effective tradition of card collecting and statistics. For the GOPPPL it was about pitting "brains (and cash)" against each other, but in a larger sense the competition was intended to create a strong relationship between the team, the local bars and the *Oakland Tribune*. This came just in time for the arrival of televised professional football in the 1960s, and all that data gave fans things to talk about in the bars and around breakfast tables and in living rooms.

It was the commercialization of the Internet that took such local clubs into the next stage of development. Again it was about providing better data for media coverage and building audiences, when CBS *SportsLine* in 1997 in tandem with the Internet service provider Prodigy launched *Fantasy Football* and *Baseball* leagues to compete with ESPN's *SportsZone*. The year 1997 became a transitional one for the Internet, not only because of technological developments but also because new kinds of audiences like sports fans were being built. The virtual game was key to making a television audience into an Internet audience, while at the same time transforming the numbers and types of people engaged with the physical game. Today, *Fantasy Football* leverages and feeds the enthusiasm of over 25 million football fans each football season. This gamified system is designed to keep professional sports fans engaged on a minute-to-minute basis throughout the season. Players role-play as managers of imaginary teams they construct. Playing in competitive leagues, they gain points from the statistics about real football players collected before, during and after a game.

The complexity and type of data that is being collected about each player and compared with others is why *Fantasy Football* is considered an exemplary application for data science. Fans have access to advanced toolsets that provide them with forecasts of performance based on a large collection of data, from play history (passes, goals and tackles) to injuries. A fan can even get an analysis of how a player will do in relation to the weather, time of day, travel schedules and team composition.

Although *Fantasy Football* is primarily about keeping fans deeply engaged, the data that is generated can profoundly affect the future of professional sports. From

Figure 2.9 Screenshot of Yahoo's *Fantasy Football* game showing player and team data.

college recruiting to game day, the visualization tools available can help coaches make better and more informed decisions about the make-up, strategies and tactics of a team.

The collection, comparison and analysis of data have become a cornerstone of 21st century existence. Gamified systems offer some of the best ways for putting data to work to meet goals and objectives. By tracking, analyzing and comparing, they can provide timely rewards, and enhanced and relevant social opportunities. Data analytics provide information for rapid feedback, enabling designers and project stakeholders with the opportunity to quickly respond to the changing dynamics of users and communities participating in the system.

GS design principle #8—data is fundamental

Gamified systems put data to work. The integration, collection and analysis of data are essential to GS design.

Emergent opportunities

> Melody, Susan and I all bought Nike FuelBands. We liked the idea of setting a goal to get us moving around, seeing how many steps we took and we liked to have a little competition going. Each night we would sync our band to our iPhones and see how the others were doing. Each week, the one who earned the most points would win a rotating trophy that I bought at a yard sale. I'd made and attached a plate that said "Nike Rock Star." Susan had an occupational advantage as she is a dog walker, so Melody was really the one I wanted to beat. One night, I'd talked to the girls about how I was going dancing with Gary and I was going to run up a big score. They said they would be at home watching a movie. I was gloating knowing that I would have the most points before the end of the night. After burning up the dance floor for nearly an hour, I noticed that the girls' points were going up as quickly as mine. I was so curious I decided to call them. They told me that they didn't want me to be the only one getting ahead, so they decided to forego the movie and play Wii tennis. Can you believe it? I told Gary "we can't stop dancing until I get more points!" Really, just having a goal, a little fun competition and someone else seeing how I was doing really spurred me to move more.
>
> —Carmella, 55, talks about her experience
> with the Nike+ FuelBand

Emergence (introduced in Chapter 1) occurs when players have freedom to take elements they discover through play and combine them in unexpected ways. This combination may lead to new and even more comprehensive structures, such as the meta-games described at the beginning of Chapter 1 about the Junior Ranger Program.

Personalization develops and on-going interest gets sustained through the process of emergence. This experience changes the nature of engagement, enabling mental space for reflection. The challenges, surprises and opportunities to play with and against others all make for memorable and repeatable storytelling. Gamified systems as a result tend to require less pre-defined or scripted narrative than games. For example, gamified fitness systems maximize this potential for reflection by leveraging the spirit of competition and camaraderie associated with sports. The Nike+ FuelBand is a sports watch that also tracks a person's daily activity, including steps and calories burned. Users can sync the band with the Nike+ FuelBand app, which provides encouraging feedback and support as the user tries to reach his fitness goal. While this is happening, friends who are also using the system can see his status updates. Real-time data-sharing makes for real-time tension. FuelBand friends can create an elaborate story worth re-telling about competing to see who can achieve their goals first. Bringing others in to encourage achievement or create obstacles all contributes to a rich and unique narrative. Participating in challenges, receiving rewards, experiencing unexpected or unforeseen events and doing so with or alongside others are the essential ingredients of emergence in gamified systems.

GS design principle #9—reflection through emergence

Challenges, surprises and opportunities to play with and against others can generate emergent behaviors, making for memorable and repeatable tales about the experience.

Pervasiveness maximizes the potential of gamified systems

Of the five concepts related to gamified systems the one that differentiates them most sharply from the traditional game spectrum of play and games is pervasiveness. Pervasiveness is about permeating or spreading the fictional worlds of game- or play-based experiences throughout everyday life. It leverages as many mechanisms as possible to affect different aspects of an individual's work and play so that the line between game and non-game becomes more important than the distinction between play and games. Gamified systems expand into an individual's life:

• Temporally.
• Spatially.
• Socially.
• Across different media.

Although these concepts are presented separately, they are in fact strongly integrated, with one affecting the other. Leveraging pervasive elements is why gamified systems remain relevant and present in our lives.

GS design principle #10—relevance through pervasiveness

Gamified systems expand into the real world temporally, spatially, socially and across different forms of media.

1. Pervasiveness > temporality

Most gamified systems maximize their usage by requiring brief moments of interaction. This is similar to what is referred to as a play session in games. A **play session** is a single continuous unit of time a player plays a game. It might be an hour devoted to playing backgammon with a friend until one player wins, or three hours playing *Guild Wars 2* with members of a guild. This session may end when an objective like a quest or raid has been completed or more abruptly, as when the player has to log off the system and attend to some other aspect of her life, like work, food or sleep. A play session could be as short as the time it takes to receive a challenge in *Words with Friends*, create a word, and send back a new challenge to the original sender. In some circumstances, like the backgammon example, the play session is synonymous with a game session, which is the entire experience of playing the game from beginning to end. As with games, gamified system sessions can vary in length of time but have a tendency to be more pervasive. Plotting a GPS location, taking a picture or entering the amount of time a player exercised takes significantly less time than participating in a lesson-plan or solving a puzzle. Because of their complexity, the latter examples generally require an uninterrupted commitment of time for a meaningful play session.

Play session

A single continuous unit of time a player plays a game. This could take ten minutes or three hours. The activity is usually marked by logging in to a session and logging out at the end.

In order to facilitate frequent moments of interaction, gamified systems as well as Facebook games like *Farmville* use what are referred to as **appointment dynamics**, requiring the player to return regularly in order to maintain his resources. Appointment dynamics utilize specific mechanics in a game system to motivate the player to return at or before a set interval of time. If a player does not return before a prescribed time, his collected resources may be diminished.

Although some gamified systems, particularly live games, rely on real-time interaction between players, many are asynchronous, meaning that users do not have to coordinate their actions in real time in order to participate. Asynchrony enables people to interact with a system on their own time, responding to the

Appointment dynamics

Appointment dynamics are generated through specific mechanics that require players to return to a game regularly in order to protect their in-game resources.

If you choose to use appointment dynamics in your design be sensitive to the addictive habits that can emerge. What gets players excited initially may end up turning them away over time.

inputs of other users or players when they can. Persistent games, like the MMORPG *World of Warcraft* (WOW) and the social networking game *Farmville*, encourage players to return frequently to see in what ways the game environment has changed.

Persistent games tend to not have a finite ending. Consequently, a **game session** could continue in perpetuity. Fitness systems, like Nike's Nike+ FuelBand, designed to promote an on-going healthy lifestyle, are meant for extended play over an undetermined amount of time. In theory, a person can use the system for the entirety of her life.

Other gamified systems are structured along the completion of specific tasks or missions, so that when a player or user has put in enough time to complete all of the activities the game session is complete. These types of gamified systems are finite in nature, and share similarities to ends or win-conditions found at the successful completion of a game. Adobe's *LevelUp* is an example of a finite gamified system. The Photoshop plug-in includes twelve sequential missions that introduce and assess important skills, tools and tasks associated with the software. Users prove their knowledge by completing projects that correspond to the different missions. Once a mission is completed, the user is rewarded and can move on. After completing the twelfth mission, he is finished with the program and has theoretically "won" by mastering all of the skills measured by the program.

The amount of time a user interacts with a system is considered a fundamental component of engagement, which is particularly important for companies using GS design to build relationships with customers. Users that interact regularly with

Game session

The length of time that a game takes from putting it into play and finishing to the final win-condition or end. Some game sessions correspond to play sessions while others because they have no clear end or win-condition are meant to continue in perpetuity.

Figure 2.10 Adobe's *LevelUp* plugin for Photoshop helps users learn specific tools and tasks.

a system are considered active participants, and often drive many of the design decisions on an on-going basis. Interacting regularly with a system over a long period of time is considered a measurement of customer loyalty, which also drives long-term decisions about the gamified system and the company.

2. Pervasiveness > spatiality

Play is often connected with space—whether the football field, the theater or the card table—but, as we have seen throughout this chapter, the boundary lines have blurred, literally so in the case of the spatial component of games. By finding creative ways to utilize physical space and movement within it, gamified systems can meaningfully expand the relationships of users and user communities to their surrounding environment. For example, the award-winning *Decoded* marketing campaign created for the release of the autobiography of the same name by the musician Jay-Z re-imagined the scavenger hunt. The game hid all of the 320 pages of the book throughout thirteen cities, and the fan who could locate the most pages would have the opportunity to win free tickets to Jay-Z concerts for life. Building off of the celebrity image of the rap star and music producer, the gestures of the game were grand. Most of the book page images were blown up to fill rooftops, subway station walls and even the bottom of a hotel swimming pool. Some of them were brilliantly hidden on less obvious surfaces like restaurant plates, inside a jukebox and on the exterior foil of a hamburger wrapper. The mix of locations from the basketball court to the hotel lobby was an inclusive gesture to the wide audience of Jay-Z fans. Because they are so motivated by the star and his vision, *Decoded* connected fans to locations and spaces in whole new ways. What was once just a billiard table in a bar transforms into a conceptual art piece in a new kind of gallery. At the same time, this space becomes a part of a much larger work. The idea of the game turns what could have been another

Figure 2.11 The *Decoded* scavenger hunt created for the release of Jay-Z's
autobiography took pages from the book and incorporated them into a
wide range of surprising surfaces. Courtesy of Droga5.

forgettable glitzy marketing campaign into a rich, thoughtful and shared exploration of an artist and his vision of the world.

Gamified systems are excellent vehicles for enriching the momentary experience of a space. Using mobile device features like GPS plotting and picture taking,
they can encourage users to dig into the stories and learning that the space offers.
Geography, natural and cultural history and contemporary life can all be experienced. Games like Google's *Ingress* create parallel worlds using a phone application,

but similarly offer real-world exploration, planned and unplanned meet-ups and of course new kinds of data for the company.

Expanding into space is also one of the best ways to get users to break themselves from what is referred to as the cocooning effect of technology. Technology separates and distances human beings from the world around them, creating a cocoon that prevents social interaction. Gamified systems leverage location to build relationships between individuals, communities and the physical world, facilitating a greater sense of the surrounding world and its opportunities for exploration and play.

3. Pervasiveness > social expansion

The success of a GS design project more often than not hinges on its ability to leverage personal and extended social networks. Building in motivations for users to encourage their friends, acquaintances and colleagues to participate drives new users to interact with a system for the first time, and to continue to do so over an extended period. One way gamified systems do this is by leveraging the invitation and peer-to-peer marketing opportunities available on social networking platforms. Any time a user can send a gift to someone else's Facebook in-box, she is reaching out to another person who can expand the experience of play. Leaderboards provide real-time updates of scores and accomplishments achieved by users, their friends and active community members. Notifications like the updates about friends' locations in Foursquare do the same thing. Although interaction can be a solo experience, these functions are an effective means of creating the feeling of playing with others.

Of course, social expansion extends far beyond leaderboards and e-mail reminders. It provides important and even critical opportunities to build, foster and leverage relationships and communities that are then associated with the system itself. This is exactly what the British newspaper the Guardian did in 2009. While it was running its investigation about the illegal expenditures by British Members of Parliament, the paper was handed approximately 460,000 documents that they were allowed to review for reporting purposes. To tackle the challenge, they enlisted thousands of volunteers to read, process, analyze these documents and report their findings. They used game elements that included top weekly finds and status of documents reviewed. Within the first eighty hours of deployment over 170,000 documents had been reviewed. Gamified systems like the Guardian's Investigate Your MP's Expenses promote crowd sourcing to accomplish very large-scale tasks. Crowd sourcing is a method for collecting information, resources or contributions from a very large group of people, but it is also a method for building a devoted and knowledgeable audience for an institution like a newspaper. In the case of the Guardian, which has successfully turned a national newspaper into a global one, crowd sourcing made it possible for the newspaper to sort through hundreds of thousands of documents and to convey the message to its global audience of readers that it values that kind of research in its reporting more generally. It is an incredibly innovative way to leverage

GS design principle #11—accomplish insurmountable tasks

Gamified systems can encourage and support crowd-sourced activities, enabling and directing the completion of large-scale tasks.

Investigate your MP's expenses

Join us in digging through the 700,000 documents of MPs' expenses to identify individual claims, or documents that you think merit further investigation. You can work through your own MP's expenses, or just hit the button below to start reviewing. Already created an account? Log in here.

We have **458,832** pages of documents. **27,093** of you have reviewed **221,538** of them. Only **237,294** to go...

Start reviewing   Please read our privacy policy to find out how we use your data. You must also read our terms of service. By reviewing pages, you are agreeing that you have read the terms of service, and that you agree to them.

Figure 2.12 Screen shot from the home page of the *Guardian*'s crowd-sourced gamified system *Investigate Your MP's Expenses*. Copyright Guardian News & Media Ltd 2009.

social networks and online communities to solve what might have once seemed impossible and at the same time to transform old institutions into dynamic 21st-century entities.

3. Pervasiveness ➢ media and devices

> Environments are not just containers, but are processes that change the content totally.
> —Marshall McLuhan, "Address at Vision 65," October 23, 1965

Transmedia leverages a variety of formats and platforms to build an experience or narrative. It is most prevalent in alternate reality games (ARGs). These games, which are explored in more detail in Chapter 6, combine material and digital content from a wide range of sources including phone messages, online content, printed material and live interactions with performers. Creating a dynamic collage of unexpected elements these games penetrate a player's life in new and surprising ways. GS design does not limit itself to any one device or media form. Through the appropriate mix of media and devices the user experience is maximized.

Transmedia

The use of multiple forms of media and technologies to develop and perpetuate a story or fictional world.

Although digital technology is commonly associated with gamified systems, the complexity of technical implementations is not always essential. In some cases, paper-based options can be just as effective for accomplishing certain goals. For instance, a trump card game based on exhibitions from the educational organization *1001 Inventions* uses a simple battle system to teach players about the concepts and objects introduced in the exhibitions. Educational productions created by *1001 Inventions* introduce audiences to important contributions made to technology, science and culture by the Muslim civilization dating back to the 7th century.

Because the game is delivered through a pack of cards not only is it affordable, but it is also extremely portable, requiring no additional set-up or infrastructure. It can be played in a classroom or car, and allows people to take time thinking about and establishing relationships between the individual pieces in the exhibitions, which paradoxically might have been difficult in the physical space of the museum itself. It also helps achieve the goal of the exhibitions, to put people on the path of learning about a subject outside of the museum space, while at the same time reminding people about their experience in the museum itself.

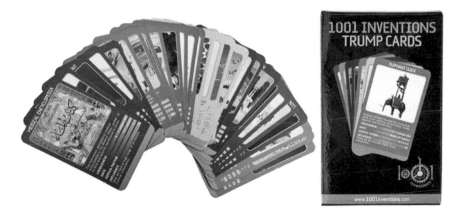

Figure 2.13 *1001 Inventions* card game. Used by permission of 1001 Inventions, www.1001inventions.com.

KEY TAKEAWAYS

- Games and gamified systems share many commonalities. However, unlike a game, a gamified system is likely to take place in ordinary life, be defined according to articulated goals outside of the game experience, and rely on external data to accomplish non-game-related objectives.
- The spectrum of gamified systems is a way of defining categories that fall between non-game experiences and games designed for entertainment only. Within this spectrum fall systems that are game-like, are part of a game layer or are Alternate Purpose Games (APGs).
- Gamified systems have identifiable characteristics, which include:
  - *External goals*—the out-of-game context goals driving the project.
  - *Game concepts and components*—elements that are associated with games.
  - *The role of data for out-of-game contexts*—how data is used beyond the game.
  - *Emergent opportunities*—the fiction associated with the game experience.
  - *Pervasiveness*—The various ways the system pervades our real lives.

EXERCISES

2.1 The spectrum

Look at any gamified system and identify where it exists on the gamified system spectrum. In what ways does the structure of the system and the messaging about it tell you if it is more or less like a game?

2.2 GS characteristics

Research and play a gamified system and identify the characteristics of a gamified system.

- What do you think the goals are of the project members?
- In what ways is the system using game concepts?
- What data is the project collecting? How do you think the data is being utilized?
- In what ways is the system pervasive? Identify the ways it is expanding: temporally, spatially, socially and through different forms of media.
- In what ways is the system encouraging an emergent experience? Is there an implied narrative or other devices that promote a fictive experience? Is there a way for users to share or build off of this?

RECOMMENDED READINGS

- *Rules of Play: Game Design Fundamentals* by Katie Salen and Eric Zimmerman, 2003. Salen and Zimmerman's book is a comprehensive and significant text about game design. Though challenging, this book is an important resource for anyone serious about games.

- *Man, Play and Games* (*Les jeux et les hommes*) by Roger Caillois, 2001 (reprint). Building off of Huizinga's *Homo Ludens*, Caillois articulates and defines a set of play forms.

- *serious.gameclassification.com* is an online database that classifies APGs, commonly referred to as serious games.

INSIDER INSIGHT

KEN EKLUND IS REDEFINING HOW GAMES CHANGE OUR WORLD

Interview granted with permission by Ken Eklund.

Game and experience designer Ken Eklund creates Alternate Reality Games that explore real-world issues through collaborative play. Eklund is known for creating the award-winning *World Without Oil*, the groundbreaking collective imagining of our next oil shock, and *Giskin Anomaly*, the cellphone adventure for museums in Balboa Park. He was the Community Lead for *Evoke*, an innovative social entrepreneurship initiative created by Jane McGonigal and funded by the World Bank Initiative. The game won the Games for Change Direct Impact Award in 2011. Eklund has made games professionally since 1988. His current project is *FutureCoast*, a game exploring climate-changed futures, for the PoLAR Partnership at Columbia University.

Figure 2.14
Ken Eklund. Ken creates "immersive stories that want to write themselves."

Can you tell me about how you developed the idea for World Without Oil?

At the time (in 2005) a few landmark Alternate Reality Games had just happened. People saw that at times these marketing ARGs had something very interesting and new going on, especially as powerful and diverse communities self-organized around a common purpose. People wondered, "When is someone going to create a game that addresses a real-life issue?"

Solving that challenge involved letting go of most of the prescripts that had arisen around Alternate Reality Games at that point. To oversimplify perhaps, you can no longer reward players with fragments of a rich story, if only because the budget for a game for good is a fraction of a marketing game. My innovation was to view this as the perfect opportunity to let go of the central conceit of the gamemaster as storyteller, and to pursue instead a new role for the gamemaster as storyframer.

What were your goals with the project?

ITVS, a media non-profit in San Francisco, awarded me the commission for *World Without Oil*; the money ultimately came from the Corporation for Public Broadcasting. So ITVS was my "client" and their goals were my goals for *World Without Oil*.

Simply put, ITVS seeks to publish the stories that you never see on mainstream media—the stories of the rest of us, I suppose you could say. So our goal with *World Without Oil* was to create a kind of "story attraction engine"—a game that would get a wide range of people to talk about their lives.

How do you think the game achieved the goals you set out to accomplish? (What did it demonstrate once up and running?)

One of our reviewers called *World Without Oil* "the most efficient story generation engine heretofore devised." The outpouring and participation were amazing during the game's one-month run.

What were some of the big surprises during and after the event?

It may seem curious, but *World Without Oil* wasn't really about oil. In my original formulation, petroleum was a narrative device, something that we all have our individual relationships with. I was looking to be a storyframer, and "what if an oil crisis started?" was an excellent frame for a story that we all could play in.

The main surprise, then, was the extent to which our players honestly engaged with questions about their relationship to petroleum energy. We noticed it immediately upon game start, and at game's end we had players writing to tell us how their lives had changed. The player engagement was deep for many players, really deep for some. One player summed up why very simply: "It was real to me," she said. I have been pursuing the game ideas set off by *World Without Oil* ever since.

You had a lead role working with Jane McGonigal on Evoke, the game funded by the World Bank Institute. Can you describe the goals of that project? Can you describe the unique aspects of the process?

Briefly, *Evoke* put a story frame on lessons relevant to learning social entrepreneurship, and created a social media platform for collaborative learning. It was a cleverly formulated blend of adventure story, academic tasks, game rewards and social media interactions, and it attracted a large global following.

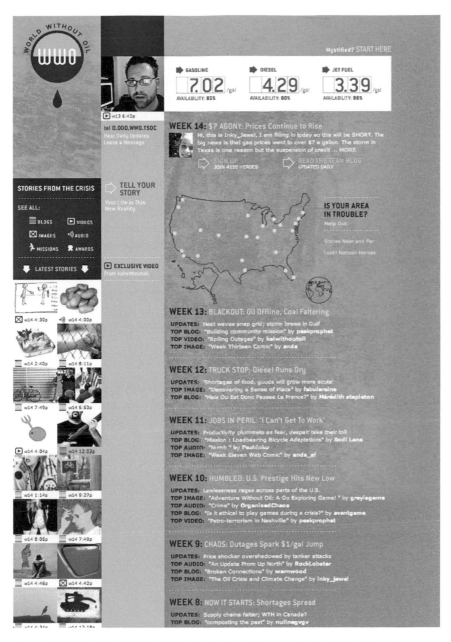

Figure 2.15 The *World Without Oil* website. Used by permission of Ken Eklund.

You clearly have a passion for ARGs. Why is this form so compelling? What does it enable that other game platforms do not?

Other game platforms have boundaries as a central element. The action takes place in a virtual world, for example, or on a prescribed court. Your interactions with other people in the game are usually defined by strict boundaries as well: you can't verbally negotiate your way to a base hit in baseball, for example, and the limitations of your interactions with other characters in videogames is a constant disappointment to many people.

Alternate Reality Games, however, don't have boundaries as a central element—quite the reverse: they are defined by their lack of boundaries. The game overlays your real life and augments it: in *FutureCoast* for example, your life goes on just the same EXCEPT that you can now take a break now and then to listen to the latest new voicemail from the future. And if you write to one of the Coasters an actual person writes you back. ARGs can be these very open and creative experiences for players, as evidenced by the number of times the players outcreate the gamemasters!

If a designer had never designed an ARG before, what advice would you give them before they get started?

Respect your players. It's their game, not yours (this is so easy to say and so hard to actually do).

Can you tell me about your current project?

By the time you read this, a truly astonishing event will have come and gone, largely unremarked. The software system of the future has sprung a space-time

Figure 2.16 The FutureCoast.org website during the 2014 event.

leak. But since it's only in the voicemail part, it takes them decades to get around to fixing it. Meanwhile, we get to listen to the messages that people leave for each other in the years 2020 to 2065—by turns banal, mysterious and terrifying.

The voicemails materialize as chronofacts—artifacts of time—appearing on earth in waves. The fourth wave of chronofalls began on February 5, 2014, and ended on April 30. People successfully located chronofacts all over the USA and in a few other countries. The good news is, in the end hundreds of chronofacts were found and decoded, and you can listen to these voicemails from the future at FutureCoast.org.

FutureCoast is a playful yet serious collaborative storytelling project about possibly climate-changed futures. At FutureCoast.org, people listened to these voicemails and speculated about the futures they must come from. At FutureVoices.net, people took on the creative challenge of recording the voicemails that truly seem to have leaked from our possible futures. FutureCoast is a member of the PoLAR Partnership at Columbia University's Earth Institute, operating with a grant for climate change education from the National Science Foundation. It's the world's first exercise in "participatory cli-fi," nominated for a Webby Award as NetArt.

NOTES

Björk, Staffan and Jussi Holopainen. *Patterns in Game Design*. Boston: Charles River Media, 2005.

Bogost, Ian. *Persuasive Games: The Expressive Power of Video Games*. Boston: MIT Press, 2007.

Caillois, Roger. *Man, Play and Games*. Champaign: University of Illinois Press, 2001. [Note: The original version of this book *Les jeux et les hommes* was written in 1958 and translated into English in 1961.]

Coren, Michael J. "Foldit Gamers Solve Riddle of HIV Enzyme Within 3 Weeks." *Scientific America*, September 20, 2011, www.scientificamerica.com/articles/foldit-gamers-solve-riddle.

Costikyan, Greg. "I Have No Words & I Must Design: Toward a Critical Vocabulary for Games." Keynote given at Computer Games and Digital Cultures Conference, Tampere University, 2002.

Crawford, Chris. *The Art of Computer Game Design*. Berkeley, CA: Osborne/McGraw-Hill, 1984.

Deterding, Sebastian, Dan Dixon, Rilla Khaled and Lennart E. Nacke. "From Game Design Elements to Gamefulness. Defining 'Gamification.'" Paper presented at MindTrek '11, Tampere, September 28–30, 2011.

Deterding, Sebastian, Dan Dixon, Rilla Khaled and Lennart E. Nacke. "Gamification: Towards a Definition." Paper presented at CHI 2011, Vancouver, BC, May 7–12, 2011.

Edery, David and Ethan Mollick. *Changing the Game: How Video Games are Transforming the Future of Business*. Upper Saddle River: FT Press, 2009.

Feldman, Lauren. "The Anti-Science of User Acquisition." *Tapstream*, February, 2014, http://blog.tapstream.com/post/76435651385/the-anti-science-of-user-acquisition.

Fullerton, Tracy, Steven Hoffman and Chris Swain. *Game Design Workshop: Designing, Prototyping, and Playtesting Games*. San Francisco: CMP Books, 2004.

Gray, Tyler. "Inside Jay-Z's Launch of 'Decoded' with Droga5, Bing." *Fast Company*, November 24, 2010, http://www.fastcompany.com/1704745/inside-jay-zs-launch-decoded-droga5-bing.

Hruby, Patrick. "The Founding Fathers of Fantasy." *Sports on Earth*, December 2, 2013, http://www.sportsonearth.com/article/64244480/#!bGSa0e.

Huizinga, Johan. *Homo Ludens: A Study of the Play-Element in Culture*. Boston: Beacon Press, 1971. [Note: The original version of this book was published in 1939 and translated to English in 1955.]

Jenkins, Henry. "Transmedia Storytelling: Moving Characters from Books to Films to Video Games Can Make Them Stronger and More Compelling." *MIT Technology Review*, January 15, 2003, http://www.technologyreview.com/news/401760/transmedia-storytelling/.

Jenkins, Henry. *Convergence Culture: Where Old and New Media Collide*. New York: NYU Press, 2008.

McGonigal, Jane. *Reality is Broken: Why Games Make Us Better and How They Can Change the World*. New York: Penguin Press, 2011.

Montola, Markus, Jaakko Stenros and Annika Waern. *Pervasive Games: Theory and Design*. London: Taylor & Francis, 2009.

Noer, Michael. "One Man, One Computer, 10 Million Students: How Khan Academy is Reinventing Education." *Forbes*, November 2, 2012, http://www.forbes.com/sites/michaelnoer/2012/11/02/one-man-one-computer-10-million-students-how-khan-academy-is-reinventing-education/.

Nudd, Tim. "Droga5 Wins Outdoor Grand Prix for Jay-Z's 'Decoded' Campaign." *Adweek*, June 21, 2011, http://www.adweek.com/cannes-lions-2011/droga5-wins-outdoor-grand-prix-jay-zs-decoded-campaign-132762.

Paharia, Rajat. *Loyalty 3.0: How Big Data and Gamification are Revolutionizing Customer and Employee Engagement*. New York: McGraw-Hill, 2013.

"Poor earning virtual gaming gold." *BBC News*, August 22, 2008, http://news.bbc.co.uk/go/pr/fr/-/2/hi/technology/7575902.stm.

Priebatsch, Seth. "The Game Layer on Top of the World." Presentation at TEDxBoston, Boston, MA, July, 2010.

Salen, Katie and Eric Zimmerman. *Rules of Play: Game Design Fundamentals*. Cambridge: MIT Press, 2004.

Walther, Bo Kampmann. "Atomic Actions—Molecular Experience: Theory of Pervasive Gaming." *Computers in Entertainment (CIE)—Theoretical and Practical Computer Applications in Entertainment*, 3:3 (July 2005): 4.

Note: There were several references to "game-like" experiences including Katie Salen's 2008 design document for Quest to Learn published by MIT Press, and Anna Daniel and Terry Flew's 2010 case study "The Guardian Reportage of the UK MP Expenses" submitted for publication to Communications Policy and Research Forum, Sydney.

Note: The idea for naming a category on the spectrum as an "Alternate Purpose Game" was derived from Ian Bogost's 2013 Games for Change talk and the article and comments that followed by Leigh Alexander on *Gamasutra*. Leigh Alexander. "Ian Bogost: Let's Make 'Earnest' Games, not 'Serious Games'." June 17, 2013, http://www.gamasutra.com/view/news/194490/Bogost_Lets_make_earnest_games_not_serious_games.php.

3 POSITIVE PERFORMANCE

INTRODUCTION

Games promote activity. When they are good, they can consume a large chunk of time and attention. Players will log in to a game regularly, often daily, for hours at time. Recently a man invested over 2,000 hours just to beat the puzzle game *Bejeweled* 2. One of the best-known examples of such a phenomenon is the devoted player community of *World of Warcraft* (WOW), which has built a loyal base of nearly 8 million players since its launch over a decade ago. Massively multiplayer online role-playing games (MMORPGs) like WOW work because they maximize the human capacity to think and care about individual and group-based activities. This chapter explores how games and gamified systems are able to engender such feelings and how that in turn promotes performance and a sense of greater meaning.

A FLOURISHING LIFE

One of the essential goals of GS design is to use game mechanisms as a way of engendering happiness. Good games and gamified systems amplify our strengths while providing opportunities to overcome weaknesses without the fear of external judgment or negative consequences. If we are content with our past, hopeful about the future, and feeling active in the present we are likely to have a positive outlook. Martin Seligman's framework for measuring personal fulfillment has sparked interest by game designers like Amy Jo Kim, who has described how Seligman's ideas offer a clear set of categories for refining and focusing design. The acronym PERMA, which will be explored in more detail in this chapter, is short for: Positive emotion, Engagement, Relationships, Meaning and Achievement.

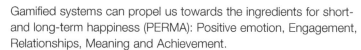

GS design principle #12—propel towards PERMA

Gamified systems can propel us towards the ingredients for short- and long-term happiness (PERMA): Positive emotion, Engagement, Relationships, Meaning and Achievement.

POSITIVE EMOTIONS

> Once you have experienced a system that is finely tuned to your emotions, you're not going to want to go back.
>
> —Nicole Lazarro, game designer and creator of the "4 Keys 2 Fun"

In many contexts the awareness or acknowledgement of the role that emotion or affect plays in every moment of our life is often downplayed or dismissed as fuzzy concepts, feelings or moods. Emotions are actually a result of an awareness of change occurring in the stimuli that surround us. It is the impact on our emotional state that determines what behaviors and activities we pursue, and the way in which we pursue them. In many cases positive affect is hard to link to one particular point of origin—we cannot be sure if we are happy because of the sunlight on our cheek, the music playing in the background, or the memory of some encouraging words from a friend the day before. But games tend to focus and organize our emotions around particular goals. The creativity inspired when we can customize our avatar, the sense of frustration we feel when we can not solve the puzzle before the clock runs out, the sense of power we feel when beating the final boss, these are feelings that gives us the momentum to achieve and continue to perform.

Through most of the 20th century, researchers were primarily interested in the study of negative emotions, the problem of being stuck within a feeling or mood, and the effects of conditions like depression or anxiety on those who suffered from them. This interest was directly related to the number of individuals suffering from the effects of wars and genocide during the same period. So it's not surprising that gamified systems are being utilized today to deal with post-traumatic stress and reintegration of military personal into civilian life. *Reinventing Michael Banks* and *Leading the Way* are both game-like systems designed to help employers, HR professionals and returning military personnel enact scenarios in the workplace to support assimilation. In addition to these projects, there's a growing interest in virtual reality technologies like Oculus Rift (2012) as a way

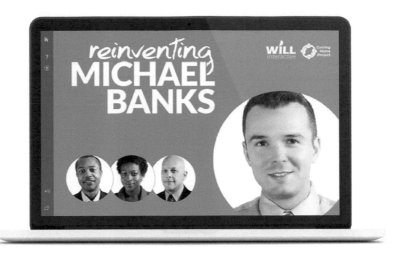

Figure 3.1 *Reinventing Michael Banks* supports the reintegration of US military members back into civilian life.

of treating post traumatic stress disorder in a fully immersive environment. In fact, a Virtual Reality Exposure therapy project led by the University of Southern California's Institute for Creative Technologies (ICT) has been implemented in over sixty sites like VA hospitals and military bases, and has shown that these therapies can dramatically reduce PTS symptoms.

Gamified systems allow for the safe exploration of a range of emotional states. Positive emotions are generally associated with the fleeting state of pleasure. And although these moments of joy come and go somewhat unpredictably they share an important relationship to the feeling of equilibrium in our lives. This balance occurs internally when our needs are met and our potential for pain is reduced. Gamified systems are both about encouraging positive emotional states and maintaining a sense of balance. They are integrated into the process of work and everyday life rather than simply "serious," "virtual" or "entertaining" interventions that take us out of the everyday. They are not about escapism, they are about engagement.

But the enjoyment of games almost always also involves a positive kind of destabilization. More precisely, they can shift our sense of balance in emotionally productive ways, "taking things to a new level" as it were. Games and play tend to be emotionally safe spaces to take leaps of faith, and we call this enjoyment.

GS design principle #13—intervention in the everyday

Through integration into the process of work and everyday life rather than simply "serious," "virtual" or "entertaining," gamified systems provide interventions that positively bridge us to the everyday.

Whether it's bungee jumping or killing zombies, by doing and achieving new things that seem beyond our current limits we stretch our ideas about ourselves. As a result of this experience of growth, we achieve a deeper and new sense of happiness that goes beyond some of the pleasurable repetitions of the everyday. Most games go back and forth between repetitive pleasure and enjoyable growth. The most obvious example of this is the level structure of many games, allowing a player to experience compounded joy each time he levels up.

> Mild positive affect, of the sort that most people can experience every day, improves creative problem solving, facilitates recall, and changes strategies used in decision making tasks.
> —Neuroscientists Gregory Ashby, U. Turken (UCSB)
> and Alice Isen (Cornell University)

Recent developments in the field of positive psychology and neuroscience have demonstrated that creative problem-solving is directly related to positive emotions. How are researchers assessing the connection between the positive feelings and creative problem-solving? Biochemically, the neurotransmitter dop-

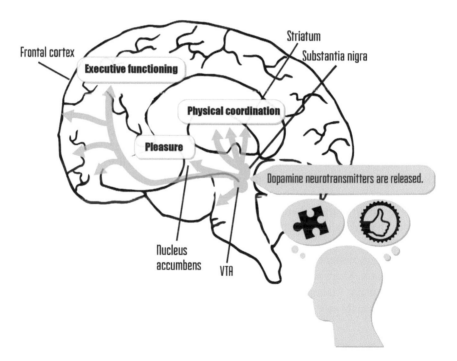

Figure 3.2 Regions in our midbrain respond to the acts of problem-solving and reward-seeking by sending dopamine neurotransmitters to activate our feelings of pleasurable emotions in the nucleus accumbens. Dopamine is also sent to the area in our brain responsible for executive functioning—the frontal cortex.

amine, which has for decades been associated with rewards and the anticipation of rewards, is also triggered when a person experiences positive feelings. Research has more recently indicated that the release of the "feel good" chemical in the brain enhances flexible thinking, demonstrating a direct link to positive emotion and decision-making.

Even moderate fluctuations in positive affect can increase an individual's aptitude and ability to integrate a diversity of information. This allows a person to enact innovative approaches to thinking and problem-solving. All of these are essential for the decision-making process involved in playing games and gamified systems.

Breaking the state of functional fixedness

This brings us to an important principle of gamified system psychology. By putting users in a positive state of mind, well-designed gamified systems jump-start, broaden and enhance creative problem-solving. There are other benefits as well, many of which can be measured, including:

- Improved accuracy.
- Reduction of rigidity in thinking.
- Innovation.
- Thoughtful and careful processing of information.
- Improved ability to organize and classify information.
- Enhanced perception of similarities and differences.
- Tasks that seem mundane are perceived as being rich and varied.

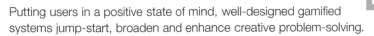

GS design principle #14—disrupt functional fixedness

Putting users in a positive state of mind, well-designed gamified systems jump-start, broaden and enhance creative problem-solving.

It is important to note that the personal resources accrued during states of positive emotions are conceptualized as durable.

—Barbara Fredrickson, Director UNC, Positive Psychology

Not only do small and subtle increases in happiness build our resources for thoughts and actions, but they also make us happier over the long term. In general, games allow people to collect such moments of happiness. Perhaps the purest example of this in the form of an actual game is *Katamari Damacy*, a Japanese videogame in which players roll and grow a giant ball of stuff. As it picks up objects that stick to it, the ball grows and builds momentum, becoming stronger and better at getting over challenging obstacles. It is the opposite of the depressing

Using gamified systems to generate positive emotions may also carry over into other aspects of a person's life. Research has shown that positive emotional moments have long-term effects, providing the ability to:

- Access multiple perspectives, to become better at shared problem-solving and negotiations.
- Be open to and interested in new and different experiences.
- Be less defensive and better able to handle negative feedback.
- Be better at coping with unexpected painful or challenging moments in the real world.

Figure 3.3 Good feelings have a snowball effect. Image reprinted with permission of artist, Alex Waskelo.

endless labor depicted in the myth of Sisyphus, in which the boulder can never be rolled to the top of the hill. In *Katamari Damacy*, positive feelings beget positive feelings, successes beget successes. The momentum can help us get beyond lingering negative emotions, help us be more resilient when confronted with undesirable experiences, and facilitate a strengthened long-term sense of well-being. Not only do we become more optimistic about the things we can achieve, but we also begin to feel a bigger sense of optimism, where it is possible to imagine that the world and its inhabitants can flourish.

GS design principle #15—broaden and build

Gamified systems can generate positive emotions that have long-lasting effects beyond the momentary.

Broaden-and-build is a theory of positive emotions introduced by psychologist Barbara Fredrickson in 1998. Fredrickson's research demonstrates that an increase of positive moments can have an impact over time, leading to an overall greater sense of personal well-being and satisfaction.

Good gamified systems promote happiness

Gamified systems thus enable feelings of happiness through both pleasure and enjoyment. These kinds of positive emotions tend to emerge in situations that are free from personal danger or adversity. In such an environment, individuals widen their perspectives, push their limits, willingly approach unknown territory and manifest the urge to play. When people are fearful or unhappy, they tend to narrow down their perceived possibility space. One of the most powerful aspects of games and gamified systems is that they can combine the simulated experiences associated with dangerous or risk-taking situations while keeping the player safe. Positive stress, referred to as **eustress**, is the capacity to respond to stressful situations with a sense of personal control and confidence. Games and gamified systems can thus create a unique kind of space, where we are consciously integrating the psychological processes associated with personal fear and danger with the persistent awareness of safety and security. The magic circle (introduced in Chapter 1) provides this protection. We can comfortably and in a balanced manner focus our ability to act in a specific situation while at the same time having access to creative problem-solving abilities associated with feelings of enjoyment.

The ways that this happens can be a crude as the repetition and achievement dynamic of a game level or as complex as the kinds of emotions usually associated with artistic forms like the novel, the symphony or the visual arts found in a museum. The feeling of happiness includes the aspects of joy, interest, contentment, pride and social bonding or love. Joy comes through new challenges

Eustress

Eustress is positive stress. It is not about the stressor, but about how one perceives stress, and responding in a way that is healthy and productive. When people feel a sense of control, motivation and invigoration they are likely to respond to a stressor with a sense of hope, optimism and meaning, ultimately leading to a greater sense of satisfaction.

Emotional engineering with the 4 Keys 2 Fun

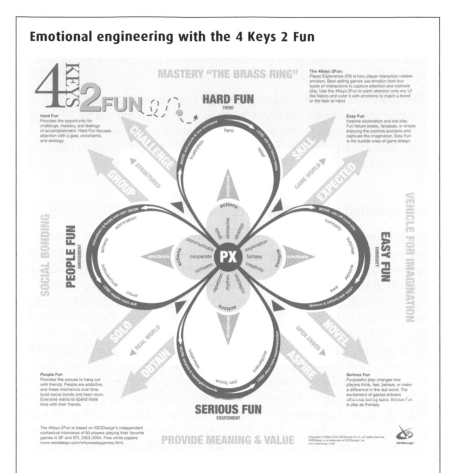

Figure 3.4 Nicole Lazarro's 4 Keys 2 Fun © XEODesign.

Nicole Lazarro's 4 Keys 2 Fun (introduced in Chapter 1) focuses on the connection between player experience and emotion. Lazarro believes that there are four categories of activity loops in games that direct emotional states: easy fun, hard fun, people fun and serious fun. These categories initiate the feelings necessary for players to make new and continued interactions in gamified systems. For instance, the curiosity, play and wonder that occur through exploration, discovery and surprise (associated with easy fun) is the best way to make players feel comfortable with initial tasks. On the other hand, when a player faces tough strategic challenges, the effect can be to generate eustress, a positive response to a stressful situation so that a player can build his skill base and his sense of confidence.

... and, the daily DOSE (dopamine, oxytocin, serotonin, endorphins)

Lazarro also proposes that game designers can help people unlock the brain states that are inhibiting their success and happiness, particularly fear. To promote these positive feelings, gamified systems should focus on activating:

- **Dopamine**—To encourage the release of the "reward" chemical get players to celebrate their achievements regularly. Keep goals small and achievable, but make them progressively more challenging.
- **Oxytocin**—This hormone only found in mammals acts like a neurotransmitter, making people more trusting. Gamified systems can support its release by building social connections, encouraging physical contact, acts of kindness and sharing.
- **Serotonin**—Associated with good moods, the imbalance of it is linked to depression. Most antidepressants work to improve mood by boosting serotonin levels. Leverage social connections and networks to help people recognize the successes of others, keeping momentum on a forward path.
- **Endorphins**—Endorphins create feelings of euphoria, reducing the sense of pain and stress. Some ways these neurotransmitters can be generated are through exercise, spicy food, laughing and crying. Consider how you can get your players moving and laughing.

Gamified systems make us happy by generating:

- Joy through new challenges, play and creativity.
- Interest through exploration, seeking and discovery.
- Emergent moments to savor.
- New experiences with friends.
- Pride through achievement.
- The desire to share and enhance relationships over time.

... and build interest by surprising us with gifts

Research has shown that, although unanticipated rewards are associated with more dopamine production than anticipated rewards, unexpected gifts actually promote the longest release of the "feel good" chemical. Although many attribute the success of social networking games like *Farmville* to their simple yet addictive interaction, perhaps it is actually the opportunity to give and receive gifts that makes them so popular.

and the opportunities to be creative. Interest may be initiated through exploration, seeking and discovery. Moments to savor, reflect upon and share these new experiences with friends can fortify contentment with the individual and collective pursuits that a person chooses to give meaning to her life. Pride is associated with achievement, which can, in turn, generate the desire to share and to pursue greater achievements in the future. Invitations, gifts, cooperative and competitive play are all methods for enhancing relationships and the sense that people care about each other. By initiating small interludes of happiness and precisely refining that sense of happiness through craft and indeed art, gamified systems can generate longer-term positive benefits.

THE BUILDING BLOCKS OF ENGAGEMENT

Chapter 1 explored the concept of engagement—the level of participation that a user has in relation to a system. For games and gamified systems engagement must be considered from both a micro and macro perspective. Not only are we concerned with the momentary input and feedback relationship between the user and the system elements and architecture, but we are also interested in the bigger conversation that happens over periods of time, often outside of the game itself. This includes the layers of social interaction occurring between individuals within online communities and social networks. The personal and collective dynamics between the users and the producer, owner or developer of the system combined together should generate what designer Amy Jo Kim refers to as an "engagement loop." As demonstrated by Figure 3.5 the engagement loop is a cyclical call to action for everyone in the system. Players hear about or are invited to play then enter through a process of onboarding, which involves the introduction to a

Figure 3.5 The engagement loop gets players playing (adapted from Amy Jo Kim's Engagement Loop). As they progress they invite new players who are in turn engaged, perpetuating re-engagement of existing players.

system's progress paths, including a glimpse into the challenges and rewards that await the player. As time persists players whose participation is waning are re-engaged by the cajoling of online friends inviting them to come back and experience new and unexplored interactions. All of this is meant to facilitate positive emotions, which in turn motivate people to share the experience and continue participating in it.

Desire to engage > embracing a game-play attitude

Before we actually engage in the act of play, we must first accept that we will be taking on psychological and possibly physical challenges that we might otherwise not undertake, all for the purpose of playing in a game system. How do we prepare ourselves to engage in game-play? Bernard Suits, the philosopher and author of the book *The Grasshopper: Games, Life and Utopia*, argues that when we decide to play a game we form a **lusory attitude**. We agree to follow the unique rules and guidelines of a game system no matter how arbitrary or eccentric they may seem. The lusory attitude can be understood as the contract with the self, other players and the system to participate so that the game, no matter how seemingly absurd, may exist. In order to engage, an individual must first submit to the parameters and constraints, like rules, procedures and requirements and boundaries of space and time.

Lusory attitude

Lusory attitude is a term coined by Bernard Suits. It refers to an individual's willingness to follow arbitrary rules and constraints in order to play a game.

Building blocks for engagement > immersion

> Immersion is the sense of being taken over by a completely other reality that takes over all of our attention, our whole perceptual apparatus.
> —Janet Murray, *Hamlet on the Holodeck*

One way that games, particularly digital games, set the stage for sustained engagement is by providing elements necessary for immersion. For players and designers immersion refers to the experience of a game world that is so involving that the actuality of it replaces that of the real, physical world. Immersion in digital environments is often measured by three factors: *urgency, agency and realism.*

Urgency

Within moments of the opening sequence of the game *Uncharted 2: Among Thieves'* the player is forced into an emergency situation. She must save the game's main character Nathan Drake from falling from a train car that is just seconds from toppling off of a mountain cliff. This is urgency. Urgency occurs when an individual has a deep sense of purpose to meet an objective or complete a task. With games, urgency often happens as a result of obstacles working explicitly against the player's goals. Diminishing resources, time restrictions and impending death each have the effect of building tension necessary for urgency.

Gamified systems often utilize obstacles to build a sense of urgency. However, some of these obstacles can be very real. Urgent problems like poverty, climate change and oil shortages may not be solved by games, but games are promoting a greater sense of awareness of these urgent issues. At the same time as they build players' initiatives to spread the sense of urgency, they try to share the conversation about problem-solving. Introduced in Ken Eklund's interview in Chapter 2, the alternate reality game (ARG) *World Without Oil* lets players experience, imagine and create the world of a global oil crisis. The plausibility of such a crisis is so likely that the game did more than just build awareness. It created a simulated environment where players put themselves into a rich collective imaginary. Blogs, videos and comics were a few of the creative formats that were used by the participants, who as a community contributed over 1,500 stories. Not only did the game generate a dialogue around ideas for improving energy policy and reducing oil dependency, but it also translated into a much greater awareness of energy use in players' real lives. This type of game builds off what Jane McGonigal refers to as **urgent optimism**. Though a problem might be seemingly insurmountable, gamified systems can enable a new perspective where solutions seem possible and achievable.

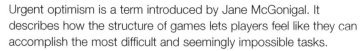

Urgent optimism

Urgent optimism is a term introduced by Jane McGonigal. It describes how the structure of games lets players feel like they can accomplish the most difficult and seemingly impossible tasks.

Agency

Unlike urgency, which seems driven by forces that are unconscious or coming from others, agency is about a desire for personal control and impact. A sense of agency is achieved when your behavior and choices impact a system. You know this because the system responds in a meaningful way. The desire for agency often comes out of the sense that the world (as a system) is not responding to your actions. The persistent display of updating points is an example of such a feedback mechanism, quickly indicating to a player that his influence matters.

Figure 3.6 *World Without Oil* promoted urgency through a plausible simulated environment of a global oil crisis. Participant Jennifer Delk created a comic for each of the thirty-two "weeks" of the game, imagining the crisis from the perspective of an urban family. © Jennifer Delk.

Multiple paths and diversity of choice are other ways that games give players a sense of agency. For instance, choosing to develop certain skills or pursue certain badges provide players with a greater sense of freedom. Functions that enable users to customize their profile, like the option to choose a picture or a nickname, are all ways to increase a player's sense of influence and agency.

With so many feedback mechanisms, games are very good at fostering the feeling of personal influence. On the other hand, because they are connected to the real world, gamified systems can enact change, giving a player a much deeper sense of impact and in turn agency. For example, the *Guardian* newspaper's *Investigate your MP's Expenses* (introduced in Chapter 2) gave its participants tools to conduct research and report findings. Everybody got to be a journalist, each contributing the hard work necessary for holding their public officials accountable for their misdeeds. The collective effort made the community true agents of change. Another example is the popular game-like *Freerice* (originally called *FreeRice*), which donates ten grains of rice every time a user interacting with the system selects the correct definition of a word from a multiple-choice quiz. Since it launched in 2007 over 160 million grains of rice have been donated around the world through the United Nations Food Program. Users continue to interact because they know that their online interactions will translate into real food for people who need it.

GS design principle #16—agency for change

Gamified systems help bring personal agency to the real world. Individuals have unique opportunities to become agents of real change.

Realism

A third point of immersion is realism. For games, this aspect is not always about mimicking the world we live in but has more to do with believability and creating a sense of internal consistency. This occurs when all elements feel like they belong to the same world, behaving according to its specific rules and parameters. Psychologically, it allows for the suspension of disbelief, giving the mind a green light for immersion. Because gamified systems primarily take place within the real world, mimicry or simulation is in many ways built into the system. Yet, we can still derive lessons from the way that games involving fictional or virtual

---

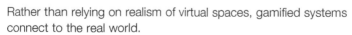

GS design principle #17—reality over realism

Rather than relying on realism of virtual spaces, gamified systems connect to the real world.

worlds encourage players to pay attention to the details and patterns in the spaces that they must navigate. Rather than encouraging connection to simulated environments, good gamified systems magnify and enhance the experience of the real world.

Sustained engagement > flow

Immersion leads to sustained engagement. Game designers refer to the sweet spot of such engagement as **flow**, a concept introduced by positive psychology pioneer Mihaly Csikszentmihalyi. Flow characterizes the sense of absorption that a person can experience when performing a task or set of tasks to accomplish a goal. It occurs when an individual undertakes challenges that are perfectly matched to her skill set as it grows (this notion is explored more in Chapter 4 in the discussion about the Zone of Proximal Development). Flow is commonly referenced in the world of game design as a shorthand for the experience of good game-play, characterizing the harmony an individual achieves stretching his abilities while overcoming obstacles progressing in difficulty. When players of games or gamified systems experience waves of peak performance, remaining safely out of reach of either anxiety or boredom, this is the state of flow. Structure, guidance, continuous feedback, increasing degrees of challenge and variety of choice are all methods that good gamified systems utilize to engender flow.

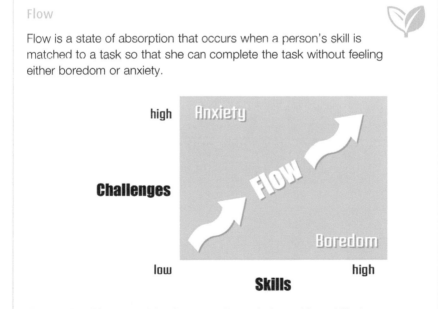

Flow

Flow is a state of absorption that occurs when a person's skill is matched to a task so that she can complete the task without feeling either boredom or anxiety.

Figure 3.7 Diagram of the flow experience (adapted from Mihaly Csikszentmihalyi).

Good gamified systems create flow through:

- Structure.
- Guidance.
- Continuous feedback.
- Increasing degrees of challenges.
- Encouragement of mastery.
- Variety of choice.

Engaging with others

> You can discover more about a person in an hour of play than in a year of conversation.
>
> —Plato

Although much emphasis in the game world has been focused on the engagement of the game system and the player or players, the world of digital networks emphasizes the social aspect of engagement, particularly the level of participation that an individual takes within an online community. Gamified systems have to take into account the ways that digital networks are simultaneously immersive, producing flow, and at the same time distracting individuals from a singular activity. They always place multiple demands on attention and energy devoted to tasks. Stepping back from this diffusion of energy, social engagement can be

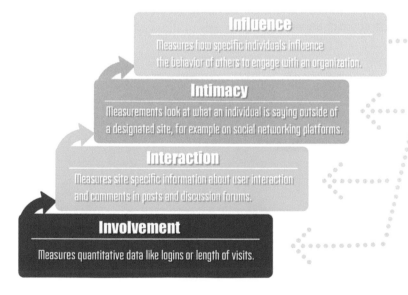

Figure 3.8 Progression of engagement (adapted from Forrester Research).

measured along a continuum according to the amount of investment an individual makes in and the level of impact he has on the community.

Illustrated in Figure 3.8, this continuum suggests four stages of progression. The first stage *involvement* measures quantitative information such as how often and long a person visited a website. The second stage *interaction* occurs when users are actively participating in forums, discussions and blog postings. *Intimacy* is when the user has a deeper connection to the community, discussing it positively in forums and social networking platforms external to the site. Finally, *influence* occurs when a user has enough status in a community to get others to actively participate.

Engagement types

The path towards influence in an online community can be characterized with more granularity than simple engagement. Online communities and social networks facilitate different people to behave in different ways. Forrester Research suggests the following categories of online community user types:

1. **Inactives**—Registered but not actively participating, these individuals may be cajoled back to an experience by friends who are more active on the social ladder.

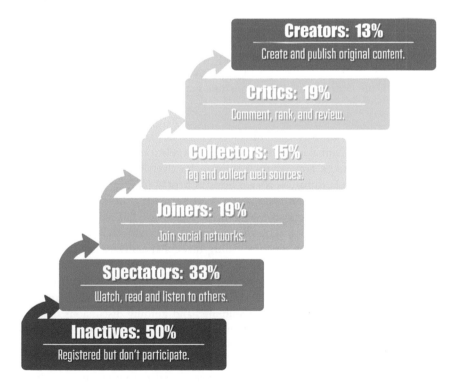

Figure 3.9 Social engagement types (adapted from Forrester Research).

2. **Spectators**—Consumption is the primary activity of this user base. They will watch, read and listen but they do not contribute anything personal or new.
3. **Joiners**—These are users who join and keep a profile. They may also visit and spectate, but they are not interacting with others.
4. **Collectors**—Collectors share content, vote, tag things and like things. They may be short of time, confidence or deep interest, but they keep information moving.
5. **Critics**—Critics are people with opinions. They like to comment on content. They are also willing to rate and write reviews about topics that are of interest to them.
6. **Creators**—Creators create, upload and publish their own content, ranging from videos and music to stories and articles. They are rare, but their participation is the point of origin for all of the other types.

> **Social engagement reaches its greatest potential when participants become creators.** Gamified systems have a greater chance of success when users create and share content.

Relationships

> Whether we like it or not, there is hardly a moment of our lives when we do not benefit from others' activities. For this reason, it is hardly surprising that most of our happiness arises in the context of our relationships with others.
>
> —Dalai Lama XIV

Humans are social animals, born into social existence and dependency on others. Because every individual is entirely unique, each relationship we enter into is rife with complex nuances. Some of these we can effectively enhance. Others we learn to carefully avoid. Fortunately, for millions of people playing around the world, games and gamified systems offer one way of narrowing these complexities. As a result, they provide navigable structures to manage this widening array of relationships. And, although achieving a state of absorption when performing a task alone can be highly productive, doing this collaboratively has been shown to be much more enjoyable. A study of professors at work illustrates this point. Although these professionals experienced a sense of flow while crafting their lectures alone, it was at the point of delivery in front of the class, which included fielding unexpected questions from students, and guiding discussions that they felt the greatest sense of achievement, engagement and absorption in their work. While constructing ideas is powerful and satisfying, it does not compare to sharing them and seeing them internalized, translated and repurposed within a larger community or group. Anyone who has ever played the same game in single-player mode and in multi-player mode knows how different the experience can be. Whether you are racing a car in *Mario Kart* or timing your body with the music and arrows in *Dance Dance Revolution*, the experience of doing these activities on your own does not compare at all to the significantly more nuanced opportunity to do them in the company of another person.

GS design principle #18—narrow complex
relationships

Gamified systems provide navigable structures to manage the widening array and complex nuances of relationships.

Social flow

Social flow describes what happens when people experience a state of absorption with others. It occurs at its highest state of intensity when there is deep cohesion within a group of equally skilled individuals. It usually requires a consensus about

---

Solo vs. social flow

A person can experience solo flow when performing a task alone. For example, playing a single-player game often requires full concentration on a task. In this state, there is no or very limited ability to converse or interact with other people. In fact, the presence of other people can break the sense of high engagement and can easily be treated as an interruption. Social flow, on the other hand, must be done with others. It can be co-active, where individuals are doing there own tasks together, like going dancing, biking or playing a racing game. Or, it can be highly interdependent, requiring significant coordination or cooperation. Soccer games, symphonies and game-based quests or raids in multiplayer games are all examples of highly interdependent play.

Co-active social flow occurs when individuals are doing tasks side by side. This type of flow can have many layers, including interdependent flow like conversation and solo flow like personal achievement.

Interdependent social flow occurs with a group or team that has relevant and often complementary skills or knowledge to accomplish a task. The cooperative survival horror shooter *Left 4 Dead* illustrates this point. Players must coordinate and cooperate efforts like deciding what room to enter and who will go first. They must also focus with a high degree of attention on what others in a group are doing, like knowing when another player is down and needs help. Getting to a safe zone together requires a collective sense of purpose, where individuals must surrender the sense of personal ego or self to the group.

the best ways to approach procedures, goals and roles. Perhaps people enjoy social flow so much because social tasks require significantly more skill and attention than most solo activities. Not only does an individual need to overcome the challenge of the task itself, but she must also do this in coordination with other individuals, all while trying to interpret and react accordingly to the verbal and physical responses of others. In addition to the shared challenge, there is the potential for a mutual victory. Because the opportunity to celebrate a win is shared, when social flow happens there is much less need for external rewards or incentives. Cooperative games maximize this potential by letting players work together to beat the game system. An example of the power of cooperative play is the board game *Pandemic*. Players work together in different roles to stop the spread of different diseases, trying to abate a pandemic. Though individual players feel the satisfaction of finding a cure on their turns, it is the joy and tension of working together and caring about each player's move that truly separates the experience.

Player types

> Play is at the foundation of all personal relationships.
> —Stuart Brown MD, *Play: How it Shapes the Brain,*
> *Opens the Imagination, and Invigorates the Soul*

In his 2003 book, *Designing Virtual Worlds*, Richard Bartle characterized the psychological motivation and characteristics of four different types of players in virtual worlds. As the co-creator of the first Multi-User Dungeon (MUD), the earliest form of multiplayer online games, Bartle knows what he is talking about. His four player types actually constitute a path of progression, including players who are entirely new to a game world (newbies) to players who have overcome all of the challenges and obstacles, but are still actively participating.

Here is Bartle's hierarchy of players:

1. **Killers**—These tend to be the newest players. They are working out the parameters of the system. Their actions against others tend to appear in the form of harassment and taunting. The presence of players aggravating others can decrease the population of all other player types.
2. **Explorers**—Explorers are familiarizing themselves with the system. Rather than focusing on achieving wins, they are exploring. Seeking and discovery enables them to reveal aspects of the system as if they were reading a good piece of literature.
3. **Achievers**—Achievers understand the system and are looking to increase their status by proving that they can overcome high-level challenges and tasks.
4. **Socializers**—Socializers are at the core of successful MMORPGs, and tend to be the players who have been around the longest and intimately understand all of the components of the system. Socializers bring people together to build fellowship and maximize social flow.

Killer   Explorer   Achiever   Socializer

Figure 3.10 Bartle's player types (killers, explorers, achievers, socializers) (based on Richard Bartle). By Alex Waskelo.

Notice how the hierarchy of players also is responsible for moving players through the different potential experiences ultimately leading to social bonding. If your gamified system is not enabling and indeed producing socializers, it is probably not going to prove very durable.

Group dynamics

Groups generate and execute plans and ideas. From governments to guilds, groups are essential for making systems large and small function. Between the various places we have each lived, studied, worked and played we have each been and will continue to be members of different groups throughout our lives. A small handful of these will be long term, intimate, tight knit and provide a sense of persistent solidarity and trust. Nuclear families, military squads and very close long-term friendships fall into this primary group category. Most other groups we find ourselves in, such as student groups, unions or classrooms, tend to be larger, shorter in duration and more goal oriented.

In games and gamified systems, groups work optimally when its members perform different roles in relation to each other, and play to their strengths. *League of Legends*, the multiplayer online battle arena (MOBA), which hosts over 27 million

---

Expect different time commitments from secondary and primary groups

Primary group members are much more likely to share personal information and stay in contact more regularly. Secondary groups tend to be larger, harder to organize and to last for shorter durations.

players a day, works by generating cross-functional teams for battle. Using what is referred to as the "meta build," players place specific champions with different roles (like mage/caster, bruiser or juggler) in different locations on the map to defeat another team in battle. As we learned with Caillois earlier in the book, role-playing is an essential aspect of game-play, freeing us from the boundaries and constraints of our everyday lives. Not only can we experience new identities through the characters we play, but we also have the opportunity to re-imagine our real-life relationships at the same time. For instance, when a 12-year-old boy gets to teach his grandfather how to get through a level of *Lego Star Wars*, the relationship dynamic is entirely flipped. The child gets to be the mentor whereas the grown-up takes the role of student. This becomes an empowering experience for the child, and a humbling one for the grown-up, offering entirely unique perspectives. Inter-generational bonding is just one way that games and gamified systems can create collaboration through difference, encouraging individuals to see themselves and the people they are playing with in entirely new ways.

GS design principle #19—collaboration through difference

Gamified systems can maximize differences between people, leveraging their distinct skills and abilities.

Groupthink

Groupthink occurs when groups make poor decisions because of an overriding pressure to maintain uniformity and harmony. This tends to happen with groups who have no clear process or rules for decision-making, and are concerned more with maintaining the balance of relationships than accomplishing a task well. On the other hand, groups that are focused on achieving specific goals rather than maintaining the status of individual group members are much better at making quality choices and decisions. Games combat groupthink by giving players specific and clear objectives and goals. For example, the game *Rock Band* unites players around the experience of performing music together. The game gives players with a range of musical abilities a unique opportunity to work as a group around the common vision of successfully rocking out.

GS design principle #20—combat groupthink

Gamified systems can loosen the fear of upsetting pre-existing relationships. By providing clear goals and challenges, structured play can facilitate idea contribution and productive conflict amongst group members.

IS THIS MEANINGFUL?

> What man actually needs is not a tensionless state but rather
> the striving and struggling for some goal worthy of him. What
> he needs is not the discharge of tension at any cost, but the
> call of a potential meaning waiting to be fulfilled by him.
>
> —Viktor Frankl, *Man's Search for Meaning*

When people ask if games are a waste of time, a form of entertainment or a kind of art, they are really asking whether playing achieves something that matters. In this regard, it is important to distinguish the difference between happiness and meaning. Whereas happiness tends to be about taking, meaning tends to be associated with giving. When we play games socially, we are in fact giving to others in a way that does not make them feel guilty about receiving a gift. This is because we are giving our time and our attention to a shared goal—playing a game. By embracing a lusory attitude, we are opening ourselves up, willingly exposing our strengths and weaknesses, and our ability to act and respond under pressure. These moments of play have the potential to build intimacy with other people, offering opportunities to create new relationships, or to change the dynamics of existing ones. By flexing our minds, our senses and our ability to do this with others under the constraints of a game environment, we may also craft new dimensions of ourselves. We experience the greatest sensation of all— joy. Consequently, we have the potential to shift our attitudes about ourselves,

---

Could playing games be the highest pursuit?

> What we need is some activity in which what is
> instrumental is inseparably combined with what is
> intrinsically valuable, and where the activity is not itself an
> instrument for some further end. Games meet this
> requirement perfectly. For in games we must have
> obstacles, which we can strive to overcome just so that
> we can possess the activity as a whole, namely, playing
> the game. Game playing makes it possible to retain
> enough effort in Utopia to make life worth living.
>
> —Bernard Suits, *The Grasshopper: Games,*
> *Life and Utopia*

Bernard Suits's protagonist the grasshopper argued that in a utopia, where all of our material needs were provided for, in our desire to reach our perfect self, game-play would be the primary activity. He considered the contemplative process found in the journey of play far more meaningful than the end-state of play.

GS design principle #21—meaningful contribution

Whereas games offer meaningful choices, gamified systems offer meaningful contributions. By playing and participating, we can add something positive to our own world.

and about others, within and outside of the game. In other words, playing games involves doing something that matters.

Games provide a variety of ingredients for building a sense of purpose, including sharing a set of values with others, and the positive feelings and sense of self-worth associated with accomplishment. While gamified systems can provide all of the opportunities for creating a sense of connection and meaning to players, they can also add another important dimension—impact on the real world. Gamified systems connect the actions of a player to something bigger than the players and the system. Earlier in this chapter the concept of agency was introduced with the example of the *Guardian* newspaper's gamified system. The project to expose the financial misdeeds of elected officials motivated thousands of people to focus on a shared purpose—exposing the truth. Reviewing financial records in unison with thousands of others gave participants real efficacy. With their malfeasance exposed, the MPs were forced to pay back their debts. The mobile game *Tilt World* is another example of meaningful contribution. As players

Figure 3.11 *Tilt World* lets players plant trees while they play. Courtesy of Nicole Lazzaro.

tilt their devices to clean up the in-game world they are gaining virtual seed points, which can then be used to help plant trees in Madagascar. Though infrastructures for donating food, planting trees and holding our elected officials accountable have existed on a much smaller scale, gamified systems have supercharged these efforts by collectively directing these efforts through the spirit of play.

Achievement

Achievement is almost always measured by meeting a standard of excellence. Rather than thinking we are good at something, we are striving to satisfy certain measurements. This is true even when we are pursuing tasks alone. For instance, if I am attempting to solve a puzzle, I have only achieved mastery when I have satisfied the conditions that determine its completion. The same idea applies when I am trying to beat a previous time or score. I am measuring myself against standards already set.

When we receive a good grade at school, get a positive review at work or beat our smartest friends at Scrabble, we know we have put forth enough effort to succeed. We have worked hard and accomplished what we set out to do. It feels terrific. Accomplishment in games works in a similar manner. Through feedback mechanisms like points, items and increased abilities, players are continuously recognized for their achievements and are then propelled to continue to pursue increasingly harder challenges. With games this also involves the engagement produced by flow. This state of total absorption is enabled through the optimal performance of skills and abilities as we are continuously challenged at a level that flexes our skill set just enough to be considered hard but yet still achievable.

GREATER COMPLEXITY LEADS TO A GREATER SENSE OF ACHIEVEMENT

Although rewards and recognition are always appreciated, we value most those achievements that have been gained through difficult and hard work. Unfortunately, many gamified systems today reward individuals for investing time in redundant or repetitive tasks. To feel a true and lasting sense of achievement, the pursuit of points, badges and other rewards needs to correspond to a progressive set of challenging tasks. Some of these may be skill based, requiring precision in achievement, like getting Pac-Man to eat dots while avoiding being captured by ghosts. Other challenges may be knowledge based. For instance, contributing important information that is not widely known by a team or group might help solve a riddle or puzzle that had seemed unattainable prior to that input. Other challenges may correspond to the amount of social interaction and social networks an individual has activated or participated in. For instance, getting other individuals to vote, rate or comment on a piece of media could provide the facilitator with unique status and access as a result of the collective feedback. As much as we love getting rewards, applause and pats on the back, everybody wants to feel like they have made a worthy investment to warrant them.

Individuals value achievements that they have worked hard for

Try to tie the bulk of your rewards system to progressively harder challenges.

WHAT ABOUT MOTIVATION?

So far we have covered the ways in which games and gamified systems promote positive and long-lasting emotions. Now, we need to understand the reasons why people choose to play and participate in these structures. Motivation combines internal and external forces, which in turn drive us to pursue a goal. Understanding the factors that create desire and momentum to act is fundamental to fields like human resources, education and consumer marketing. Though these might be the most obvious, understanding motivation is actually relevant to every field that relies on human decision-making. And, of course, this applies to the field of GS design as well.

Intrinsic motivation

It should come as no surprise that intrinsic motivation, doing something that is innately interesting, leads to much higher levels of learning, creativity and flow. Although extrinsic motivators, like good grades or more points, may get us to put forth an effort, it is only when we enjoy the processes we pursue for their own sake that we commit to doing them for an extended period of time without any foreseeable reward. There are three important ingredients to intrinsic motivation:

1. Autonomy.
2. Mastery.
3. Relatedness.

Autonomy

Autonomy is characterized by the freedom to make choices and to do things in your own way. Montessori schools, where students get to choose the work they do each day, succeed because of this idea. Independent game developers circumnavigating the traditional game industry are also in pursuit of this type of freedom. Although school children and game developers are still measured by external standards, like tests or revenue, it is the sense of personal freedom during the process or journey that ultimately becomes more meaningful and motivating than the end-game. By promoting agency, gamified systems succeed when they enable individuals to have the freedom to engage on their own terms. This usually involves multiple paths of discovery and progression as well as options that let users participate on their own schedule, using the device of their choosing.

Mastery

Mastery relates to achievement. It is often considered the highest level we can reach when learning a skill. Stuart and Hubert Dreyfus, both professors at UC Berkeley, described the path towards mastery through five stages of skill acquisition. According to the Dreyfus brothers, everyone learning a new skill begins as a *novice* (or newbie). This is the first point of acclimation, where an individual is being introduced to the context, and has no emotional connection to the pursuit. In a game environment this usually involves figuring out how to move a character, vehicle or camera from one place to another. Through instructions and trial and error experimentation individuals reach *competence*. If I have used my controller to move forward and to jump, I will likely try to see what happens when I do both at the same time. In this way I can confidently move a character up and across platforms. Competence enables an understanding of the constraints and capacities of a system. Through greater exposure and increased performance an individual reaches the stage of *proficiency*. At this point, once I have learned how controls are mapped to a game environment I am thinking significantly less about the controller in my hand and the rules and constraints of the environment. From here I begin to develop a sense of meaning for my actions, seeing the ways they correspond to long-term goals. I can now set values to my actions based on these goals, focusing energy and time on those aspects. The majority of people trying to master a new skill or system do not progress beyond *proficiency*.

Before an individual reaches proficiency he must rely on instructions, guides and rules to learn. At the stage of *expertise* an individual has so much experience with a system, knowing how to respond in a variety of situations, that he can rely increasingly on intuition. For games and gamified systems, a sense of

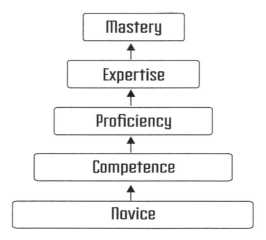

Figure 3.12 The five stages of mastery.

technical and structural limitations gives way to new possibilities, enabling greater opportunities for feeling an enhanced sense of loyalty and personal ownership. At this point, players and users can teach their knowledge to others. For example, Khan Academy encourages and rewards its experts to participate in the system by teaching and supporting less skilled members of the community. Finally, *mastery*, the ultimate goal, occurs when the expert reaches a state of total confidence where performance requires very little effort and no additional support.

The pursuit of a goal is most important when it contributes to something greater than the specific task at hand. Relatedness is about the emotional connection we make to the things we are doing. Big meaningful endeavors, like curing cancer or HIV/AIDS, give us a very good reason to spend hours playing games like *Foldit*. We set a substantial value to our work because we can relate it to a big picture—promoting scientific research and curing diseases. Gamified systems have demonstrated that they can excel at relating our tasks to big meaningful endeavors.

The concept of relatedness also extends to relationships. The more we can build and enhance relationships through shared pursuits and interests the more valuable these relationships become. In the pursuit of big real-world goals, gamified systems can bring people together to pursue and build shared values and interests. For example, Simple Energy's software-as-a-service platform for utility providers combines game concepts like badges, leaderboards and team challenges with data analysis to help communities work and play together to reduce their energy consumption. When San Diego's Gas & Electric piloted the program, customers and city residents reduced their energy usage by half in a period of three months. The greater an individual feels a sense of relatedness, like saving energy, the more likely she is to bring in her social circles, like friends and neighbors, to share in the benefits of the experience.

Small tasks need to be clearly tied to a bigger picture

Users are likely to be more willing to perform a seemingly small task if is related to a bigger purpose that supports their values. Inform prospective players and remind active ones about the connection to objectives beyond the system.

The motivation continuum

Though external and internal motivations might seem antithetical, it turns out that they are actually two sides of the same coin. As Figure 3.10 illustrates, *amotivation*, or total uninterest, and intrinsic motivation, or internal drive, sit on opposite sides of the motivation continuum. The process of moving from uninterest, through a state of acceptance and finally to a point of valuing a task for its own sake is called *internalization*. Although external influence tends to get a

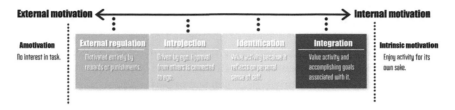

Figure 3.13 A taxonomy of the human motivation continuum.

bad rap, it is extremely common for the values we set on tasks to derive through the influence of others. For instance, if I surround myself by friends who work hard to get good grades, I might over time also place value on work. Then, eventually, I might actually work just because I enjoy the process of learning. This is when *integration* happens. I now value the work for its own sake, and do not need any external prompting to continue my pursuits. Social encouragement like gifts and invitations, public achievements and contextual leaderboards are all ways that gamified systems facilitate integration. These concepts are explored in more detail in Chapters 6 and 7. Although rewards may be what initially motivate a user, building internal motivation takes a significant amount of handholding and creativity.

Motivation and rewards

Stickers. Happy faces. Gold stars. We have been conditioned since we were small children to pay attention and perform low-interest tasks for external rewards. Although some behaviors may continue without these rewards, many will drop off when the rewards are no longer a motivating factor. In many cases, giving rewards can reduce autonomy, and prevent the internalization of a task. It is important to understand how to use rewards effectively. For instance, *task-contingent rewards*, which are given when a person completes an objective, tend to be perceived as controlling. The message "Do X and you will get Y" is clearly one that does not support choice or autonomy necessary to embrace a task for its own sake. On the other hand, *engagement-contingent rewards* are granted merely for

---

Know how rewards and their contingencies impact internalization

- *Task contingent:* Rewards given when a person completes an objective are perceived as controlling.
- *Engagement contingent:* Rewards granted for participating in a task. Has the effect of a gift given by surprise.
- *Performance contingent:* Rewards for a doing an activity well deliver feelings of personal pride.

being involved in a task. This type of reward can be considered much more along the lines of a pat on the back or a surprise gift. The player is not expecting anything, and may thus get a sense of unexpected pleasure or delight from the surprise. The most effective rewards are those that are *performance contingent*. These are only received when a person reaches a certain level of competence or mastery. Special abilities, items and privileges when tied to performance deliver individual pride and status within a community.

Expert perspectives: how gamified systems motivate

For Gabe Zichermann motivation is rooted in status, access, power and stuff. Zichermann, the author of *Gamification by Design* and the CEO of Gamification Co., argues that our primary motivation is derived through social contexts. According to this premise, it is our pride and sense of self-worth in relation to others that drives us forward and perpetuates engagement. He believes that users of gamified systems are driven by four fundamental desires. He abbreviates these in the acronym SAPS, which represent these desires according to their order of importance:

1. **Status**: Social standing provides people with a sense of value relative to others. With gamified systems, users who have made a bigger investment in terms of accomplishment and engagement over time expect to have a higher level of social capital than newer users.
2. **Access**: Status often translates into special permissions or access. For instance, the VIP section of a nightclub only permits people who are deemed "very important." In order for them to feel special, it must mean that others must be kept out, making the right even more socially desirable.
3. **Power**: Letting more experienced and engaged users have some control over what less engaged players can do or get is a way to keep everyone in a community motivated.
4. **Stuff**: The desire to receive and consume is tied to many desires far beyond our ego. Rewarding users with items, and letting them share or trade with others, is a way of making them feel important and welcome.

Using SAPS for analysis and design

When designing or conducting analysis of gamified systems you can use this formula to understand and consider how to generate external motivations.

*   Level systems, ratings, rankings, special badges and unique privileges are all components that *promote a sense of status*.
*   Special privileges like early access or special access to functions, elements or rewards are all ways to *make highly invested users feel special*.
*   Systems that let users or players take on leadership roles or editorial functions can *give certain users the feeling that they have influence and power*.

- Providing inventories, virtual goods, discounts, movie tickets or free coffee are all examples of the kind of stuff Zichermann believes make *players feel appreciated.*

Scott Nicholson's RECIPE stresses integration

Scott Nicholson, the Director of the Because Play Matters Game Lab at Syracuse University works with library and museum educators to create gamified systems intended to foster long-term engagement, community and a love for learning. Because external motivators (like badges or stickers) when removed can stall or abort a desired behavior, like developing a love of reading, Nicholson and his partners must find other approaches to drive these longer-term goals. Nicholson's RECIPE for meaningful gamification is meant to capture what he argues are the essential elements that gamified systems can incorporate to facilitate integration and internal motivation:

1. **Reflection**: The possibility of telling a story about an experience is what separates the meaningful from the mundane. The idea of reflection is also related to the way that activities, behaviors and choices reflect or validate a person's sense of self. For Nicholson it is "the point where a user makes connections between activities in the gamified system and aspects of his or her life." Building conceptual bridges between what is happening in the gamified system and what is happening in a user's life is a way to make the experience personal and give the system deeper and longer-term meaning.
2. **Exposition**: Presenting a narrative layer to the user can make them interested in learning about the back-stories and motivations of characters, environments and scenarios. Creating the desire to reveal a story over time can build a deeper connection between the user and the specific context. Dramatic elements can also help support, validate and contextualize the different game elements included within a design.
3. **Choice**: The introduction of choice into a gamified system gives the user freedom to decide how he or she engages with the system. Giving a user choice manifests the experience of agency, which in turn builds autonomy, an essential characteristic of internal motivation. Rather than having a single ordered set of activities, the user should have choices as to what to engage with (or to choose not to engage at all).
4. **Information**: Information can be thought of as facts or data that are provided or learned through a system. It can also be thought of as a concept or idea that is conveyed but not clearly articulated, forcing an individual to make his own connections to the content. Information enables exposition. Users become more involved in the "whys" and "hows" rather than the amount of points something is worth.
5. **Play**: Nicholson describes play as the optional exploration of a bounded space, where the key element to play is the choice to interact with and cross

boundaries (for more on play see Scott Eberles's interview at the end of this chapter).

6. **Engagement**: Nicholson emphasizes engagement and interaction between people. Connecting participants in a gamified system can generate peer groups and communities of interest. Interdependent social flow, where people are working closely to overcome obstacles, is the highest form of engagement.

Using RECIPE for analysis and design

When either designing or conducting analysis of gamified systems you can use this formula to answer the following questions:

- How do players reflect upon what they are doing and the choices they have made?
- How are dramatic or narrative elements used to help players connect the game activities to the real world?
- Are the players given a choice of different paths or activities?
- What ways are players provided with feedback about their actions? How is information revealed so players are interested in their purpose and back-story?
- What elements of play let players cross the boundaries between the game and the real world?
- How are the players being encouraged to interact with each other?

Which approach should I use?

Both approaches have the goal of helping gamified system designers understand ways to drive participation and satisfy immediate and longer-term desires. Zichermann's SAPS can be leveraged for satisfying the ego-driven desires of players. Giving devoted participants the many benefits associated with status, like access, power and stuff, is a way to reward and encourage continued investment. Nicholson's RECIPE also has a place in gamified systems. Thinking about reflection, exposition, choice, information, play and engagement is important for creating systems that can sustain themselves beyond rewards.

KEY TAKEAWAYS

- PERMA, which stands for Positive emotion, Enagagement, Relationships, Meaning and Achievement, provides a clear set of categories for analyzing and refining gamified systems.
- Well-designed gamified systems facilitate positive emotions to improve accuracy, reduce rigid thinking and jump-start, broaden and enhance creative problem-solving.
- Engagement is derived from many vectors including a lusory attitude, immersion (agency, urgency and realism), personal and collective absorption.

- Though singular flow is engaging, social flow, either co-active or inter-dependent, is preferred, and is considered more enjoyable, leading to longer-term play and increased loyalty.
- Although good games offer meaningful choices, good gamified systems can offer meaning by allowing players to contribute to the real world.
- Bartle's four player types (killers, explorers, achievers, socializers) in virtual worlds are a path of multiplayer game progression where socializers are critical for long-term player commitment.
- Internal motivation is driven by three characteristics: autonomy, mastery and relatedness.
- It is common for the values we set on tasks to derive through the influence of external factors, like other people in our lives.
- The process of moving from uninterest, through a state of acceptance and finally to a point of valuing a task for its own sake is called *internalization*.
- Rewards and reward contingencies affect internalization. *Task-contingent* rewards given when a person completes an objective can be perceived as controlling. *Engagement-contingent* rewards granted for participating in a task can be surprising and encouraging. *Performance-contingent* rewards are connected to a sense of achievement and pride.
- Gabe Zichermann's SAPS (*status, access, power* and *stuff*) and Scott Nicholson's RECIPE (*reflection, exposition, choice, information, play, engagement*) are both useful approaches to consider when designing for external and internal motivation.

EXERCISES

3.1 PERMA

Study a gamified system and identify the ways that it aligns to Seligman's PERMA categories (positive emotion, engagement, relationships, meaning, achievement).

3.2 Immersion

Evaluate a game and a gamified system, and identify how they instantiate the three points of immersion (agency, urgency, realism).

3.3 Reward schedules

Review a gamified system and look at the ways it utilizes the three different types of rewards for different contingencies (tasks, engagement, performance).

3.4 Motivational design

Using Zichermann's SAPS and Nicholson's RECIPE identify the different methods that a gamified system utilizes to generate both external and internal motivation.

RECOMMENDED READINGS

* *Drive: The Surprising Truth About What Motivates Us* by Daniel H. Pink, 2011.
  Daniel Pink explores the fundamental drives behind motivation, encouraging readers to reconsider traditional ideas about the role of rewards and punishments.

* *Flow: The Psychology of Optimal Experience* by Mihaly Csikszentmihalyi, 2000 (reprint).
  Originally written in 1990, psychologist Csikszentmihalyi details and describes the optimal experience of flow.

* *Play: How it Shapes the Brain, Opens the Imagination, and Invigorates the Soul* by Stuart Brown MD and Christopher Vaughan.
  Play is an accessible and compelling work about the science, biology and psychology behind play.

INSIDER INSIGHT

SCOTT EBERLE STUDIES PLAY

Interview granted with permission by Scott Eberle.

Scott G. Eberle, PhD, is Vice-President for Play Studies at the National Museum of Play, and the editor of the *American Journal of Play*, which explores the history, science and culture of play. Dr Eberle has a PhD in Intellectual History, and is the author of *Classic Toys of the National Toy Hall of Fame* and other works on American history, culture and play. His "elements of play" framework is highly regarded by the behavioral science community as an effective tool for understanding and explaining the concept of play.

Figure 3.14
Scott Eberle.

Can you tell me why you are so interested in play? How did you get here?

Personally, I'm drawn to studying play because I have a mischievous streak; professionally, because play knits together so many historical, psychological and philosophical threads. Also, play has proven to be the ideal rubric to contain and explain the vast collections at the Strong, in its National Museum of Play.

What makes play so valuable historically and in contemporary society?

It is not possible to explain play without reference to history because play itself is a process. Play unfolds, and as such cannot be understood separate from the passage of time. Over the long haul play is deeply a part of our species history, as it's important to understand the rise of our graduating class, mammalia. And, unless something went very wrong with our infancy and childhood, play is crucial in our own personal development and history. And then our cultural histories and our sociologies are intimately entwined with play. When you know what a culture enjoys, you learn what makes it tick. When you examine the rules we promulgate to constrain and prolong competition, you've opened the door to understanding a society's value system. You cannot study play without encountering the largest questions most central to the society that has produced it: race, class and gender, for example, or questions of identity and safety, of fairness and transgression, or of individuality or cooperation. Sherlock Holmes solved one case by the absence of a clue—a dog that did not bark. And when play is deliberately suppressed, as in the disgraceful case of Romanian orphanages, or when play is neglected, as is the case at contemporary schools that eliminate recess, something has gone radically wrong with human relations.

You have a framework that walks through the process of play. Can you describe it?

Play begins with *anticipation*, in an imaginative, predictive, pleasurable tension. This state of readiness, whether mild or intense, already feels rewarding as it makes way for play. Anticipation gives rise to the next element, *surprise*, when, as Charles Darwin observed, "the novel or incongruous idea breaks through a habitual train of thought." *Pleasure*, the third element, functions as the keystone or hub of play, both as a defining trait and an incentive to play some more. As we play, pleasure mixes with anticipation, surprise, understanding, strength and—if we are lucky— poise. While playing, we experience pleasure in intensifying shades of satisfaction, buoyancy, gratification, joy, happiness, delight, glee and fun. Play would not be playful if it were not fun. And because pleasure offers its own reward and because play entails pleasure, play perpetuates itself. But pleasure is mostly momentary. "Pleasure passes like a fleeting shade," Voltaire reminded us. This is another reason why pleasure applies more easily to play—a process rather than a static thing. *Pleasure* drives play.

Understanding points to insight and sensitivity as rewards of play. When we understand strength as devotion or creativity, we feel the power of this sort as pleasure. And the luckiest players experience poise in increasing dimensions of dignity, grace, composure, ease, wit, fulfillment, spontaneity and balance—all pleasurable feelings. By investing us in play and by inviting us to play some more, pleasure enlarges the physical, intellectual, emotional and social dividends that accrue. We appreciate the last three elements of play—*understanding, strength and poise*— as physical, intellectual, emotional and social pleasures. Other avenues present themselves as paths toward education, vigor and self-assurance, but none is quite so much fun as play. We play because it is fun, to be sure, but we reap short- and long-term benefits thereby mostly unknowingly. As Karl Groos, the pioneering observer of play, put it, "Animals cannot be said to play because they are young and frolicsome, but rather they have a period of youth in order to play."

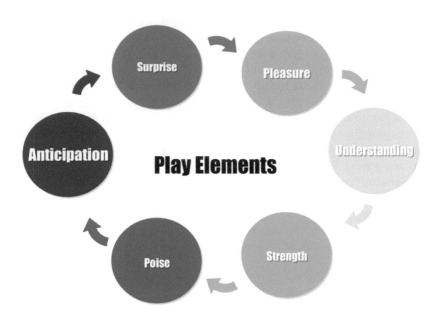

Figure 3.15 The play elements according to Eberle. Based on "elements of play."

How do you think designers can apply this process to enrich people's experiences and interactions in their daily lives?

All play, and all great ideas as a matter of fact, begin in anticipation. The designer looking at a blank screen, the painter contemplating the newly gessoed canvas, the chemist or the mathematician looking for balance all must explore, combine and recombine, and transform their ideas. They play with possibility. Designers always look for surprises. They take pleasure in the pursuit. They forge and formulate new understanding of their media and their audience. They nurture their creativity. And they cultivate spontaneity and ease in their designs.

What do you imagine a future based on play might look like?

I'm not sure what a future based upon play will look like. (Perhaps our cars will drive themselves while we play *Angry Birds?*) But I know what it will feel like. Fun.

NOTES

Ashby, F. Gregory, Alice Isen and U. Turken. "A Neurophysiological Theory of Positive Affect and Its Influence on Cognition." *Psychological Review*, 106:3 (July 1999): 529–550.

Bartle, Richard. *Designing Virtual Worlds.* San Francisco: New Riders, 2003.

Biron, Lauren. "Virtual Reality Helps Service Members Deal with PTSD." June 11. 2012. DefenseNews.Com. http://archive.defensenews.com/article/20120611/TSJ01/306110003/Virtual-Reality-Helps-Service-Members-Deal-PTSD

Brown, Stuart. Play. New York: Avery, 2009.

Buckner, Clark, with Nicole Lazzaro. "Four Chemicals That Activate Happiness, and How to Gamify Them." TechnologyAdvice Podcast, July 24, 2014. http://www.xeodesign.com/4-chemicals-that-activate happiness-and-how-to-gamify-them/.

Csikszentmihalyi, Mihaly. Flow: The Psychology of Optimal Experience. New York: Harper Collins, 2008. [Note: This book was originally published in 1990.]

Dreyfus, Hubert L. and Stuart E. Dreyfus. "A Five-Stage Model of the Mental Activities Involved in Directed Skill Acquisition." Research document funded by the Air Force office of Scientific Research and UC Berkeley, Berkeley, CA, February, 1980.

Drummond, Katie. "Virtual Rx: how Oculus Rift could revolutionize mental health." The Verge, April 22, 2013, http://www.theverge.com/2013/4/22/4251926/oculus-rift-virtual-reality-therapy-mental-health.

Eberle, Scott. "The Elements of Play: Toward a Philosophy and a Definition of Play." American Journal of Play, 2014: 214–231.

Flato, Ira, with Jane McGonigal. "Could Gaming be Good for You?" Interview on Science Friday, NPR radio, February 18, 2011, http://www.npr.org/2011/02/18/133870801/could-gaming-be-good-for-you.

Forrester's NACTAS Q4 2006 Devices & Access Online Survey, 2006.

Forsyth, Donelson. Group Dynamics. Belmont: Thompson Wadsworth, 2006.

Frankl, Viktor. Man's Search for Meaning. Boston: Beacon Press, 1946.

Fredrickson, Barbara. "Positive Emotions Broaden and Build." Advances in Experimental Social Psychology, 47 (2013): 3–40.

Kim, Amy Jo. "Smart Gamification: Seven Core Concepts for Creating Compelling Experience." Presentation at Casual Connect, Seattle, WA, July 2011.

Kim, Amy Jo. "Players Journey: 5-Step Design Framework for Longterm Engagement." October 19, 2013, http://www.slideshare.net/amyjokim/players-journey 5step-design-framework-for-longterm-engagement?related=1.

Lazarro, Nicole. The 4 Keys 2 Fun. White paper posted on March 8, 2004, http://www.xeodesign.com/category/the-4-keys/.

McGonigal, Jane. "Gaming Can Make a Better World." Presentation at TED, Monterey, CA, February, 2010, http://www.ted.com/talks/jane_mcgonigal_gaming_can_make_a_better_world.

McGonigal, Jane. Reality is Broken: Why Games Make Us Better and How They Can Change the World. New York: Penguin Press, 2011.

McMullen, Samuel P. Stereo 3D: A Study on Urgency, Agency and Realism and Their Effect on Video Game Immersion, A study conducted for Fergason Patent Properties, 2004.

Murray, Janet. Hamlet on the Holodeck: The Future of Narrative in Cyberspace. New York: Free Press, 1997.

Nicholson, Scott. "Two Paths to Motivation Through Game Design Elements: Reward-Based Gamification and Meaningful Gamification." Paper presented at iConference, Fort Worth, Texas, February 12–15, 2013.

Pink, Dan. "The Puzzle of Motivation." Presentation at TED, Monterey, CA, 2009, http://www.ted.com/talks/dan_pink_on_motivation.html.

Salamone, John D. and Merce Correa. "The Mysterious Motivational Functions of Mesolimbic Dopamine." Neuron, 76:3 (November 8, 2012): 470–448.

Seligman, Martin. "Flourish: Positive Psychology and Positive Interventions." Presentation given at the Tanner Lectures on Human Values. University of Michigan, Ann Arbor, MI, October 7, 2010.

Seligman, Martin. "Flourish." Presented to the Royal Academy of Arts, London, UK, July, 2011, http://www.thersa.org/events/video/archive/martin-seligman.

Smith, Emily Esfahani and Jennifer L. Aker. "Millennial Searchers." *New York Times*, November 30, 2013, http://www.nytimes.com/2013/12/01/opinion/sunday/millennialsearchers.html?pagewanted=all&_r=0.

Sterling, Jim. "Man Beats Bejeweled 2 after Three Years—Was It Worth It?" *Gamesradar*, April 30, 2010, http://www.gamesradar.com/opinion-man-beats-bejeweled-2-after-three-years-was-it-worth-it/.

Suits, Bernard. *The Grasshopper: Games, Life and Utopia*. Peterborough, ON: Broadview Press, 2005. [Note: The original version of this book was printed in 1978.]

Walker, Charles J. "Experiencing Flow: Is Doing It Together Better than Doing It Alone?" *Journal of Positive Psychology*, 5:1 (2010): 3–11.

Zichermann, Gabe and Christopher Cunningham. *Gamification by Design: Implementing Game Mechanics in Web and Mobile Apps*. Sebastopol: O'Reilly Media, 2011.

4   FUN IS LEARNING

CHAPTER QUESTIONS

At the end of this chapter, you should be able to answer these questions:

- What is the connection between fun and learning?
- What are the principles of constructionist learning?
- What is Bloom's Taxonomy, and how does the framework apply to our practice?
- What is cognition and memory?
- How does the Zone of Proximal Development relate to gamified systems?
- What is scaffolding, and how do game structures utilize it to support the process of learning?
- How can gamified systems help create cognitive apprenticeships?

INTRODUCTION

> The word "fun" comes from the Middle English word "fon," which translates roughly as "to be a fool." Later, by the 17th century the word became synonymous with cheating. Now of course we associate fun with pleasure derived from participating in activities we enjoy.

Culturally, we are often suspicious of "fun." The word itself does not have the most respectable origins. But today, the idea is associated much more with enjoyment derived from overcoming new challenges, rather than foolishness or trickery. Over the past few years a handful of game designers have tried to develop a new paradigm for fun. In *A Theory of Fun for Game Design*, Raph Koster makes a strong connection between the process of learning and the feeling of fun experienced while playing a game. The idea that games promote enjoyment by stimulating the learning process may seem relatively novel, but in fact it mirrors and confirms ideas proposed over the past century by some of the brightest minds in the fields of education, computer science and human psychology. This chapter shows how games teach, helping us construct ideas, solve problems and learn new skills by directing attention, supporting memory development and providing essential guidance and feedback.

HARD FUN

> Fun in games arises out of mastery. It arises out of comprehension. It is the act of solving puzzles that makes games fun. Fun is just another word for learning.
> —Raph Koster, *A Theory of Fun for Game Design*

We are infovores. Our brains love assimilating new information. When our minds recognize novel patterns that can be processed and compared with pre-existing knowledge, they release the reward drug dopamine. Making connections among information, we experience the "click of comprehension" and, when we do, the brain rewards us by releasing endorphins. With every new piece of information that comes in we become better at predicting what new kinds of differences will emerge. We experience glee as we get faster and better at processing, comparing, comprehending and performing. By maximizing our skills in novel and unexpected ways, frameworks for challenging us through play engender the physiological states of joy we call fun.

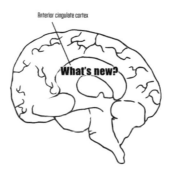

Figure 4.1 The anterior cingulate cortex is the part of our brain whose mission is to look for novelties.

It's a craving that begins with a preference for certain types of stimuli, then proceeds to more sophisticated levels of perception and cognition that draw on associations the brain makes with previous experiences. When the hunger becomes even moderately starved, boredom sets in.
—Neuroscientists Irving Biederman and Edward A. Vessel

Gamified systems can satisfy our brain's desire for richly interpretable experiences by provoking novel forms of pattern recognition.

More importantly than simply consuming information, we love to master the skills involved in deploying it. This is called **hard fun**, and it is at the core of most game experiences from answering questions in a quiz show to winning a game of horse with a basketball. Seymour Papert, founder of the MIT Media Lab and pioneer in the field of artificial intelligence, became fascinated by this concept of hard fun. "Everyone likes hard challenging things to do," writes Papert. "But they have to be the right things matched to the individual and to the culture of the times." And so for our most profound experiences of fun, we seek mastery. Hard fun in this way pushes us beyond our perceived potential.

Hard Fun

The phrase used by game designers like Nicole Lazzaro is rooted in Seymour Papert's observations about how children applying themselves to appropriately challenging tasks experienced joy.

Papert has also been at the forefront of constructionist learning, which suggests that the best way for an individual to understand the world is to construct her own models of how it works. And this is what happens as you achieve mastery. You build up information and skills that allow you to produce, define and manipulate a system that effectively engages with the world. According to this

Figure 4.2 *Lego Mindstorm*, which lets users build and write scripts for programmable robots, is derived from the Logo programming language.

approach, the most effective learning happens when people actively make tangible objects. The Logo programming language, which Papert co-created, exemplifies this idea of *learning by doing*. It enables children to build games and robots all while being introduced to the logic and processes of computer programming.

How do games, gamified systems and the technologies that they leverage encourage hard fun? According to Papert, technology can help us make and do things that we cannot achieve in the real world. An example of *technology as building material* is the wildly popular game and world-building tool *Minecraft*. The game's endless space and extensive crafting capabilities enable opportunities for construction that would never be possible in the non-digital world. In fact, *Minecraft* exemplifies the constructionist principles at the core of hard fun. The game, which is increasingly being embraced as a teaching tool for subjects ranging from history to architecture, emphasizes *learning by doing*, the idea that active and participatory learning occurs when we construct artifacts and ideas by choice. Autonomy (introduced in Chapter 3), the cornerstone of intrinsic motivation, is the essential component here. The freedom implied by the game structure lets learners and players take charge of their own learning process.

Individuals cannot always learn something at a specific time or under specific time constraints. Taking time ensures that learning a new skill or concept can be done according to a learner's own clock. Time is essential, as is failure. According to Papert, "you can't get it right without getting it wrong." Failure is fundamental

Zone 5: Shapes

Figure 4.3 *MinecraftEdu* is a modification of the popular world-building game designed for classrooms. Courtesy of Joel Levin, MinecraftEdu. By encouraging exploration, resource-gathering, building and collaboration, *Minecraft* exemplifies constructionist ideals. The game as a learning tool supports the personal connection to knowledge gained through play.

GS design principle #22—promote hard fun

Gamified systems generate hard fun by:

- Enabling what is not possible in the non-digital world.
- Tools that let players create knowledge.
- Freedom from imposed time limits.
- Maximum opportunities for experimentation.
- No punishment for failure.

Figure 4.4 *Wonderful World of Humanities* was built in *MinecraftEdu* by middle school social studies teacher Eric Walker to support and supplement in-class learning of ancient history, and the texts and culture.

to learning. The first time a player fails to build a structure that protects him through the night in *Minecraft*'s survival mode is the best way to learn why and how to build a better structure that will keep him safe when the sun goes down again.

BRAIN GAIN

> One must learn by doing the thing, for though you think you
> know it—you have no certainty until you try.
>   —Sophocles, 5th century BCE

Over the past decade, several research studies have validated what players and designers already knew—games are optimal environments for learning precisely because they promote hard fun. According to a recent Gates Foundation analysis of over 60,000 studies, players of learning-based digital games make significantly higher cognitive gains relative to comparative traditional learning environments. This "brain gain" coincides with higher levels of confidence as well as improved attitudes towards learning. Whether it be *Minecraft* or *Teach with Portals*, a modification of the first-person puzzle game *Portal 2*, educational gamified systems have repeatedly demonstrated their capacity at enabling skill acquisition, procedural knowledge, declarative knowledge and retention of these abilities after the fact.

How do games do this? The best ones push us up the learning ladder. The division of learning into types is usually referred to as a taxonomy, the most famous one being that designed in 1956 by University of Chicago professor of education Benjamin Bloom. *Bloom's Taxonomy* is a system for understanding the stages of learning and for classifying the different categories of knowledge that occur during the process. Though the framework has been slightly revised over time (one current taxonomy is displayed in Figure 4.5), it remains an accessible and useful method for understanding how we learn. The revised version of cognitive progression includes: memory, comprehension, application, analysis, evaluation and creation. To move up the framework to higher-order thinking skills (HOTS) an individual must first demonstrate competence at the earlier stages of lower-order thinking (LOTS).

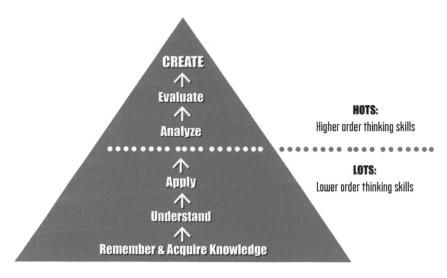

Figure 4.5 The revised version of Bloom's Taxonomy includes the six progressive stages of learning.

Stage 1: Memory and knowledge acquisition

This initial stage corresponds to learning declarative knowledge, such as facts, dates and events. To pass through this stage, learners need to prove their ability to recognize or recall information. Identification and labeling demonstrate this stage in the process.

Stage 2: Comprehension

A learner proves her ability to comprehend an idea by showing that she can take her knowledge gained in stage 1 and expand upon it. Demonstrations include comparison and predictions of outcomes.

Stage 3: Application

By solving problems or performing tasks, learners demonstrate that they can apply knowledge and abilities gained previously.

Stage 4: Analysis

Analyzing means recognizing patterns, rearranging and classifying parts of larger systems. In this stage, learners actively look for meanings hidden beneath the surface. Organizing, classifying and differentiating are all analytical tasks.

Stage 5: Evaluate

Evaluation occurs when we take our analysis of a situation and draw conclusions. At this stage, learners make predictions based on their ability to generalize their knowledge of the domain. Critiquing, making value judgments and discriminating between the merits of approaches and alternatives to tasks are all parts of evaluating.

Stage 6: Create

The peak of the process is to take all of the knowledge and procedural skills gained in earlier stages to innovate and invent new ideas. Creative work involves ideating concepts, generating designs, making unique products and finding novel solutions.

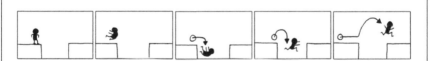

Figure 4.6 Playing through Bloom's stages.

Do Bloom's stages sound familiar? When a player interacts with the mechanics within a game system, he works through the different stages of Bloom's Taxonomy. First, he must combine prior knowledge with the experience of immediate feedback to learn the basic information about the mechanics and imagery presented to him. Next, experimentation and trial and error move him through the stages of analysis and application. System feedback enables him to evaluate and assess, and then finally create new solutions. This leads to combinations of mechanics in new ways, where he can develop new strategies to achieve short-term and long-term goals.

CATEGORIES OF KNOWLEDGE AND DOMAINS OF LEARNING

When creating a gamified system, it is important to think about what kinds of knowledge you want to emerge from the experience of interaction. One approach is to focus on categories of knowledge. These can be understood best as the content of what is being studied during the different of stages of learning. **Factual knowledge** is the basic set of facts and terms related to any domain. Labels, names and dates are all examples of factual knowledge. This piling up of facts can have real-world dimensions, such as Fantasy Football, or can be purely fictional, such as the seemingly endless variations of Pokémon. Much of the pleasure of these kinds of games does not come from the simple mathematics and mechanics of the play itself but instead emerges out of conversations about the different game elements, comparing stories about collection and acquisition.

Conceptual knowledge occurs when an individual forms generalizations about the relationships of basic elements. Understanding why certain dates or names are studied together is conceptual knowledge. In a classic game like Risk, for example, there is a certain enjoyment in putting the pieces of the continent together, thinking strategically about the relationship between the various regions. Likewise, almost all online learning systems use the concept of "modules." This groups not just bits of information but overarching concepts associated with that information.

The third category **procedural knowledge** is about putting conceptual knowledge into action through practice. In most games, some of the enjoyment comes from actually learning and following the rules, performing a skill or employing a domain-specific technique. When people say "I'm working on my free throw" or "practicing my backhand" they are not only trying to gain mastery but also reveling in the development of a particular game skill. Likewise, when a debate erupts over whether someone has violated the rules, part of the fun is actually knowing what the rules are, pulling out the rulebook and looking them up.

Finally, **meta-cognitive knowledge**, the most abstract form of knowledge is about self-awareness, and occurs when an individual is consciously thinking about her methods for building strategies. Planning how to approach a learning task is an example of this concept. Many gamified systems designed for instruction and learning combine the four areas of knowledge in an effort to reach the meta-cognitive. Try Objective-C teaches the programming language necessary for developing apps for the iPhone and iPad by first taking users through badges and a leveling system with nostalgic arcade-style graphics. This teaches the factual and conceptual knowledge associated with the language. But the gamified system also provides structure for users to demonstrate their capacity to put this knowledge to use. Writing programmable code in the iOS development language necessary for developing apps for the iPhone and iPad, learners showcase their ability to carry out procedures, and to plan and strategize best solutions throughout the different levels of the course.

But learning can also be approached through domains of experience. Bloom divided this into three kinds of domains: thinking, doing and feeling. Thinking

Types of knowledge:

- **Factual**—Sets of facts like labels, names and dates.
- **Conceptual**—Overarching ideas that clarify relationships of factual data.
- **Procedural**—The application of factual and conceptual knowledge to perform a task.
- **Meta-cognitive**—Thinking about learning strategies and the best ways to apply factual, conceptual and procedural knowledge.

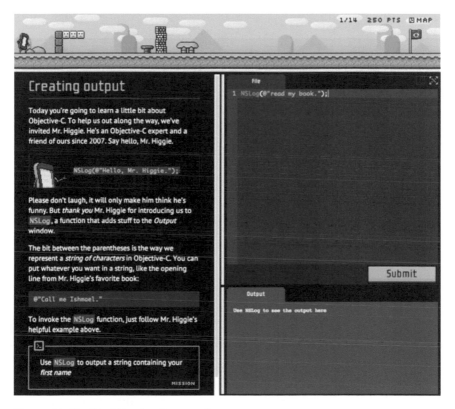

Figure 4.7 The *Try Objective-C* screenshot.

or the **cognitive domain** is where mental skills are developed, and most educational endeavors focus their energies and assessments here. The emphasis is on learning facts, concepts, techniques and methods, and applying these to create new ideas. *Minecraft* and *Try Objective-C* are just a few examples of this domain.

Doing, or physical activity, involves the performance of manual skills. The **psychomotor domain** uses technique, time and precision as measurements of dexterity and coordination. Doctors playing "twitch" games requiring rapid response and precision as a preparation for surgery is one example of how psychomotor skills can be applied from games to the real world.

Finally, feelings and emotional development comprise the **affective domain**. It is measured by the ways that we interpret and read, respond to and cope with different social situations. *Dojo*, an immersive biofeedback game (described below), demonstrates how gamified system (GS) design can support important social learning skills.

GS design for affective learning

Figure 4.8 *Dojo* develops affective learning.

Dojo is an immersive biofeedback game meant to help players recognize modulations in their physiological and emotional states, learning to regulate emotional reactions in a variety of scenarios over time. The game takes place in a secret temple below a subway system, where the player encounters dojo masters who guide him through challenges meant to teach emotional control. During a play session the fingers of the player are attached to a device that measures both skin conductance and heart rate. The data coming through the device is then interpreted into an algorithmic layer, which is translated into interactive and graphical feedback in-game. *Dojo* is being used in urban high schools and the juvenile justice system to help young people manage impulsive behavior during stressful situations.

Learning domains

- **Cognitive**—Corresponds to the mind.
- **Psychomotor**—Relates to physical dexterity and abilities.
- **Affective**—Applies to emotional capacity to respond in a social situation.

HOW WE THINK

Creating hard fun requires knowing what kinds of knowledge and mastery you are aiming to produce, but creating an environment in which hard fun is possible requires an understanding of cognition. Cognition is the act of thinking and knowing. It is the convergence of perception, language, reasoning and understanding. We create and assign meaning to things in our world by transforming and constructing our thoughts in specific ways. Cognition comprises both passive and active thinking. Intelligence, memory, attention, problem-solving and learning are all associated with this idea about how we use our brain to process data.

Cognitive adaptability is the ability to utilize pre-existing knowledge to develop innovative solutions to problems. This competency is essential for high-stress jobs like those performed by doctors, military personnel and aviators. All of these require quick and strategic thinking, and the ability to try out different strategies to solve problems while quickly reflecting on and responding to dynamic feedback. Its strength depends upon focused attention, reassessing the parameters of a problem, goal orientation, experience and creative thinking.

Games and gamified systems are one way of enhancing and maintaining these kinds of competency. Recognizing this, the US military conducted a study watching personnel play through *Portal 2*, a first-person puzzle game that requires players to negotiate and navigate a shifting environment. Using a portal gun, players create paths from one room to another, often defying three-dimensional logic. The study identified game features optimal for promoting cognitive adaptability. One aspect noted was how the game requires players to adapt quickly to the changing and expanding parameters while the complexity of play increases. In addition, players demonstrated that they were able to use the implicit cues they discovered by paying attention to the environment feedback that they received when attempting to overcome an obstacle. This process forced players to constantly re-evaluate this information to meet the changing requirements. Researchers recognized the cognitive value of *shifting implicit rules and reinforcements* that governed and modulated how a player could and could not interact with the world. Because each level generates new conditions that demand constant re-assessment, the *shifting environments* produce similar gains amongst players. Finally, the study found that the experience of *open-endedness* within each level gave players enough autonomy to freely experiment and construct their own concepts about the space.

Figures 4.9a and 4.9b *Shifting, dynamic rules and open-ended environments are what makes Portal 2 (shown here) so valuable as an environment for learning.* © Valve Corporation.

In part as a result of such studies, *Portal 2* has also been repurposed for use in education, particularly for teaching subject matters that require intensive cognitive processing like geometry or physics. Discussed in the book's introduction, the *Teach with Portals* modification of *Portal 2* is being actively used by teachers for its exceptional capacity at supporting the instruction of complex and abstract learning concepts including geometry, spatial visualization and physics.

Directing attention

One of the most important goals of gamified systems is to direct attention towards a task. It is well known that games often have the effect of focusing attention, but they also have the ability to shift perception. Perception results from the way we direct our attention, mentally engaging with a particular piece of information. Because so much information competes for our attention at all times, we tend to have different levels of awareness of these different data streams. **Continuous partial attention**, a term defined by the psychologist Linda Stone, refers to our capacity to pay attention to incoming information from simultaneous sources. Games, because of their immersive properties, reduce these data streams. Gamified systems actually maximize them. Game-layer systems, in particular, require short bursts of attention when appropriate, recognizing that, though it is impossible to perform more than one reflective task at a time, play structures can help players selectively orient their attention to complete a task while continuing on when finished with others.

Continuous partial attention

Coined by the psychologist Linda Stone, this concept describes how we process incoming information from simultaneous sources.

GS design principle #23—maximize continuous partial attention

Good gamified systems are often designed to support the needs to regularly change and re-focus attention. Visual and auditory clues orient us towards important elements, ideas or activities, enabling individuals to fixate and sustain their attention to solve a problem.

Figure 4.10 Warning signs direct our attention.

Enhancing memory

> Memory is the mother of all wisdom.
>
> —Aeschylus

The way that gamified systems focus attention and shift perception through the experience of play also can have the side effect of enhancing memory. Memory is the capacity to retain, store and later access information. We actively use memory to match interactions in the past with present situations, looking for aspects that are similar and distinguishing those that are different. Doing this allows us to adjust our expectations or behaviors accordingly, to repeat successful performance, and make modifications for variation. We conduct strategic thinking and analysis with our **working memory**, integrating a variety of information sources to navigate and discover both conventional and fantastic worlds. The ability to access and use our memory cannot be understated. It is essential for every activity we perform.

Good gamified systems provide the mechanics and structures to support memorable dynamics, ultimately leading to emergence and reflection. The Alternate Reality Game (ARG) I Love Bees, which was created to promote the launch of Microsoft's game Halo 2, is noted in ARG history for creating such distinct

Figure 4.11 The ARG *I Love Bees* encoded itself in the memories of players and ARG history when it used payphone booths and live operators in the game. © Andrew Sorcini.

Encoding

Encoding occurs when information stored in short-term or working memory is transferred to long-term memory. It involves:

- **Working memory**—a process that accesses and manipulates memories. To function it relies on both long-term and short-term memory.
- **Long-term memory**—information that is stored and can be retrieved.
- **Short-term memory**—information that is retained for on average twenty seconds and then forgotten.

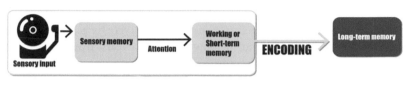

Figure 4.12 Encoding.

reflective opportunities. One of the most dramatic and memorable moments occurred when the game masters (the individuals running the game) decided to incorporate telephone booths into the game. Players had to find specific telephones, wait for them to ring, and then respond to live operators giving seemingly improvised instructions over the phone lines. By enabling positive feelings associated with particular activities, players are able to **encode** their experiences, transferring short-term memory to long-term memory. By attaching the feelings of warmth and intimacy with these activities, they become stored as **episodic memory**. Associated with a unique personal experience, this type of memory is the most accessible and meaningful.

Support the memory process

To promote encoding GS design should provide sustained tasks, repetition and discrepant, memorable moments distributed sequentially and over time.

HOW GAMES TEACH

> All aspects of the learning (game) environment . . . are set up
> to encourage active and critical, not passive learning.
> —James Paul Gee, *What Video Games Have to*
> *Teach Us About Learning and Literacy*

In his book *What Video Games Have to Teach Us About Learning and Literacy*, James Paul Gee describes the kind of active learning that allows for hard fun and at the same time shifts and enhances how we think. Active learning occurs when individuals engage in higher-order thinking and problem-solving. Introduced earlier as meta-cognition, this process of learning requires an individual to think about what she does while performing a task. It is marked by involvement, focused attention and exploration. Games and gamified systems support players by providing adaptive feedback that responds to input, helping individuals learn from their mistakes and keeping them from becoming frustrated and stuck.

Gee proposed thirty-six learning principles associated with playing games. While they are each significant, a few are particularly relevant for our purposes. One of these is the **active learning principle** and describes how environments of games are set up to encourage active learning. It is a variation of the "learning by doing" idea introduced by Papert. Returning to the example of *Minecraft*, players construct knowledge through the activity of building their own objects and environments.

Active learning is perpetuated by the **amplification of input**. Players know that simple mechanics combine to form secondary and more complex behaviors, which means that their continued efforts will be increasingly rewarded. The artful skill of generating new combinations of moves (combo moves) in a fighting game like *Street Fighter* are examples of this kind of expanded reward set. Experienced players of the game can artfully move the joystick in a chain of forward and down motions at exactly the right moment to strike the powerful and famous "Shoryuken" power attack. The rising dragon fist is only possible because of amplified input.

Though the possibilities for performance and reward are compounded over time, the introduction is incremental. Gee's **incremental principle** describes how challenges are staged in complexity to build off of pre-existing skills over time. This idea is fundamental to the practice of level design. When defining a space and its obstacles, designers must also identify the skills that a player needs to overcome them. These skills must be obtained and practiced in earlier levels (these ideas are covered in greater detail in Chapter 6).

Distributing information incrementally relates to feedback. In order to overcome a new challenge or untested skill a player should be provided with **explicit information on demand and just-in-time**. Good games and gamified systems provide necessary information at the most optimal time for understanding and applying it. The black and white illustrations displayed prominently at the beginning of each level of the first-person puzzle games *Portal* and *Portal 2* provide an example of this type of explicit instruction, letting players know at the outset what the goal is to complete that level.

Incrementally distributed information given on demand and in-time keeps players in the **regime of competence**, which occurs when players are always working at the edge of their abilities. This idea is explored more in this chapter in the discussion about the Zone of Proximal Development. Good design ensures that players have the skills they need to complete a challenge. However, an obstacle may require that a player combine these skills in new and unexpected ways.

Because games are inherently forgiving, players can take risks without experiencing any real-world consequences of their actions. The **psycho-social moratorium** highlights the emotional side of getting it wrong before we get it right. In the game world, bad grades, illness or haunting debt don't follow us no matter how poorly we performed or acted while playing. The success of the *Grand Theft Auto* (GTA) series is rooted in this concept. Players can freely misbehave, stealing what they want and driving as carelessly as they can without any fear of the consequences of breaking "the law." Games give us the freedom to fail and misbehave without suffering any real-world consequences.

Gee's learning principles

Six important principles for gamified systems:

- **Active learning principle**—Game environments encourage learning by doing.
- **Amplification of input**—Complex behaviors emerge through simple mechanisms.
- **Incremental principle**—Challenges are staged to build off of proven skills.
- **Explicit information on demand and just in time**—Provide necessary feedback at the appropriate time.
- **Regime of competence**—Players work at the edge of their abilities.
- **Psycho-social moratorium**—Misbehavior and failure is allowed and expected.

GETTING TO THE ZONE

Although learning may not always be the overt goal, by applying noted methods for structuring learning, games and gamified systems can move players through the **Zone of Proximal Development** (ZPD). Introduced in the 1930s by Russian psychologist Lev Vygotsky the ZPD is actually the foundation for Gee's "regime of confidence" principle. Players learn because they are working at the edge of their abilities. According to Vygotsky, the ZPD is the distance between a learner's current capacity (what he can do without support) and what can be achieved with additional support.

Figure 4.13 The Zone of Proximal Development.

By carefully ordering information and allowing players to incrementally build off of previous knowledge gained, games and gamified systems keep players continuously in the ZPD. As we play, we process the knowledge we are ready to learn with support and feedback from the system. Through this, we internalize lessons, bringing into our knowledge set what was once coming through external help from others. Skills that we can perform near the end of playing would not have been possible without earlier levels. According to Vygotsky, moving learners through the zone towards internalization and expertise occurs in four cyclical stages.

Stage 1: Assisted performance

In the first stage, a person learns a new subject matter or skills. To do this, an individual requires help from someone with greater knowledge than her own. This is where adaptive feedback triggered by repetitive failures or partial successes becomes essential in gamified systems.

Stage 2: Unassisted performance

The next phase occurs when a person attempts the learned task from Stage 1 without the help of a support structure. Adaptive feedback is low here in order to give a sense of autonomy and personal achievement.

Stage 3: Internalization

In this stage, the learner takes control of his knowledge. Play and experimentation happen, and new ideas emerge. Learners should have more access to tools that can hone or expand their skill set and creative works.

Stage 4: Recursion through earlier stages

This last stage enables learners to repeat earlier performances with confidence and become a part of the support structure for new learners. Social recognition is important here, because it infuses old tasks with new meanings.

Scaffolding

> Scaffolding refers to the steps taken to reduce the degrees of
> freedom in carrying out some task so that the child can con-
> centrate on the difficult skill she is in the process of acquiring.
> —Jerome Bruner

Reducing complexity and funneling attention, gamified systems can constrain
player focus to solve problems in a player's immediate sphere of ability. Like the
temporary structures this concept is named for, *scaffolding* supports learners
through the ZPD. Regulating task components, and progressively disclosing small
bits of information at appropriate moments, players perform just beyond their
solo abilities. By promoting exploration, gamified systems provide players the
freedom to organize and construct concepts and knowledge on their own terms.
Originally created in 1991, Sid Meier's *Civilization* game, now in its fifth incarna-
tion, lets players build empires while exploring territory, conducting research
and trading, competing and fighting other civilizations for dominance. Though
the turn-based strategy game is challenging enough to keep a grown-up busy for
months at a time, it is nevertheless like *Portal* and *Minecraft* being utilized as an
Alternate Purpose Game (APG) in middle school classrooms. Though it is an
extremely complex game with hundreds of options for building and protecting
civilizations, it provides the right amount of scaffolding so that novice players
are never left to their own devices to be overwhelmed by too many choices. In
the first play session, once inside what will be their civilizational world of
expansion, players are directed to perform their first task. A kindly female voice

Figure 4.14 Scaffolding provides critical supports to accomplish challenging and
complex tasks.

encourages building, announcing "this is a good place to found a city." As play progresses this type of support continues with new tasks, but is removed for tasks that have been proven and repeated. Consequently, players have the opportunity to discover and construct relationships, and assign their own personal meanings to incoming information and emerging abilities.

Games and gamified systems scaffold learning in a variety of ways. Introducing achievable tasks early is a good way to boost self-confidence, to lower frustration and motivate players to continue to advance forward. Though options at the beginning of a turn will expand significantly over time, at the beginning of *Civilization V* players are only required to make one choice at a time. They must choose their leader and then select a small area of land to begin exploring. This approach makes players feel that, when they are presented with more challenging tasks, like choosing a social policy, or deciding whether to engage in combat, they will have the knowledge and support they need to make meaningful choices. As a large set of options is revealed to players, guidance and feedback become essential. Direct instruction, asking questions, reassurances and reinforcement are all methods that games like *Civilization V* use to scaffold the experience. Good games and gamified systems should support a player until she has proven through recursion (repeated tasks) that she has mastered a skill. With enough repetition, initial support structures become unnecessary, and can gradually be removed.

Figure 4.15 *Civilization V* relies on scaffolding to help players manage the many decisions available for learning this complex system. Sid Meier's *Civilization V* screenshot courtesy of Firaxis Games, 2K Games, Inc., and Take-Two Interactive Software, Inc. All Rights Reserved. No part of this work may be reproduced in any form or by any means—graphic, electronic or mechanical, including photocopying, recording, online distribution,or information storage and retrieval systems—without the written permission of the publisher or the designated rightsholder, as applicable.

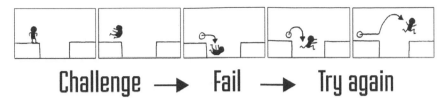

Challenge ➔ Fail ➔ Try again

Figure 4.16 The "challenge > fail > try again" cycle.

Scaffolding enables the "challenge > fail > try again" cycle of game-centric skill development. Players understand that failure is a part of the learning process as well as the process of knowledge creation. At the same time, the gamified system ensures they will not be overwhelmed with unnecessary information until the time is appropriate. This gives players ample time to build a skill, practice using it, fix and analyze misconceptions, develop the most accurate hypotheses and finally re-apply this knowledge over time.

Scaffolding players through the Zone of Proximal Development

GS designs can provide scaffolding through:

1. *Direct instruction* from a character, animated guide or more experienced player. If done in an appropriate way these messages can become an important part of the emergent narrative.
2. *Opportunities to model expert behaviors* or tasks through demonstrations by character, guide or more experienced player. By watching an expert perform a task players can organize their skills and become more efficient over time.
3. *Immediate feedback*, either oral or written to *assess performance* and *provide guidance towards improvement*.
4. Guides, characters or system messages *ask questions* of the player to *assess or assist performance*.
5. *Reassurance and reinforcement* should be introduced for partially understood concepts. Hints can let a player know when he is close and has completed portions of a task correctly.
6. When players get a task partially correct but not entirely, *redirect them* to other opportunities for learning and proving skills.
7. *Opportunities for recursion*. Get players to solidify knowledge by occasionally repeating tasks they have already successfully completed.
8. *Shared goals* to encourage collaboration amongst players. Frustration and alienation can be reduced when critical thinking, problem-solving, and decision-making are performed together.

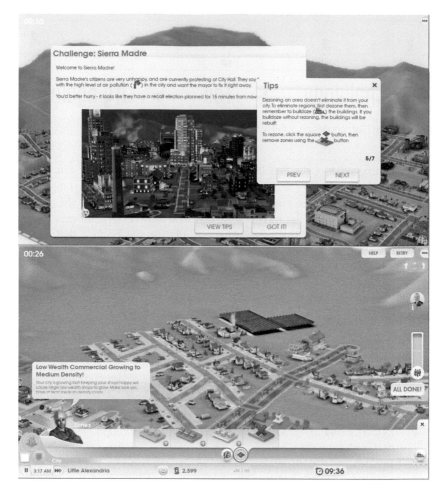

Figure 4.17 *SimCityEDU*, a modification of the *SimCity* game, provides guides, feedback and direct instruction through a variety of design approaches to help students while learning new skills. Courtesy of Katie Salen Institute of Play.

Cognitive Apprenticeship & Situated Learning

> It is quite possible to acquire a tool but to be unable to use it. Similarly, it is common for students to acquire algorithms, routines, and decontextualized definitions that they cannot use and that, therefore, lie inert.
>
> —J.S. Brown, A. Collins and P. Duguid,
> *Situated Cognition and the Culture of Learning*

Before institutions of learning (like schools) became widespread and available to a larger range of the population, apprenticeships were the way the majority of people experienced necessary training to perform a task. Individuals interested in learning a specific skill or craft would spend several years with a master, learning the tools and methods associated with a particular trade. Although such personalized training has been replaced by more standardized and scalable approaches, modeling experts while they perform their trades or tasks still remains one of the most valuable and relevant approaches to learning. Gamified systems provide a range of opportunities for cognitive apprenticeship, exposing at different layers of intensity processes and interactions that replicate a variety of aspects associated with an authentic experience.

Cognitive apprenticeship provides models and practice for problem-solving in real-world contexts. It engenders what is known as situated learning, which involves making the parts of any process explicit and visible. The game-like school Quest to Learn is built around the principle of situated learning. As its creator Katie Salen describes at the end of this chapter, the entire school semester is structured around game concepts like missions and quests, all leading up to a two-week boss level. During this time, students are required to re-engage and apply all of their learning, and collaborate together to perform high-level tasks required of an expert in a professional field. For instance, students who utilized the game SimCityEDU to learn about urban planning, local governance and environmental science may have to take on the roles of city planners, local politicians, business owners and research scientists. At the end of this two-week intensive, students must present their work to a board of real experts who work for actual cities demonstrating how they can transfer the knowledge they gained in the virtual world to the real one.

Although modeling the practices in-person with real-world experts is optimal, this approach is not always feasible. Simulations, best understood as imitative representations of real-world processes, provide opportunities for cognitive

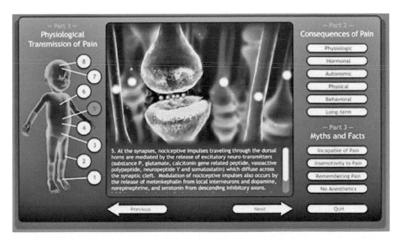

Figure 4.18 *NursingAP.com* is a gamified system built by the University of Texas designed to help nurses gain valuable knowledge by working with 3D infant patients.

apprenticeship in lieu and in addition to the support of human models. Because they can amplify or mimic different scenarios, while controlling and reducing other factors, simulations enable learners to make hypotheses and predictions about the effects of their actions. The use of simulations is widely used in the field of nursing because of the potential to improve problem-solving and critical decision-making without risking injury or harm to actual patients. One example is the University of Texas's award-winning research project, which asked, "Can game play teach student nurses how to save lives?" The project's design team built NursingAP.com, a 3D game-based simulation, which let nursing students support the lives of infant patients. Role-play is combined with a time-sensitive mini-game to build the skills necessary for healthcare providers in emergency scenarios. The system demonstrated that it could encourage empathy of the nurse while maximizing critical decision-making under pressure.

KEY TAKEAWAYS

- By provoking novel pattern recognition, gamified systems can satisfy the brain's desire for richly interpretable experiences.
- Constructionist learning is based on the idea that we learn best when we build our own knowledge. Seymour Papert, who pioneered the idea, believed that constructionist learning required the following ingredients: *hard fun, learning by doing, technology as building material, learning to learn, taking time* and *accepting failure as an essential part of the learning process.*
- Games and gamified systems provide potentiating environments where there are plenty of hard, interesting things to do, and it is accepted as normal, appealing and fun that everyone regularly gets confused and fails at tasks.
- *Bloom's Taxonomy* is a framework for understanding the progressive process of learning, identified by six levels of progression: *memory, comprehension, application, analysis, evaluation* and finally *creation.* It provides one way of understanding how the stages of play support different areas of learning.
- By using familiar devices, control mappings, and relying on a small handful of core mechanics, games and gamified systems support the variety of cognitive processes required to maximize working memory.
- In his book *What Video Games Have to Teach Us About Learning and Literacy*, James Paul Gee articulates thirty-six principles about how games and gamified systems promote active learning. Good gamified systems focus attention and encourage exploration to engage players in higher-order thinking and problem-solving.
- Games and gamified systems move players through the Zone of Proximal Development. Defined by Lev Vygotsky, ZPD is the distance between unsupported ability and what can be achieved with additional support. At each step of the design process, the ZPD is a way of mapping what is already known to the player and what is being introduced by the gamified system.

- Scaffolding is a concept introduced by Jerome Bruner, relating to the changing and dynamic support structures necessary to move individuals through the ZPD.
- Gamified systems can provide scaffolding through a variety of means including appropriate and timely feedback, expert modeling, asking questions, reassurance, assisting performance, recognizing success and providing redirection. Scaffolding should also encourage and enable group problem-solving and provide opportunities to re-use learned skills in recursive tasks.
- Cognitive apprenticeship provides models and practice for problem-solving processes that can be found in real-world contexts. This creates situated learning making the parts of the process explicit and visible.

EXERCISES

4.1 Hard fun

Study a gamified system and identify the ways that it aligns to Papert's requirements for constructionist learning: hard fun, learning by doing, technology as building material, learning to learn, taking time and accepting failure as an essential part of the learning process.

4.2 Taxonomy of learning

Using Bloom's revised taxonomy, evaluate the types of knowledge and learning occurring in a game or gamified system. What kind of knowledge is being gained; what kinds of skills? What domains (cognitive, affective, psychomotor)?

4.3 Scaffolding

Review a gamified system and look at the ways it provides scaffolding through feedback, modeling, collaboration and recursion.

4.4 Situated learning

Review a gamified system that demonstrates the principles of cognitive apprenticeship. How is the system using expert modeling and other support structures to encourage players to learn to be proficient at the skill and knowledge required to succeed?

RECOMMENDED READINGS

- *A Theory of Fun for Game Design*, by Raph Koster, 2013 (reprint).
  Koster's comic-filled book distills the important connections between the experience of learning and the joy of playing games.

- *What Video Games Have to Teach Us About Learning and Literacy*, by James Paul Gee, 2003.
  Through his thirty-six principles Gee demonstrate how games facilitate and encourage active learning.

KATIE SALEN CREATED A GAME-LIKE SCHOOL

Interview granted with permission by Katie Salen.

Katie Salen locates her work in the field of game design and is the founder of a non-profit called the Institute of Play that is focused on games and learning. She is also Professor of Games and Digital Media at DePaul University. Salen led the team that founded Quest to Learn in 2009, a sixth- to twelfth-grade public school in New York City, as well as ChicagoQuest, a 6–12 charter school that opened fall 2011 in Chicago. Salen is co-author of *Rules of Play*, a textbook on game design, *The Game Design Reader*, *Quest to Learn: Growing a School for Digital Kids*, and editor of *The Ecology of Games: Connecting Youth, Games, and Learning*, all from MIT Press. She has worked as a game designer for over twelve years and is a

Figure 4.19
Katie Salen.

former co-editor of the *International Journal of Learning and Media*. She was an early advocate of the then-hidden world of machinima and continues to be interested in connections between game design, learning and transformative modes of play.

*   *   *

Game designers traffic in the space of possibility. They design systems that define rules and thus give rise both to play and to a sense that anything is possible. As a game designer, I believe in the value of such spaces. The design of Quest to Learn thus began with an inquiry into the idea of possibility.

What, for example, my team asked, might be made possible for kids if we found a way to conceive of school as just one kind of learning space within a network of learning spaces that spans in school, out of school, local and global, physical and digital, teacher led and peer driven, individual and collaborative?

What might be made possible for teachers if their creativity around how to engage kids were deeply valued and they were supported with resources—such as collaborating with game designers—to really understand what engagement around learning can look like?

What might be made possible for communities if school were to become a catalyst for activating a network of mentors, partners, peers and leaders who are focused on helping kids figure out how to be inventors, designers, innovators and problem-solvers?

What might be made possible for students if they were challenged to teach others how to do the stuff they know how to do, and content was treated as an actionable resource rather than something to be memorized?

What might be made possible if kids not only were able to use games and media and models and simulations as drivers of their learning, but were also able to design them, too?

What might be made possible for the world if we were able to support kids to be curious, to have ideas and build theories around those ideas, to fail often and early as a strategy for learning how something really works, to be given an opportunity to interact with the larger world in ways that feel relevant, exciting and empowering?

What might be made possible if we treated school not as a problem to be fixed or complained about, but as a partner in the learning lives of our kids, our parents and our communities?

What might actually be possible?

Quest to Learn

New York City was willing to hedge its bets and see what would be possible when a school stopped talking about technology as a learning solution and instead looked to kids as the centers of innovation. Quest to Learn was the result of this bet, a new sixth- to twelve-grade public school that opened its doors in fall 2009 with seventy-six extremely excited sixth graders.

It is important to be clear about something now in order to address any possible misconceptions. Quest to Learn is not a school of videogames or a school where kids play videogames all day. Games are one important tool in the school, most certainly, but they represent something more than a resource. They are the basis of a theory of learning that is both situated and game-like. As a result, we designed the school around an approach to learning that draws from what we know games do best: drop kids into inquiry-based, complex problem spaces that are scaffolded to deliver just-in-time learning and to use data to help players understand how they are doing, what they need to work on, and where to go next. It is an approach that creates, above all else, a need to know—a need to ask, why and how and with whom?

Teachers in the Quest schools work with game designers to create ten-week-long "missions." The missions pose difficult and often enigmatic challenges for students to solve. Quests of one to five weeks in length break down the bigger challenge into smaller ones whose solutions contribute tools, knowledge and skills to the larger mission. Here's a good example.

A mission called Ghost vs. Ghost challenges seventh graders to grapple with the question of how it could be possible for a group of individuals to experience the same event but come away with competing points of view. A group of fictional ghosts of various lineages, all present at the events surrounding the founding of the American colonies, are trapped in the sub-, sub-, sub-basement of the Natural History Museum. They are fighting over the "correct" interpretation of historic events. The question posed is a critical one: How might someone know what and who to believe when everyone's story is different?

Over the course of the mission—which connects history, social studies and writing, and tackles a robust set of required learning standards—students dig into primary documents to uncover evidence supporting various versions of the contested events. They write individual memoirs from the point of view of their favorite colonial ghost, and they ultimately produce persuasive essays that are grounded not only in a respect for the rigors of narrative and history, but also in the power of empathy to allow for the co-existence of competing points of view.

Creating opportunities for learners to fail productively—to discover what they need to know through a process of trial and error—is a trait shared among inquiry-oriented teachers and game designers. One key property of these types of experiences is that they require that individual expertise be applied within a collaborative context. Members of a team must work together on a problem by contributing different forms of skill and expertise. The idea that teamwork and collaboration are skills critical to success in the 21st-century workplace is not new, of course, but game-like learning has some potential to become a key space for these skills to develop. Here's an example, to illustrate this point.

The New York City Math Olympiad Tournament provides teams of middle school students from schools around the city with the chance to demonstrate their not-insignificant mathematical chops. Teams meet weekly throughout the year to practice and come to the tournament prepared to compete. In 2010, Quest to Learn first fielded a team of sixth and seventh graders, in contrast to the mostly eighth grader make-up of the other teams. Members of the team had come to Quest from different elementary schools across the city and all shared a passion for math.

Traditionally, teams focus their practice sessions on individual training—in the competition students compete as individuals in the initial rounds, so individual performance is critical. But because of Quest to Learn's focus on game-like learning, members of the team were also trained in collaboration as part of their regular classes. As a result, participants had deep experience in what might be called "teaming and competing": groups of individuals working together to achieve both individual and group success.

Quest's team won the Olympiad and most who witnessed the victory said simply, "They were the team who worked together best." Quest has gone on to win the Olympiad every year since.

A starter set: guiding principles of game-like learning

These kinds of successes have shown that game-like learning has the potential to enable new engagement models that not only support learning with academic, civic and career implications, but also cultivate peer exchange and the building of mentor networks. These models include teaming and competing structures that mix collaborative and competitive elements, real-time data to support just-in-time learning, rewards and incentive structures that are communally defined and reinforced, and multiple, overlapping expressions of recognition and reputation. But are there larger ideas that help hold these various elements together in ways that move them beyond a kind of "gamification" of the classroom? Are there design principles that can underlie the Quest model? What are the rules, in other words, that organize the play of learning at Quest to Learn?

Following are a set of seven guiding design principles that have bubbled up as we've iterated on the early ideas of the school. Embedded within each of the principles are several design features; these features point to specific elements that can be designed in support of the larger guiding principle. Design features represent our thinking on the types of mechanisms that need to be present to support realization of the larger principle within a designed learning context.

Seven guiding principles of game-like learning

1. Everyone is a participant

Create a shared culture and practice where everyone contributes, which may mean that different students contribute different types of expertise. Design learning experiences that invite participation and provide many different ways for individuals and groups to contribute. Build in roles and supports for teachers, mentors, outside experts and instructors to act as translators and bridge-builders for learners across domains and contexts. Make sure barriers to entry are low and that there are opportunities for students, especially new students, to lurk and leach (i.e. observe and borrow); peer-based exchange, like communication and sharing, should be made easy and reciprocal. Develop a diverse set of resources to support teaching and mentorship activities. Consider developing challenge-based experiences that invite networks of experts in to collaborate with students; design problem sets in ways that capitalize on global expertise.

2. Feedback is immediate and ongoing

Create structures for students to receive on-going feedback on their progress against learning and assessment goals. Feedback should include structures for guidance and mentorship, which may take place via the online communities associated with the curriculum, or in classroom, afterschool or home settings. Create ways for this feedback to increase in depth and richness as the types of contributions students make or the roles they take on grow and change. Provide opportunities for students to take on leadership roles, based on expertise and interest. Make sure there are plenty of ways for them to share their work with their peers, solicit feedback, teach others how to do things, and reflect on their own learning. One key aspect of this is allowing every student's contribution to be visible to everyone else in the group. Utilize the tools associated with the school's social network platforms to enable communication and exchange between peers, who may or may not be part of the same group or setting.

3. Challenge is constant

One of the more powerful features of challenge-based experiences is that they create a need to know by challenging students to solve a problem whose resources have been placed just out of reach. Students must develop expertise in order to access the resources. They are motivated to do so either because the learner finds the problem context itself engaging or because it connects to an existing interest or passion. Make sure that learning activities support situated inquiry and discovery so that students have rich contexts within which to practice with concepts and content. Consider including "gates," levels or other structures that limit access to highlight opportunities for advancement. As students advance against a challenge provide a diverse array of opportunities for them to build social and cultural capital around their progress. Explore teaming and competing structures like competitions and collaborations that mix collaborative and competitive elements in the service of problem discovery and solving.

4. Learning happens by doing

Learning is participatory and experiential. Students learn by proposing, testing, playing with and validating theories about the world. Challenge-based learning experiences should be designed around performance-based activities that give rise to authentic learning tasks. Make sure that learners have access to robust mechanisms for discoverability; resources supporting problem discovery and solving are easy to find, diverse, and easily shareable across networks. Peer-produced tutorials, FAQs and other materials should be easy to find, use and share. Think of ways to situate problem sets within a context that has meaning or relevance for participants, be this peer, interest or academic in orientation. Provide students with multiple, overlapping opportunities to interact with experts and mentors who model expert identities associated with the problem space. Allow students to collaborate in many different ways, as they explore different roles or identities related to the design project at hand.

5. Everything is interconnected

Students should be provided with multiple learning contexts for engaging in game-like learning—contexts in which they receive immediate feedback on progress, have access to tools for planning and reflection, and are given opportunities for mastery of specialist language and practices. Create infrastructures for students to share their work, skill and knowledge with others across networks, groups and communities. These channels might take the form of online public portfolios, streamed video or podcasts, student-led parent conferences, or public events where work is critiqued and displayed, to name but a few. Allow students to make interest, peer and academic-based identities, status and achievement visible across settings of home, school, afterschool and peer group. Build in roles and supports for teachers, mentors, outside experts and instructors to act as translators and bridge-builders for learners across domains and contexts. Provide diverse forms of recognition and assessment, which might take varied forms, including prizes, badges, ranking, ratings and reviews. A social network platform can play a key role in supporting this principle.

6. Failure is celebrated as iteration

Create many opportunities for students and teachers to learn through failure. All learning experiences with a game-like learning model should embrace a process of prototyping and iteration, based on a game design methodology: students work through multiple versions of any idea or solution, integrating on-going feedback into the learning process, and developing debriefings that identify strengths and weaknesses of both process and solution. In some cases, students may choose to build on previous solutions or approaches of other students, seeing themselves as contributors to a larger body of collaboratively generated knowledge. Participants build both cultural and intellectual capital as a result.

7. It kind of feels like play

Create learning experiences that are fundamentally engaging, learner-centered and organized to support inquiry and creativity. Rules create limits: learning experiences invite interaction and inquiry into the limits and possibilities of the platform, tools, problem spaces or media in which students are working. Challenges organize inquiry so that learning experiences pose challenges for participants to overcome in ways that are engaging and aligned with interest and ability level. Support learners in defining goals that structure the nature of their interaction and inquiry from moment-to-moment, as well as longer term. Align core mechanics with learning goals. In other words, the ways in which participants interact with the learning environment—the mechanics or "verbs" of their interaction—align with core learning outcomes. Action is therefore never not in the service of the learning taking place. Design choice to be meaningful: participants power movement through the experience via choices they make along the way. Help students reflect on the choices they are making in the design or transformation of a system—empower them to see themselves as agents of change.

Table 4.1 offers a view of the seven principles at-a-glance.

Closing the Loop

Designing for effective game-like learning requires a mindset that sees the various spaces of formal and informal learning opportunities as integrally linked. A designer's job, as creator of the contexts, activities and connectors linking each, be they assessment or credential systems, mentor networks, communities or tools and technologies, is to create feedback loops that place the above design principles in conversation with each other, so that the whole becomes greater than the sum of its parts.

Table 4.1 The seven principles of game-like learning

Design principle	Supporting design features	Guiding reflections
Everyone is a participant.	• Low barriers to entry and access. • Varied participation opportunities and ways to contribute. • Diversity in level and type of expertise supported. • Sharing is easy and reciprocal. • Incentives and rewards for learner support. • Integrated professional development programming.	• Do all students have a role to play, which allows them to contribute? • Is peer-based exchange like communication and sharing easy and reciprocal? • Are a diverse set of resources to support teaching and mentorship available?
Feedback is immediate and on-going.	• Guiding feedback and mentorship. • Increasingly rich feedback and support for specialization. • Leadership development opportunities. • Visibility of contributions enables communication and exchange between peers.	• Are students using data as a tool to inform their learning? • Are there opportunities for students to take on leadership roles, based on expertise and interest? • Are contributions visible to everyone in the group?
Challenge is constant.	• Challenges create a "need to know." • A need to share enables peer exchange. • Embedded infrastructure for sharing across individuals, groups and communities. • Structured access. • Contributions organized around a shared culture, knowledge base or purpose. • Infrastructure to support collaborations and competitions.	• Is a "need to know" created by organizing learning around solving complex problems set in engaging contexts? • Does the design of the challenge create both a reason and an opportunity for sharing? • Is a shared interest being pursued via the challenge? • Do students have opportunities to both team and compete?
Learning happens by doing.	• Participatory and experiential contexts. • Performance-based and authentic task design.	• Are students involved in hands-on inquiry? • Are students being challenged to tinker, explore,

	• Robust mechanisms for search and discoverability. • Abundant learning resources organized around challenges. • On-going interaction with experts and mentors. • Varied opportunities to build social capital.	hypothesize and test assumptions? • Does the learning experience allow students to show understanding in multiple ways? • Are support resources linked to challenges and easy to find and share? • Do students have access to mentors who are modeling best practices within the domain?
Everything is interconnected.	• Diverse forms of recognition and assessment are visible across communities. • Cross-site sharing mechanisms for credentialing, mentoring and assessment. • Feedback loops reinforce activity across spaces and sites. • Support multiple, overlapping pathways toward mastery.	• Does the experience build in opportunities for authority and expertise to be shared and made reciprocal among learners/mentors/teachers? • Is there a way for students to share their work, skill and knowledge with others across networks, groups and communities? • Are adults helping students to make connections across contexts and communities?
Failure is reframed as iteration.	• Easy to use prototyping tools. • Numerous structured opportunities for reflection. • Student-level controls for making work public. • Low-risk "messing around" spaces afford opportunities to see many examples of possible outcomes. • Rubrics are leveled through novice, apprentice, senior, master stages.	• Are students prototyping and iterating to improve ideas and understanding? • Do students have control over when and to whom they share their work? • Are students allowed to remix and build on the work of others to meet a shared goal? • Is evidence of progress towards goals visible to students?
It kind of feels like play.	• Rules create limits. • Challenges organize inquiry. • Goals provide purposeful interaction. • Choice is meaningful. • Core mechanics align with learning goals. • Reflection is integrated throughout.	• Is the learning experience engaging, learner-centered and organized to support inquiry and creativity? • Are students making choices that matter? • Are students given opportunities to reflect on their understanding of the current and future state of a system?

At Quest to Learn, a set of feedback loops create intentionally redundant and overlapping learning opportunities, such as an afterschool program, which supports students in learning how to create videos, an integrated math/science class where the creation of video tutorials is the primary form of summative assessment, and which includes a specially designed social-network platform called QLink, allowing students to post, rate and review each other's tutorials and video remixes against assessment-oriented rubrics.

This kind of feedback loop—one made up of various learning contexts across which kids move—is almost always reinforcing. Youth have opportunities to practice and synthesize content and skills in varied contexts that have been intentionally designed to point to other spaces to learn.

And then there is the rise. Structures and experiences emerge from the system because attention has been paid to the possibilities the spaces afford. Feedback loops act like connective tissue between the "bone" of state standards and core literacies. And when designed well, feedback loops can give rise to the kinds of supplementary, passion-based learning we know help kids excel.

We need to do a better job of giving kids opportunities to rise, which means designing systems that enable the rise—that enable kids to move across networks and to engage in really hard problems with resources to solve them.

Games are all about creating spaces of possibility, where players feel that they can do anything. I believe schools can aspire to design these kinds of spaces, too.

* * *

For more information and resources on game-like learning, visit www.instituteofplay.org. We've developed a set of tools, videos and curriculum resources that show the principles described in the text above in action.

NOTES

Benyon, David, Phil Turner and Susan Turner. *Designing Interactive Systems: People, Activities, Contexts, Technologies.* Harlow, Essex: Addison-Wesley, 2005.

Biederman, Irving and Edward Vessel, "Perceptual Pleasure and the Brain." *American Scientist,* 94:3 (May–June 2006): 247–253.

Bloom, Benjamin. *Taxonomy of Educational Objectives: The Classification of Educational Goals: Handbook I, Cognitive Domain.* Edited by Benjamin S. Bloom. New York: Longmans, 1956.

Brown, John Seely, Allan Collins and Paul Duguid. *Situated Cognition and the Culture of Learning.* Report 6896 for BBN System and Technologies Corporation, 1988.

Bruner, Jerome. *Toward a Theory of Instruction.* Cambridge: Harvard University Press, 1966.

Chaiklin, S. "The Zone of Proximal Development in Vygotsky's Analysis of Learning and Instruction." In *Vygotsky's Educational Theory and Practice in Cultural Context.* Edited by A. Kozulin, B. Gindis, V. Ageyev and S. Miller. 39–64. Cambridge: Cambridge University Press, 2003.

Clark, D., E. Tanner-Smith and S. Killingsworth. *Digital Games, Design and Learning: A Systematic Review and Meta-Analysis.* Report for SRI International, Menlo Park, 2014.

Flavell, J. "Piaget's Legacy." *Psychological Science*, 7:4 (1996): 200–203.

Gallagher, Shane. "Can Playing Video Games Improve Cognition and Adaptability." *Advanced Distributed Learning Blog*, November 19, 2012, http://www.adlnet.gov/from-adl-team-member-shane-gallagher-can-playing-video-games-improve-cognition-and-adaptability/.

Gallagher, Shane and Shenan Prestwich. "Cognitive Task Analysis: Analyzing the Cognition of Gameplay and Game Design." Paper presented at Interservice/Industry Training, Simulation, and Education Conference, Orlando, FL, 2013.

Gee, James Paul. *What Video Games Have to Teach Us About Learning and Literacy*. New York: Palgrave, 2003.

Kapp, Karl. *The Gamification of Learning and Instruction*. San Francisco: Pfeiffer, 2012.

Koster, Raph. *A Theory of Fun for Game Design*. Phoenix: Paraglyph Press, 2004 [updated version 2010].

Mercer, Neil. "Neo-Vygotskian Theory and Classroom Education." *Language, Literacy, and Learning in Educational Practice: A Reader*. Edited by Barry Stierer and Janet Maybin. 96–97. Buckinghamshire: Open University, 1994.

Papert, Seymour. *Eight Big Ideas Behind the Constructionist Learning Lab*. 1999. http://sylvia martinez.com/tag/seymour-papert/.

Prestwich, Shenan. "The Cognition of Gameplay." *Advanced Distributed Learning Blog*, December 19, 2012, http://www.adlnet.gov/from-adl-team-member-shenan-prestwich-the-cognition-of-gameplay/.

Salen, Katie, Robert Torres, Loretta Wolozin, Rebecca Rufo-Tepper and Arana Shapiro. *Quest to Learn: Developing the School for Digital Kids*. Cambridge: MIT Press, 2011. [Based on the design document originally written in 2008.]

Shafer, David Williamson. *How Computer Games Help Children Learn*. New York: Palgrave Macmillan, 2006.

Shanker, Stuart and Talbot J. Taylor. "The House that Bruner Built." *Jerome Bruner: Language, Culture and Self*. Edited by David Bakhurst and Stuart Shanker. 50–54. Thousand Oaks: Sage, 2001.

Sheldon, Lee. *The Multiplayer Classroom: Designing Coursework as a Game*. Boston: Cengage Learning, 2012.

Shelton, Brett E. "Designing Educational Games for Activity-Goal Alignment." *The Design and Use of Simulation Computer Games in Education*. Edited by Brett E. Shelton and David A. Wiley. 106–110. Boston: Sense Publishers, 2007.

Squire, Kurt. *Video Games and Learning: Teaching and Participatory Culture in the Digital Age*. New York: Teachers College Press, 2011.

Stager, Gary. "An Investigation of Constructionism in the Maine Youth Center." PhD dissertation, 2007.

Stone, Linda. "Continuous Partial Attention." *Linda Stone's Blog*, http://lindastone.net/qa/continuous-partial-attention/.

Vygotsky, Lev. *Mind in Society: The Development of the Higher Psychological Processes*. Cambridge: Harvard University Press, 1978.

Vygotsky, Lev. "Extracts from Thought and Language and Mind and Society." *Language, Literacy, and Learning in Educational Practice: A Reader*. Edited by Barry Stierer and Janet Maybin. 45–58. Buckinghamshire: Open University, 1994.

Note: For information about the *NursingAP* simulation see http://www.utdallas.edu/news/2012/4/19-17251_ATEC-Nurse-Training-Simulations-Singled-Out-for-Aw_article-wide.html.

II THE TOOLBOX

5 WHAT IS GAMIFIED SYSTEM DESIGN?

CHAPTER QUESTIONS

At the end of this chapter, you should be able to answer these questions:

- What is GS design?
- What skills are required to be a gamified system (GS) designer?
- What transferable skills can individuals trained in either game design or user experience (UX) design bring to the practice?
- What are the steps in the design process?
- What is Agile, and how is it translated into the Scrum framework?

INTRODUCTION

While gamified systems use concepts or entities from the game world, what really sets them apart are the goals, articulated throughout the design process.

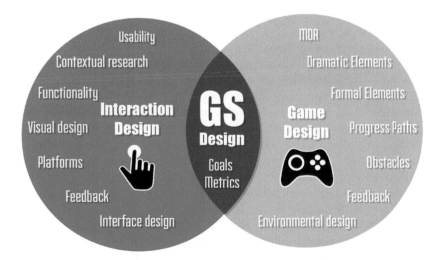

Figure 5.1 GS design combines skills from game design and interaction design.

These extend beyond the specific interaction that the player experiences during play. GS design meets these articulated goals using elements and concepts associated with games and play. It also involves defining the mechanisms for incorporating and generating data to support and measure these goals. As a practice, gamified system design brings together the fields of game design and interaction design. Given how new the practice is, most designers today are likely to be have been trained in either the field of game design or in the field of Human Computer Interaction (HCI). Although game and interaction design tend to be separated in the academy and in industry, they actually both fall under the larger category of user experience (UX) design, which can be understood as the design of content and form to meet a certain set of human behaviors. With the public's overwhelming receptivity to social media gaming, casual gaming and now gamified system designs, it seems inevitable that the lines between these two disciplines will continue to intersect. Through this evolution, gamified system design will continue to benefit from the confluence of skills related to creating interactivity and game play.

THE CONVERGENCE OF GAME AND INTERACTION DESIGN

The design of gamified systems includes a large range of activities. And, although some methodologies and skill sets differentiate the areas of game and interactive design, the overlaps are significant. In terms of work process, both practices utilize similar approaches, including cross-functional teams, iterative design method-ologies and Agile development, a product development philosophy described in more detail later in this chapter. They also share many of the same technical implementations. Finally, these practices are heavily impacted by similar audience acquisition strategies and monetization choices as well as their use of metrics and analytics to measure effectiveness and improve design.

In *Rules of Play: Game Design Fundamentals*, Katie Salen and Eric Zimmerman define the practice of game design as: *designing game play, conceiving and designing rules and structures that result in an experience for players.* This definition describes the essential practices involved in game design, which creates rules and resources for players. And, while game design is traditionally intended for the boundaries of the magic circle, the practice nevertheless emphasizes design for human experience. The game designer must measure the success of the rules and structures she creates by the experience players have playing his game.

Like game design, interaction design focuses on enhancing the human experience. Jenny Preece, Yvonne Rogers and Helen Sharp, in *Interaction Design: Beyond Human-Computer Interaction* (2002), have a good working definition: *designing interactive products to support the way people communicate and interact in their everyday and working lives.* Although interaction design is about supporting the needs of everyday existence and game design is traditionally understood as external to daily life, both emphasize the role of design in crafting optimal opportunities for people to make meaningful and informed choices, often through technology and digital artifacts.

Looking at the overlaps and distinctions between the two definitions can help us to generate our own description of this new practice. A definition of GS design could be:

Combining game concepts with non-game-related structures to create interactive and play-centric experiences that serve goals outside of the game context.

GS designers combine the need to create great game-play structures like procedures, rules and materials with the desire to support the needs and requirements of every day digital and non digital existence. While online and multiplayer game designs must incorporate UX design, interface design and communication functions, these tend to act in a type of supporting role to play-oriented elements (like characters and environments). With gamified systems, however, particularly those considered to fall in the game layer category, these interactive functions tend to be the core or foundation of the system. They thus have as much priority as the game elements. GS design must carefully balance play with functionally for the purposes of meeting goals that reside outside of the specific game-play experience.

REQUISITE SKILLS OF A GS DESIGNER

The GS designer must manage a large set of changing concerns and issues throughout the various stages of design, implementation and assessment. Having the right set of skills could make the difference between a great usable project and one that never gets off the ground. Abilities needed on the job include:

*   **Collaboration and communication:** Working productively with a cross-functional team of individuals often having different perspectives and agendas.
*   **Design:** Applying patterns from a wide range of game genres to design game elements that satisfy goals external to the game context.
*   **User-centered approach:** Studying and empathizing the people who will be using your system. Understanding the activities and contexts where they will be used.
*   **Technical knowledge:** Understanding the technologies, devices and materials that can be leveraged for implementation.

Collaboration and communication

GS design is a balancing act. The out-of-game goals drive design decisions. These in turn get measured and refined through feedback from the users or players. The designer must act as a bridge on the development team, negotiating between business development, marketing, finance, engineering and art departments. At the same time, he must work closely with one or more content experts, often from outside the organization itself. In some cases these will be specialists in specific fields, which will vary depending upon the project. For instance, Try Objective-C (introduced in Chapter 4) required the participation of programmers deeply versed in the programming language Objective-C. The atmospheric puzzle platformer Never Alone (Kisima Ingitchuna) is another excellent example of this type of collaboration. Experienced game designers worked hand in hand with a team of forty Alaskan Native elders to design a richly textured game that shares and educates players about the Iñupiat heritage and culture. In other scenarios, particularly in the case of business and marketing, expertise comes from clients who know their product or concept better than anyone else. In most cases, there will be a combination of different but equally valuable and valid perspectives driving the project goals, which will each need to be addressed in some way during research, design and implementation.

A key part of the designer's role is to listen closely to the needs and perspectives of the content experts and/or client and translate these into a design that the development team can implement so that an audience will respond positively. An example of this type of collaboration happened when the American Legacy Foundation's Truth campaign conducted a project with students and professors at the Savannah College or Art and Design. The initiative brought together students and faculty with the non-profit's research scientists and marketing team. Together we developed a gamified loyalty program for teenagers to promote the Truth brand and subtly promote its anti-smoking message. The design team worked with the organization's key personnel and gathered feedback from real teenagers about their reactions to designs and implementations. GS design requires constant collaboration and an essential capacity to work with a wide range of people inside and outside of an organization.

Working through an iterative development process the designer must re-adjust the project measuring inputs from content experts and users against those coming from the rest of the development team, particularly in regards to technical feasibility. Programmers and developers are ultimately the team members who answer the question "Can it be built?" It is almost always the job of the designer to listen to the varied and diverse inputs of constituents, and identify creative solutions that can mitigate potential implementation and design issues down the road.

Ultimately, the key to success is to establish clear goals that drive the team forward. Creating a mission statement usually comes out of the marketing planning process (this will be covered more in Chapter 9). This can be one clear sentence that everyone on the team, if asked, can repeat. As the team goes through the process of gathering goals and objectives, sometimes referred to as requirements, it's important that the designer boil these down to be actionable and coherent. While each member of the team is working on his or her own set of tasks, it is your job as the designer to keep everyone moving along the same path, reminding them of the bigger picture and promise you are working towards.

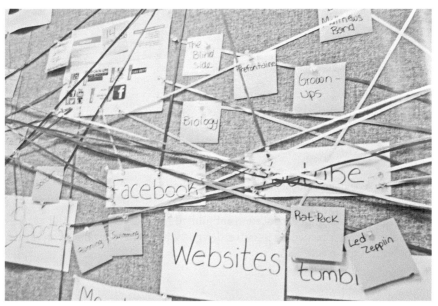

Figures 5.2 and 5.3 Images from the Truth loyalty program include the final project design and the brainstorming and research that went into it. Source: Legacy for Health. Used by permission.

Design

Designing gamified systems involves research, innovative thinking, ideation and the ability to turn these skills into written specifications and workable prototypes. Beginning with the creative process, the designer must take the goals and objectives defined by content experts and clients, and then match these to game elements like feedback, rewards, obstacles and mechanics. She must be able to craft these concepts so that they are able to generate measureable data. Screens for play, management tools and data dashboards must also be designed. These interfaces must satisfy the needs of the target audience, and the technologies that will be utilized to deliver the experience. As ideas take shape, sketching and then more detailed documentation, either paper or digital, need to be developed. The designer is ultimately responsible for making sure that these specifications effectively detail the system that the development team needs to build.

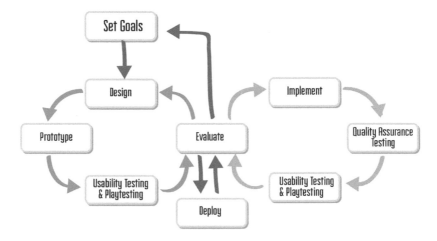

Figure 5.4 A diagram of the iterative design process.

GS design is a dynamic process combining design, development and analysis. We refer to this practice as iterative design, which is a continuous cycle that includes:

1. Setting goals.
2. Design & ideation.
3. Prototyping.
4. User testing (usability and playtesting).
5. Evaluation.
6. Implementation.
7. Testing (quality assurance, usability and playtesting).
8. Deployment.
9. More evaluation . . . repeat the cycle.

This approach is about rapidly getting to workable prototypes that can be tested early and often by the target audience. This input is then used for refinement as the cycle continues. Once a deliverable is achieved the process continues with the evaluation being driven by metrics (measureable data) and feedback from users or players about the live site or playable experience.

Usability

Successfully achieving project goals requires accurate and up-to-date knowledge about the different audiences that will be interacting with the intended system. This means having a clear and definitive articulation of the knowledge and skills that a user or player brings to the prescribed task. Spending time with members of the target audience is essential for understanding their capabilities and their limitations. Designers must also test these designs with the target audience. A powerful gamified system leverages the collective conversation occurring between the different technologies and devices in a user's life. The outcome of these usability tests should direct the refinement of the product for more testing.

Designing gamified systems is about crafting an experience filled with meaningful choices and clear objectives so that these in turn can satisfy external goals. Doing this well means having a keen creative sensibility combined with a strong capacity to understand, interpret, implement and guide the many perspectives influencing the direction of a project. You must create something that is both fun and playable for an audience, which works within the available technical infrastructure, all while serving the bigger mission of the project. Achieving all of these objectives is no small task and can in fact be very challenging. Good GS designers use the game world for brainstorming, and must be familiar with the materials used for games including board games, live gaming events, mobile, single and multiplayer console and computer-based games. This is why successful gamified systems have received so much attention and why GS designers are so increasingly valuable to organizations. Examples mentioned throughout this book all demonstrate that innovation and success, while challenging, is achievable.

LAYING THE GROUNDWORK

Because gamified systems can differ so much in terms of goals and implementation, there is not one specific process for design, development and implementation. Yet, certain basic steps are generally conducted in a structured way, a process that could be reasonably applied to most projects. These initial steps include:

1. Setting goals.
2. Conducting research.
3. Identifying target behaviors.
4. Developing "Key Performance Indicators" (KPIs).

Figure 5.5 Diagram of the GS development process.

Setting goals

Each project should begin by defining the project goals. Though these will continue to be modified, every project needs an agenda and directive dictating the approach taken. Based upon the context of the project, these goals and objectives will likely come from a variety of people, each focusing on his own priorities.

Let's take an example of a consumer brand company designing a new product and developing a marketing plan for it. While a product designer would primarily want feedback from customers about features and functions, a marketing professional would want to build consumer awareness of the new product. On the other hand, a Chief Financial Officer might want to know how a project will generate revenue. For this set of divergent goals, the designer would have to produce a system that generates feedback, builds an audience, and delivers sales. No matter which objectives you and your team define, the envisioned goals will ultimately drive specific types of engagement and target behaviors. Goals and objectives are as wide ranging as the projects implemented to serve them.

Conducting research

After clarifying goals and objectives, exploratory research ensues. Defining the target audience is the most important part of the research process. This first phase, often conducted by members of product and marketing teams, involves the collection of data about the people who will be using your product. If these prospective users are defined too broadly, the rest of the product definition process will suffer from lack of clarity. Building this picture requires secondary and primary research. **Secondary research** is the collection of information about audience demographics (age, gender, income, education level), consumer behaviors, preferences and technical skill level. This research tends to be more quantitative in nature. **Quantitative data** is numeric, and usually involves the collection of large and measureable data sets. An example might be the average income within a county or zip code. **Qualitative data**, on the other hand, is descriptive, and is a collection of perspectives and insights from different individuals that can be observed but not measured. With secondary research, you are likely to get lots of good general information, but it will not be very specific. For this reason, it is important to get quality data by interacting directly with people from the target audience. This gathering of information directly from an audience is known as **primary research**. A common approach for conducting **primary research** is a practice derived from the field of anthropology known as **ethnography**. Observing people in the environments where they would be using your system is at the core of design ethnography. **Contextual inquiry** adds the interview process to this observation. Sitting down with individuals and listening to them describe their experiences and share their opinions in the moment can provide very specific, detailed information. Contextual research is excellent for understanding aspects of a target audience that might seem so obvious to them that they remain unarticulated in another setting. It is also a good way to begin to explore new ideas and refine goals. Finally, focus group tests and surveys are broader tools of primary research that can be used to gather information about the audience. They are particularly good for testing out responses to proposed concepts.

Primary research

Data collected through interactions with individuals. Produces qualitative data, which is descriptive in nature.

Secondary research

Involves research of materials like articles, databases and census reports to collect quantitative data about the market being targeted. This tends to be conducted as the first phase of the process.

Market research is essential for understanding and defining your user base. This information can be used to create personas, which can best be understood as profiles of hypothetical users. Personas are a way of personalizing the combination of data collected about members in the target audience. This fabricated image of a person usually involves an anonymous person's photograph, a name you have assigned to the person in the photograph and a comprehensive story about her life story, particularly as it relates to the use of your system. The story will likely include information about her occupation, her relationship status and how she spends her work time and free time. It might also cover details about the games she might play and the devices that she uses, and detail their frequency of use. Like many of the other parts of the design process, the specific details will change depending upon the context and goal of the project. Personas are an external point of reference for the design team, providing a practical tool

Empathy through ethnography

> Our goal is to see people's behavior on their terms, not ours. While this observational method may appear inefficient, it enlightens us about the context in which customers would use a new product and the meaning that product might hold in their lives.
> —Ken Anderson, Anthropologist, Intel Research

To understand your audience you must develop empathy. Some ethnographic methods you can use to gain this critical frame of reference include:

- *Observation*—Watching people perform tasks in the anticipated environment.
- *Contextual inquiry*—Sitting with members of a target audience and letting them talk through their decisions and behaviors as they perform tasks.
- *Longitudinal studies*—Archiving and assessing insights recorded over an extended period of time by your audience. Text, audio or video journals or diary entries kept for weeks or months can provide this type of information.

Use surveys to monitor early reactions

Surveys are an excellent method for getting feedback from a large number of people in a target audience. Online survey tools like SurveyMonkey or Google's Consumer Surveys can provide a quick, affordable and effective way to collect specific information from target audience members on the web and through social networking platforms.

to keep the team focused on the needs of the audience. They are meant to remind project members that their perspectives, approaches and ideas need to be driven first and foremost by the needs, desires and aspirations of the people who will be using the system.

Research also involves developing a deep understanding of competitive or similar product offerings. A study of the landscape of products and projects that can inform design and implementation decisions should happen in this early stage. Your research is likely to span a variety of games, interactive systems, products and gamified systems. Derived from product marketing and entrepreneurship, this exploration is often referred to as competitive analysis. Through the evaluation of a range of systems and products, a picture of their strengths and weaknesses should emerge. This product review should help to inform the

"My kids are ready to think about college. I'd like to help."

Family: Married, two children
Goals: Help my kids find a college and financial aid.
Computer experience: Comfortable with web basics and apps.

Rebecca Hamilton

Age: 47
Employment: Attorney
Education: Graduate school
Frequency of use: High
Duration of use: On-going
Computer use: High
Web use: High
Apps used: e-mail, banking, mobile games, social media.

Introduction

Rebecca is an attorney that works full time. Her husband is also an attorney and works as much. They have two twins who are interested in very different things. One is very good at art, but not great at math and science. The other excels at all academic areas, particularly science.

Motivations

Though she doesn't have much time, she would like to have some way of helping her daughters through the process of choosing the right college, and through applying and looking for funding opportunities like scholarships and financial aid,

Task objectives

Rebecca would like to research colleges for different daughters based on their interest when she has time. She would like her daughters to get a sense of the schools they are looking at. She wants a way to find out regularly about on campus and off campus events, like lectures, film groups, music performances, and museum exhibitions.

Potential frustrations

She can is likely to get overwhelmed with information and frustrated if she does not have the right amount of support. If the app does not find a way to prompt her to come back she is likely to not remember to return.

Figure 5.6 This example persona is a hypothetical profile that includes a picture, demographic data and some details about an individual's personal story, motivations and relationship to the task the system is expecting the user to perform.

Using personas can provide important benefits to a project

Personas are excellent tools for:

- Guiding research to understand the target audience.
- Crystallizing the target audience to help the team define a clear product definition.
- Providing important information about user behaviors.
- Learning if the target audience understands the tasks being required of them to use the system.
- Exploring the merits of different design choices, and making decisions that match the expectations and attitudes of the audience.

---

direction of your project. Not only can bad decisions be circumvented, but good ones can also be emulated, modified or improved upon.

Finally, research means having a general familiarity with the field for which the project is designed. Designers are not expected to be experts in fields other than design. Yet, they must be able to work with experts who are intimately familiar with their product, services, organization or subject matter. During this phase, effective communication between the designer and these specialists is necessary to ensure information is meaningfully integrated into the design. For instance, if you were hired to gamify a museum exhibit, you would probably be working with the curator responsible for developing the show. She would be the person who knows all of the important information and interesting details that you might be able to include in your designs. In Chapters 8 and 9 we will discuss the role of this type of expert in greater detail.

During the research phase, you are likely to perform these activities:

- **Primary and secondary research**—Gathering data about the target market and collecting feedback and insights from members from the target audience.
- **Product landscape survey**—Studying, playing and interacting with a variety of systems that can influence your design.
- **Subject matter research**—Gathering information from experts and specialists related to the field.

Defining target behaviors

What behaviors are you trying to motivate? Are some of these measureable? These questions will obviously be directly tied to the goals of the project. From the user or player's perspective you should consider what the primary task is that she wishes to accomplish by using the system. For instance, let's imagine we are designing a fitness system. Let's call it Fit-Shtick. Let's imagine that our hypothetical app relies on humor, jokes and comedy to support users through the process of trying to get in shape. Let's assume that one of the primary goals of the hypothetical GS design is to help users manage their weight. In this situation, the system may need to encourage people to input their daily calorie intake and their weekly weight. To facilitate this scenario or user story, target behaviors for a user might include:

- Register and create an account.
- Enter height and initial weight.
- Enter fitness or weight loss goals.
- Log in daily.
- Enter calorie intake daily.
- Enter weight once per week.

This core set of behaviors can drive even more behaviors. For example, a player might invite a friend to compete against him in a weight loss challenge to lose five pounds in a month. This might lead to secondary fitness goals like running five miles each week or giving up ice cream. Core tasks should be flexible enough for this kind of scalability. Once you have a list of the core tasks and the target behaviors that support these, you can then rank these in order of importance. This list of priorities will help determine design and implementation decisions in the later stages of development and analysis.

Don't forget social behavior

Facilitating social behavior is at the core of most successful gamified systems. Consider the ways you want your players to motivate each other to participate. Once you determine which social behaviors you want to encourage, rank them in order of importance, and then define the target behaviors that support them. Some social behaviors you may want to promote:

- *Inviting* others to play.
- *Welcoming* friends, new and returning players.
- *Helping* other players learn the system and accomplish personal and collective goals.
- *Gifting* friends in and outside of the system.
- *Sharing or exchanging* information, content and rewards.
- *Viewing* content or media shared by other players.
- *Liking* information, content or media shared by other players.
- *Commenting* on information, content or media shared by other players.
- *Voting* for publicly shared content or media.
- *Rating* publicly shared content or media.
- *Reviewing* information, content or media.
- *Curating* the display of information, content or media.
- *Making editorial decisions* about the display of information, content or media.
- *Competing* against other players or against the system with other players.
- *Cooperating and coordinating* efforts with other players.
- *Challenging* other players.
- *Bantering, chatting and joking* with other players or human performers.

Defining key performance indicators

Given that gamified systems have goals outside of the game context, it makes sense that these should be measured in some way. Key Performance Indicators (KPIs), introduced earlier in Chapter 2, are quantifiable measurements that are set before the project is introduced. They are a means of defining what success means for a project. For some gamified systems, the most important KPIs might

> ### Return on Investment (ROI)
>
>
> A measure of the benefits returned by investing in a project or venture.

be based upon the number of total monthly users. For learning-based gamified systems, it might be about educational performance, like the number of players who demonstrate proficiency at a certain skill set. In product companies, KPIs may focus on product sales or product referrals. In such cases, the designer and team will want to show a **return on the investment** (ROI) of the project. If the project must generate or save money for the company, return needs to be greater than the investment required to create, run and monitor the project.

ITERATIVE DESIGN

With the goals defined, research on target audience and competitive landscape completed, target behaviors articulated and KPIs selected, the design phase can begin in earnest. Because in systems design each project is unique, no exact prescription exists for how to do this. Iterative design, in which the process of design uses feedback to continuously refine all of the elements in the design process, is a method that has emerged precisely because of this aspect of uniqueness.

Iterative design > using inputs and outputs

One way to begin this phase is to think systemically and articulate what the inputs and/or outputs will be for the system. For example, in the case of our humor-based fitness program, the design team would prioritize the measurement of daily and weekly activity of a player. The design would likely require players to input specific data, and in response report back information to the user about these changes over time. Social behaviors that encourage this activity are likely to be necessary elements of the system. Design choices about how to motivate and reward target behaviors can then be determined.

Iterative design > defining the core experience

Another way to begin the design process of a system is from the inside out. This involves defining the "core experience," which refers in games to the essential experience that the player should have while playing. It may revolve around a fictive narrative, like experiencing being a medieval knight on a quest in a historically inspired world. However, the idea of the "core experience" can be expanded to include desired behavior related to emergent game-play.

Keep brainstorming loose

There are many ways to begin the process of brainstorming and ideation. Whichever approach or approaches you choose for getting started should be open to experimentation. Choosing to use materials like sticky notes, whiteboards, paper and pen keeps this activity open, participatory and dynamic.

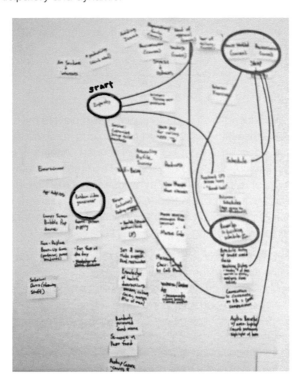

Figure 5.7 Brainstorming with sticky notes, paper and pen.

For instance, in a system that creates a high level of secrecy, taunting or mischief between players could fit into a variety of forms including scavenger hunts, mysteries and territorial acquisition games. Using this method is a helpful way of defining progress paths and the player journey, which is the path a player will take from the beginning to the end of a game. With the core experience defined, the appropriate inputs and outputs for data can be chosen. The process of defining the core experience, also referred to as the aesthetic experience, and game elements to accompany the experience are detailed in Chapter 6.

Use the GS spectrum

A third approach, which might be called classificatory, involves using the GS spectrum to define the nature of your system. Knowing target behaviors, data inputs and outputs, and how these will tie into the core experience, is the foundation for envisioning your project and understanding where it fits on the GS spectrum (game-like, game layer, Alternate Purpose Game). Where the idea fits in the spectrum should elucidate how the more undefined characteristics of the system might manifest. This is the point where game components (explored in Chapter 6), interface ideas, emergent and reflective opportunities and pervasive elements can begin to be imagined.

Imagining opportunities for emergence

Emergence (introduced in Chapter 2) occurs when players have freedom to take the elements provided to them and combine them in unexpected ways. This might lead to unintended patterns of interaction or forms of play. It might also lead to interesting and memorable moments that become worthy of re-telling later. With an idea about the core concept and the player journey, it is possible to begin imagining the different types of emergent behavior you might encourage amongst your audience. To do this, ask yourself some of the following questions:

- How do I want the experience to be reflected upon by the player or user during and after the experience?
- How would a meta-game tie together individual components? How might it increase engagement and foster relationships?
- How will personal achievements translate into personal stories for sharing with others?
- How do I want social interaction to translate into stories shared by the player community over time?

Though you cannot dictate exactly what players will experience or how they will talk about it with their friends, crafting a vision about potential moments of reflection should help you back into features, functions and game concepts that are most likely to facilitate them.

Even for the ambitious blue-sky creative, feasibility must be at the forefront of any iterative design process. Every project has constraints that determine design choices. Knowing what these are can actually be very constructive and liberating from a creative standpoint. The first of these are the resources allocated to the project, like money and staff. Most projects have a deliverable date, which dictates how much time the project has for design, implementation and testing. In addition, although some projects will begin by using a pre-existing technology

Ideating pervasive elements

Pervasiveness was covered in Chapter 2, and relates to the way a fictional world or game experience touches other aspects of our everyday life. Consider the ways your system will utilize pervasive concepts. Brainstorm how your designs will leverage:

Temporality

What type of time requirements do you imagine your system will demand? Will the interactions be short, long or vary in length depending upon the task? If it is a game layer system, will it be functioning in the background of other tasks? If so, when would you imagine that the system might make contact with and provide feedback to the player?

Space and location

Is this going to leverage physical and/or virtual locations? Are the physical locations tied to a specific place, like one of the many hiking trails in Yosemite National Park, or will they reference any location that fits the criteria, like a hiking trail. If you are creating a virtual environment, what sorts of real and virtual points will you use for reference points?

Social expansion

How might the experience extend socially into a player's world? Will it involve family, friends, work associates or people living in the same city or community? Will these other people participate knowingly or unknowingly?

Different forms of media

Will this be a digital or analog experience? Perhaps it will include aspects of both. If it is digital, what devices will you be considering? How can you maximize what they each do well separately and in combination? If you are not using digital technologies, what sorts of materials will you be using? How can you leverage their intrinsic values to create a meaningful experience?

infrastructure, many will have to be developed or modified for the specific project. These variables are likely to determine the technology choices made, which will in turn affect the data that will be utilized and measured as well as the overall player or user experience.

Learn to love constraints: be ambitious but realistic

Figure 5.8 The iron triangle.

The iron triangle (or project triangle) represents the three competing constraints of any project: 1) Time, 2) Scope and 3) Resources. In order to build a quality product, all three parts of the triangle need to effectively serve each other. A project that is large in scope must have ample resources (like money and people) and enough time for the project to be well produced. If any one of these attributes are reduced or increased, another must shift to compensate. For instance, if a project budget needs to be cut, the scope must also be reduced. Even at the ideation phase of the project understanding the iron triangle is a way of managing the vision.

AGILE DEVELOPMENT

Once you have generated the basic parameters of your system by understanding inputs and outputs, and core experience, and know where they lie on the GS spectrum, you are ready for development. One of the most common methods for the iterative design of systems is Agile development. Agile development is a philosophy about software development. Created by programmers, it replaces the traditional "waterfall method" of product development, where each stage in the process of development occurs in order. Instead, Agile starts from the premise that technology-based projects cannot be entirely designed before construction of the application begins. Because unanticipated changes in design and technical implementations occur throughout a project's development, this alternative approach to development embraces change from the beginning, reducing unnecessary anxiety and expectations. Agile emphasizes iteration in design and constant interpersonal communication within a project team. The goal is to move away from over-reliance on preproduction documentation, and, instead, move

Figure 5.9 Agile envisions a continuous cycle of development, testing, reviewing and planning.

quickly to prototyping, building, revising and testing. Agile development sets and prioritizes feature requirements and lets the developers get to work.

The Scrum framework

Scrum is the most popular implementation of the Agile approach to development, because it emphasizes communication and process. Self-organizing teams work in incremental time frames from two to four weeks, which are known as sprints. These work periods end with tested working product features. Incremental release dates significantly reduce the need for documentation, which is only generated immediately before a sprint period. Daily meetings, planned reviews and retrospectives are typical ways of incorporating feedback.

The Scrum framework is made up of three core components. The first is about defining roles: defining who has overall responsibility for the entire project (the project owner), which people are responsible for implementation (the Scrum team) and the person who is responsible for making sure implementation happens according to plans (the Scrum master). Second, a "backlog" made up of "user stories" defines aspects of the project that can be prototyped and implemented. The backlog is essentially a list of all of the requirements remaining to be implemented before the entire project is complete. Finally, events are the third part of Scrum. Events organize time in "sprints," and they help keep track of "burn down," or how much of the backlog is finished. Understanding how to develop a backlog and how to structure a sprint are the most important parts of the process.

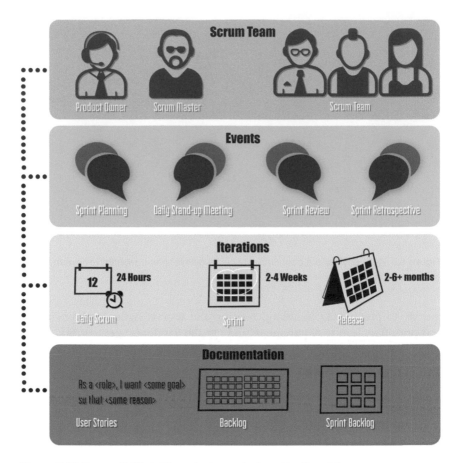

Figure 5.10 Scrum distilled. Character icons designed by Freepick.com.

The backlog: user stories

User stories are at the cornerstone of Scrum. A user story quickly captures from the perspective of a user a specific task he needs to accomplish when interacting with a system. A template for a user story looks like:

"As a <*role*>, I want <*goal/desire*>."

Returning to Fit-shtick, our hypothetical fitness system, if a player was on a team competing to lose more total weight than another team, an example user story might be "As a player, I want to see how much total weight my team has lost to date." A long list of user stories will be developed at this time. These will later be translated to the various features, functions and mechanics that make up the system. The user story list will likely grow and be modified throughout the project. However, at this point, the project leaders, content experts and clients

JTBD: an alternative to user stories

Harvard Business School Professor Clayton Christensen introduced the *Jobs To Be Done framework* in 2007. Increasingly embraced by user experience designers it emphasizes the story from the user's perspective. This new structure highlights the situation that an individual finds herself in, the motivation or goal this situation triggers, and the outcome or objective she wishes to accomplish.

The structure of a JTBD story

When <event or situation occurs>, **I want to** <motivation/desired behavior> **so I can** <expected outcome>.

Example job story

When I am *on a diet* I want to *track my exercise* so I can *monitor my weight loss*.

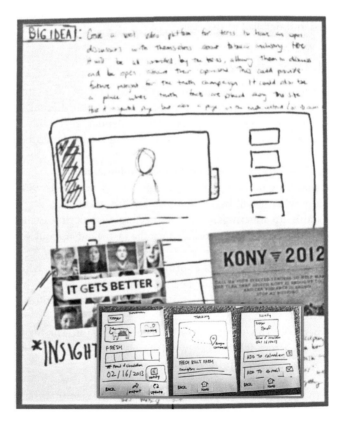

Figure 5.11 Sketching allows for experimentation and quick ideation.

should have enough information to set priorities. These prioritized user stories will directly impact how the development schedule proceeds. As the Scrum team finishes features, new user stories are introduced from the product backlog, the home of the prioritized user story list. These new stories are to be translated into design specifications so that they can be built.

User stories should identify the features and elements you decide to pursue first. Utilizing Agile methods, a set of the highest-priority user stories will be defined for development. Working through the backlog, this process will be continued throughout the project in a series of two- to four-week increments, known as sprints. High-priority elements will be clarified here. These include: game concepts and components, interfaces and information design, data collection, storage and analysis, pervasive expansion (time, space, social, technology) and opportunities for emergence. These definitions should at this point include detailed descriptions of functionality, which will differ according to the feature being described. In some cases, sketches or wireframes of interface components are most appropriate. In other cases, it may be necessary to include flowcharts diagramming how and when data is collected and stored in the database. In essence, anything presented to the user base within the system and as an extension of it via social networking platforms or communication technologies like e-mail are described and detailed at this point.

The sprint: from prototype to release

With initial design specifications from the first set of user stories, full-on development can begin through the prototyping of different user stories. Prototyping in Scrum occurs in sprints. On a calendar, preferably one that can show simultaneous bands of development, the following should be identified:

- **Sprints**: Two- to four-week periods of implementation.
- **Sprint planning meetings**: When the project owner meets with the team to determine what it will be working on for the sprint.
- **Daily stand-up meetings**: A short meeting that occurs each morning to review work that has been done since the last stand-up and work that will be done before the next one.
- **Sprint reviews**: At the end of a sprint the Scrum team meets with the product owner to review what has been accomplished. At this meeting it is determined what is shippable and what needs to be modified, changed or removed.
- **Retrospective**: This event marks the end of a sprint. The Scrum team gets together to assess what went well during the sprint and what could be improved so the next sprint runs smoother.

Prototyping begins early so you can test out your ideas with the target audience and the project stakeholders. Prototyping can take on a variety of forms. Low-fidelity paper-based concepts can easily provide enough information to get

Figure 5.12 Low-fidelity paper prototypes are an affordable and accessible way to quickly test out ideas with your audience.

valuable responses about design ideas. They will also provide an opportunity for this group to make early recommendations to the design team. High-fidelity prototypes enable a greater resemblance of the actual experience, which not only provides a means to collect initial feedback and recommendations, but can also provide information about the usability of the system design. There is a variety of game engines and prototyping tools that can be leveraged for these tasks (for an updated guide about these visit this book's supplementary website, www. gamifiedsystems.com). Prototyping occurs throughout the design and implementation phases. The cycle of iteration, which takes valuable user feedback and translates these into meaningful changes, creates and refines quality systems for the marketplace.

At some point a project needs to be delivered in some useable form to its intended audience. This should happen when the product is feature complete, tested thoroughly and reviewed and approved by the core constituents of the team. Many games and applications are released before they are considered entirely complete. This gets a product out early with the opportunity to test with a wider audience. Most releases like this prominently display the "alpha" or "beta" label, giving the audience fair warning that bugs and incomplete features are to be expected. It is also common to encourage feedback so that users feel like their interactions can contribute to a better final product.

Product analysis

Data collection is more often than not the primary goal of a gamified system. Once a system is working and people are using it, a massive amount of data can be collected and analyzed, and new kinds of potential for data collection will be

Data analytics is a continuous feedback loop where data is collected, then analyzed for identifiable patterns. The information provided, such as whether or not a project is meeting its KPIs, can be used to improve and optimize a system.

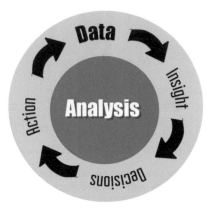

Figure 5.13 The data collection and data analysis cycle.

revealed. Analytics is a means of discovering patterns about data. By looking at different patterns, organizations can make better predictions of future performance. This can help inform and shape important decisions like pricing and marketing. In addition, it can help designers understand how users are responding to their system so that they may optimize and improve it.

In some cases the collection of data may not be delivered through a database or an accompanying tool set enabling accessible information. Paper-based games, Alternate Reality Games and Alternate Purpose Games might all need a different type of assessment. In learning environments, assessments usually take the forms of tests, papers or projects. This is a way for an instructor to see whether or not the student actually learned knowledge or skills through the process. Other contexts might use more traditional marketing research methods like surveys and interviews. The goals and development phase of the project will already have produced a number of questions that designers will want answers to once the project is accessible to users or players. Though the tools and techniques for collecting data may vary, the effort is essential for achieving goals and validating your project.

KEY TAKEAWAYS

•   As a practice, gamified system design (GS design) falls under user experience design (UX design) and combines the skills associated with both game design and interaction design.

- GS design can be defined as: *Combining game concepts with non-game related structures to create play-centric experiences that serve goals outside of the game context.*
- To be a GS designer, one must possess the ability to: collaborate with a cross-functional team, understand both game design and interactive design, be able to conduct research about users and turn that into enjoyable or playable designs, and have a good understanding about technologies and their appropriate applications in the field.
- The process of designing a gamified system includes: defining objectives, conducting research, establishing target behaviors and key indicators, creating and testing out designs, implementation and analysis.

EXERCISES

Exercises provided in this chapter are meant be treated as the initial phases of a larger project that will continue for the duration of the book. Tasks suggested at the end of each chapter are meant to support you through the process of designing a gamified system. Choose from one of the three hypothetical client projects below. Utilize the material provided in this book as well as the supplementary materials available at the book's website, www.gamifiedsystems.com, to help you complete your work.

5.1 Choose a client project

Below you will find three hypothetical design projects, each in need of a GS designer. These projects span a range of different type of clients, including:

1. Your city zoo.
2. A national chain of supermarkets.
3. A major record label.

You are being asked to craft a gamified system for at least one of these clients. To begin, read the profiles of each potential client, and the primary goals they have identified for their project. They will also tell you about the audiences that they are targeting. In addition, they will let you know about any constraints or parameters that need to be kept in mind as you go through the process.

Once you understand the needs of your client, it is time to begin your research. Use the information provided in this chapter to better understand the audience and to begin to envision an appropriate system. As you go through the rest of the chapters in this book you will continue to develop and revise your initial plans.

Clients in need of a great GS designer:

Your city zoo

Your city zoo wants to create a system to encourage more residents and tourists to visit. They are also looking to give visitors something fun and interesting to do while they are at the zoo. Nearly all visitors come with their mobile phone on them, and many use their phones to take pictures of the animals. The zoo has over ten animal areas, which can be accessed by foot or by the special zoo train. It prides itself on the treatment of its animals and the opportunities visitors have to experience them. There is a large gift store, many ice cream stands, and a restaurant surrounded by a glass wall that looks on to the penguin habitat. The zoo also employs specialists who educate visitors every hour about the many species and habitats on site. These tend to coincide with a particular animal's feeding time.

- *Audience profile*: Children between the ages of five and ten are the primary audience for this group. The secondary audience are the grown-ups who are chaperoning them for the day, most of whom are parents.
- *Primary constraints*: The system you create must have a digital component and an analog or printed component so that visiting school and camp children can also play.

National supermarket chain

A national supermarket chain is trying to retain its customers and compete with specialty markets and other stores more commonly associated with organic food and healthy lifestyles. At the same time, they are trying to reach out to other customers who are looking for easy-to-make affordable meals that are alternatives to fast food restaurants. The company has over 2,000 stores throughout the United States, and has over 700 convenient stores.

- *Audience profile*: The supermarket chain's primary target audience is women between the ages of thirty and forty-five. Most have a family income averaging at about $75,000 annually. The majority are mothers with at least two children at home. They are comfortable using mobile devices, and tend to favor smart phones.
- *Primary constraints*: The system you create must have a digital component. It should also be appealing to children so that they can encourage their mothers through social networking or communication technologies to purchase their favorite foods. The company is also open to generating revenue from advertising products sold in the stores.

Major record label

This client is a large, respected record label with shrinking profits. The company is interested in exposing its audiences, particularly college students, to up-and-coming bands. By doing this, the label hopes to increase music download purchases and live performance ticket sales. In addition, because it has had to reduce its number of music scouts, it is looking for a new method for identifying promising talent and exposing them to the audience.

- *Audience profile*: College students between the ages of eighteen and twenty-four are the primary audience. They are extremely comfortable with technology, often setting trends in usage and uptick of new applications and devices.

- *Primary constraints*: The implementation has to appeal to a hip, trend-setting crowd that embraces DIY (Do-It-Yourself) and experimentation. They do not want to have anything to do with the idea of the music label as a corporation. They need to have a sense of ownership over the direction of the project. You have the freedom to include or feature any of their more famous artists. You should also find a way to direct players to venues, shows, festivals and concerts.

Perform initial tasks:

5.2 Research

Begin your project by finding out as much as you can about your audience and the games, gamified systems and technologies currently available to help them complete the tasks you are trying to address. For this phase of the project you should conduct the following activities:

- Collect market research.
- Develop personas for your primary and secondary target audiences.
- Study the product landscape.

5.3 Clarify goals

Use this part of the process to articulate your goals, identifying what you want your users to do and how you will measure success. Here you will:

- Define initial user stories.
- Define initial target behaviors (for the individual, for social interaction).
- Identify KPIs.

5.4 Ideation

Begin to brainstorm and develop ideas about the overall experience and the design concepts and devices that will deliver it. For this stage you should:

- Define your core concept.
- Identify important data that needs to be collected.
- Imagine the pervasive components (temporal, social, spatial, devices).

5.4 Do a reality check

Though this project is hypothetical, you should still have a sense of whether your plans will contradict the constraints that your client has placed upon you. Make sure that you are applying the lessons of the iron triangle.

RECOMMENDED READINGS

- *The Agile Pocket Guide: A Quick Start to Making Your Business Agile Using Scrum and Beyond* by Peter Saddington, 2012.
  This book is a solid introduction and resource for those who are new to Agile and Scrum development.

- *IDEO method cards: 51 ways to inspire design* by IDEO, 2003.
  From the design company responsible for producing the first commercial mouse, *IDEO method cards* are a toolkit for approaching creative problem-solving challenges.

- *Universal Methods of Design: 100 Ways to Research Complex Problems, Develop Innovative Ideas, and Design Effective Solutions* by Bruce Hanington and Bella Martin, 2012.
  Universal Methods of Design is an excellent and highly usable reference guide covering a hundred research and design methods used by top designers.

INSIDER INSIGHT

A BUSINESS PERSPECTIVE FROM BUNCHBALL FOUNDER RAJAT PAHARIA

Interview granted with permission by Rajat Paharia.

Rajat Paharia is the founder of Bunchball, which provides a cloud-based gamification technology platform and service for over 300 major corporations including Adobe, Clorox, Urban Outfitters, Wendy's, USA Networks, Cisco and Ford. Paharia is at the forefront of gamifying business, and is recognized for coining the phrase gamification. He is the author of *Loyalty 3.0: How to Revolutionize Customer and Employee Engagement with Big Data and Gamification*, a book that underscores the importance of data in gamified systems.

Figure 5.14
Rajat Paharia.

*   *   *

In my book, I present a definition of gamification for use in business, which is: *The use of the data-driven motivational techniques from video games to drive business objectives.* Let me share with you some other phrases that we use when we describe it to people: "measure and motivate," "recognition and reward," "loyalty," "reputation," "guiding and amplifying high-value behavior." I don't think that anyone would disagree that these are good things, and smart businesses have been doing many of them very effectively for years to drive meaningful business outcomes.

And the core theme that runs through these is this idea of motivating people through data.

Do you know what game designers do? They make games. They start with a blank sheet of paper and they create something out of nothing, an experience whose sole purpose is to engage and entertain. Gamification, however, is not a game design problem—its purpose is not to entertain, but to drive a business outcome. And you rarely, if ever, start with a blank sheet of paper. You start with something—a customer community, a marketing campaign, a sales force automation system or an e-commerce site, and you integrate gamification mechanics into it to capture the data that your participants are generating as they interact with that experience, and then present that data back to participants in a way that motivates them to perform better.

This goal-shift is the fundamental difference between game design and gamification design, and why game designers often have no interest in designing gamification programs, or don't have the proper mindset to succeed at it. Gamification is less a game design problem, and more a fundamental interaction design problem. Your users are raising their hands and telling you something about themselves with every action that they take—*how do you listen and utilize that data to create a more engaging user experience that motivates better performance, drives better business results and leads to a competitive advantage?*

If it's not a game design problem, then why is it called gamification? Although gamification isn't about making games, it does leverage the data-driven motivational techniques that videogame designers have honed and refined for years. When you think about it, it makes total sense—from *Pong* in the 1970s to *Call of Duty* now, when you play a videogame you are immersed in a digital world where every single thing you're doing is throwing off data. Videogame designers were the first people to have access to this kind of incredibly rich set of user activity data, so of course it makes total sense that they were the ones who first figured out how to leverage and utilize that data to their advantage. First by keeping score, then by enabling players to level up, giving them goals to accomplish, badges to indicate achievement, fast feedback so they could learn and evolve strategy, and more. All with the goal of engaging players and motivating peak performance.

For a long time, that rich data set was limited to video games, so that was the only place these mechanics could be effectively used. What has happened in the last few years is that increasingly our "real life" is becoming more digital—everything that we do is being mediated by technology (Facebook, Salesforce, iTunes, Gmail, Skype, etc.) and is now throwing off quantities of user activity data that rivals that of video games.

So if you're trying to learn how to motivate people using this data, where would you turn? You'd look to the 40+ years of experience from the videogame industry, and you'd pull the best practices and ideas from there and use them in this new hybrid real/digital world that we're all living in. And that is what gamification is, and what you'll need to learn how to do if you're going to be successful at it.

NOTES

Anderson, Ken. "Ethographic Research: A Key to Strategy," *Harvard Business Review*, March, 2009, https://hbr.org/2009/03/ethnographic-research-a-key-to-strategy/ar/1.

Benyon, David, Phil Turner and Susan Turner. *Designing Interactive Systems: People, Activities, Contexts, Technologies*. Harlow, Essex: Addison-Wesley, 2005.

Christensen, Clayton M., Scott D. Anthony, Gerald N. Berstell and Denise Nitterhouse. "Finding the Right Job for Your Product." *MIT Sloan Management Review*, 48:3 (spring 2007).

Cooper, Alan, David Cronin and Robert Reimann. *About Face 3: The Essentials of Interaction Design*. Indianapolis: Wiley, 2007.

Fullerton, Tracy. *Game Design Workshop: A Playcentric Approach to Creating Innovative Games*. Third Edition. Boca Raton: CRC Press, 2014.

Fullerton, Tracy, Steve Hoffman and Chris Swain. *Game Design Workshop: Designing, Prototyping, and Playtesting Games*. Berkeley: CMP Books, 2004.

Kim, Amy Jo. "Engagement Style in Social Games." Posted to Slideshare on May 10, 2011, http://www.slideshare.net/amyjokim/engagement-styles-in-social-games?qid=5091 4b87-85f8-4546-be41-8a81a88421b8&v=default&b=&from_search=6.

Klements, Alan. "Replacing the User Story with the Job Story." *Alan Klement.com*, September 20, 2013, http://alanklement.blogspot.com/2013/09/replacing-user-story-with-job-story.html.

Martin, Bella and Bruce Hanington. *Universal Methods of Design*. Beverly: Rockport, 2012.

Paharia, Rajat *Loyalty 3.0: How Big Data and Gamification are Revolutionizing Customer and Employee Engagement*. New York: McGraw Hill, 2013.

Preece, Jenny, Yvonne Rogers and Helen Sharp. *Interaction Design: Beyond Human-Computer Interaction*. Third Edition. Hoboken: Wiley, 2011.

Rubin, Kenneth. *Essential Scrum: A Guide to the Most Popular Agile Process*. Boston: Addison-Wesley, 2012.

Salen, Katie and Eric Zimmerman. *Rules of Play: Game Design Fundamentals*. Cambridge: MIT Press, 2004.

Silverstein, David, Philip Samuel and Neil DeCarlo. *The Innovator's Toolkit*, Second Edition. Hoboken: John Wiley & Sons, 2012.

6 APPLYING GAME CONCEPTS

CHAPTER QUESTIONS

At the end of this chapter, you should be able to answer these questions:

- What is the MDA framework?
- What are some techniques that can be used to design a player journey that evolves over time?
- What are the different point structures and how can they be leveraged for gamified system (GS) design projects?
- How have badges been used meaningfully over time to designate achievement?
- What lessons can we apply from different game genres?
- How can we use dramatic and formal elements to define and organize our game components?

INTRODUCTION

Points, badges and leaderboards (referred to in unison as PBLs) are the game elements most commonly associated with gamified systems. But there is a host of dynamic, rich and varied game concepts that can be explored and applied to our practice in addition to PBLs. As gamified systems continue to grow more commonplace and evolve, they increasingly require innovative approaches towards design and implementation. Not only can we learn from what is effective in current gamified systems, but we can also gain a significant amount of knowledge and insight by understanding what makes videogames, social networking games, mobile games, pervasive games and table-top games successful. This chapter investigates game design concepts and their application in GS design.

THE MDA FRAMEWORK

Developed by Robin Hunicke, Marc LeBlanc and Robert Zubeck, the Mechanics-Dynamics-Aesthetics (MDA) framework is a formal structure for analyzing and

Figure 6.1 The MDA framework articulates the different perspectives and relationships that the designer and the player bring to a game system (adapted from the original MDA diagram).

understanding games. MDA simultaneously enables user-driven "bottom up" and software architecture "top down" approaches as ways of understanding how the functional elements of a game match the emotional and emergent responses intended by the designer. MDA treats game systems as artifacts or tools in environments rather than linear narratives like traditional media such as film, focusing primarily on the interactivity between the player and the system.

Mechanics

Mechanics are the granular functions that enable player action. For instance, in the classic *Mario Bros.* games, because the player must make Mario run and jump to dodge and overcome obstacles, running and jumping are the primary or "core" mechanics. Mechanics are the actions that are defined by the rules. They are best imagined as verbs and are often described as what the player "gets to do." Systems utilize these mechanics over and over again, thus providing the basic means for players to attain their goals. For the player, mechanics manifest as a kind of interactive toolkit. Players can choose the ways in which they utilize, avoid or combine them in order to progress within a game.

Mechanics are not the same as feedback

A game's core mechanic contains the experiential building blocks of player interactivity. It represents the essential moment-to-moment activity of players. During a game, core mechanics create patterns of repeated behavior, the experiential building blocks of play.

—Katie Salen and Eric Zimmerman, *Rules of Play: Game Design Fundamentals*

Figure 6.2 A diagram of a system shows how players are rewarded with badges and points for taking pictures. Here, the mechanic is the act of taking a picture. All of the other elements in the system are either processing or updating that input (adapted from Andrzej Marczewski's *Gamasutra* article "Game Mechanics and Gamification").

PBLs are not mechanics

A mechanic instantiates or changes the system in some way. For instance, clicking a button may increase the number of points a user has, and then that number of points could in turn effect the receipt of a badge, and possibly update a score on a leaderboard. In this example, as in most gamified systems, it is the action the user takes that is the mechanic. The points, badges and leaderboards are actually feedback mechanisms and visual cues to let the user have a general sense of his progress.

Dynamics

In the world of physics, dynamics relate to the energy, action or change that is instantiated through an external force. In games, these variations are the interplay between the moment-to-moment interaction between players and the game

Being in the moment

Dynamics provide the moment-to-moment interplay between an individual, a community and a system. They are the foundation for rich, emergent aesthetic experiences.

Gamified systems can instantiate dynamics like:

- Momentum to overcome challenging obstacles.
- Problem-solving alone or with others.
- Competing against other players or the system to accomplish a goal.
- Cooperating, negotiating or trading with others.
- Surprise when something new or unexpected occurs.
- Seeking information.
- Making a discovery.
- Avoiding a trap.
- Improvised social behavior.

system. They are the effect that individual mechanics and combinations of mechanics produce at any given time during play. For instance, if a player has to get her character from one side of a screen to another before a clock runs out, she will experience the dynamic of time pressure. If she must do this in conjunction with another player, this will combine the dynamics of both time pressure and social pressure.

Aesthetics

Aesthetics in the world of philosophy deals with the reflection or judgment of a work of art, which is derived through the experience of the senses. In games, aesthetics are the emotional responses that a game should conjure in a player. These are derived from the dynamics of a play system. Aesthetics correspond to the core concept or the main idea or theme associated with a game or gamified system. As the designer, ask yourself a few questions about the player's motivations. What will the player be playing for? Does he want to experience a fantasy? Who will he be performing as? Will he be plundering ships as a pirate or perhaps rescuing people from burning buildings as a fire fighter? According to MDA, the aesthetic experience manifests itself initially through the mechanics and subsequently through the dynamics of the game.

Ultimately, the appeal of any game or gamified system comes from the promise of this emergent aesthetic experience. Some of the dominant tropes for aesthetics as applied to gamified systems include:

- **Exploration**: Gamified systems like the Junior Rangers Program encourage the pursuit of knowledge and discovery through exploration. Location-based games like scavenger hunts and geocaching are also excellent vehicles for this type of experience.
- **Empowerment**: Good gamified systems can provide the opportunity to prove ability and expertise. This might translate into the reward of system-wide status, like being the highest ranked player. Or, it could be more localized within specific circles of influence, like becoming a leader of a guild. The *Guardian* newspaper empowered its readers to review government documents, and then recognized those that made significant contributions.
- **Fellowship**: Ultimately, it is the opportunity to bring people together to solve problems and overcome challenges that make gamified systems so appealing. Through collaboration and competition, gamified systems can initiate and enhance relationships.
- **Expression**: The chance to play a role from a different perspective enables players to flex themselves socially and intellectually. This may happen in a variety of environments. Some may be fantastic, whereas others may be entirely reality based.
- **Heroics**: This is the virtual experience of heroism, often lacking in everyday life. As in the ancient performances of Homer's *Iliad*, players get to feel what they may never have actually experienced, including death. "Let me not then die ingloriously and without a struggle, but let me first do some great thing that shall be told among men hereafter."

Of all these tropes, which largely reflect different aspects of the self, heroics may be the most important. To unselfishly help others through grand and dangerous measures is the foundation for many familiar narratives, from epic poetry to video games. Many game designers have read or heard about Joseph Campbell's *The Hero with a Thousand Faces*, which provides a breakdown of the different aspects of what a hero's journey entails (see Figure 6.3). Although many gamified systems won't have obvious narrative and fiction elements, there remain plenty of avenues for heroics to surface through design. While entertainment-based games like *Legend of Zelda* might let us rescue princesses, gamified systems like *Recyclebank*, which rewards participants for making and performing ecologically beneficial activities in our daily lives, like reusing sandwich bags or reducing our daily energy consumption, let us play a small but seemingly tangible role in the world. Though both experiences provide an opportunity for heroic behaviors, they play out in different ways as a result of their implementations.

The hero's journey is a well-known formula used in narrative forms because it provides a structure for character growth. The gamified system takes on the role of the supernatural here, bringing players across the threshold of transformation. The space of play is also the space of the unknown. Campbell's is modeled after the five-act structure of a play, with action rising to a catharsis and then falling back. Games are typically very good at highlighting the line between the known and the unknown, like the curtain going up and down at the theater.

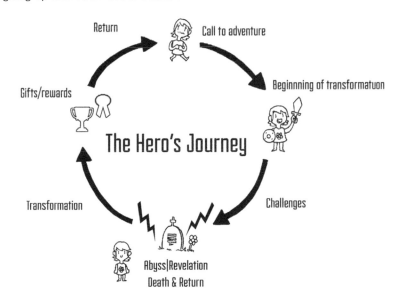

Figure 6.3 A simplified diagram of the hero's journey. Dragon icon designed by Freepik.com and Alex Waskelo.

- **Invention and nurturing**: To build something new or to nurture something to growth and prosperity generates pride and personal ownership. With over 30 million copies sold, the popularity of the sandbox game *Minecraft* (introduced in Chapter 4) provides a solid testimony to this proposition. Players don't just want to explore the world of *Minecraft*, they also want to build buildings, spaces, objects and game modifications, and share them with the world. Nurturing is another widely popular aesthetic experience. Since the success of the virtual pet toy *Tamagotchi*, followed by *Neopets*, *The Sims* and Zynga's *Farmville*, it is very clear that taking care of virtual entities for the sake of seeing them grow and change is a satisfying endeavor for many players because it provides the essential of intrinsic motivation—purpose, autonomy and relatedness. What's more, they provide some of the most compelling kinds of feedback for players whose personal actions and progress are immediately and visually manifest.

Aesthetics → dynamics → mechanics

When defining game concepts consider starting with the intended aesthetic experience. Then work your way backwards through dynamics. Finally, develop the specific actions or mechanics you want players to take.

CREATING A JOURNEY

We often associate the notion of a journey with something long, enduring and mythic. Taking us from one space (or state of mind) to another, a player journey enables a sense of progression, keeping us on a path filled with surprises along the way that inspire us and propel us forward. The video game *Journey* is an excellent example of this idea. Players must guide their player character through a densely rich but lonely landscape filled with challenges, puzzles and surprises. Without words or text, a player must find her way. Other players may offer limited support as they intersect along their own challenging journeys. Though many gamified systems are not finite in structure and are not always focused on developing a rich virtual environment, the absence of a clear win-condition or an imaginary space does not preclude the meaningful moments that can be produced by finding creative ways to get players to pursue a set of goals.

The concept of onboarding, introduced in Chapter 2 and explored more in Chapter 7, suggests that gamified systems must provide the right structure to engage people initially and then introduce progress paths and feedback loops to keep them invested over time. In Chapter 3 we covered the ways in which the process of achievement took an individual on a path of progression from novice to master. Gamified systems support onboarding, achievement and progression by providing motivational opportunities matched to the player's abilities and attitudes related to the experience. With a novice player, it is the responsibility of the system to hold his hand to make him interested, feel welcome and supported. Once a player gets more proficient at the task and understands the environment, maintaining interest requires frequent and indeed regular surprises. Finally, a player who has proven his commitment by investing time and recruiting others will need to feel special to continue to loyally participate and return. Whether you are utilizing a leveling system or an intriguing storyline that reveals its intricacies over time, your job is to choose the most appropriate forms to continuously drive your players forward.

Feedback must satisfy different player needs throughout the journey

Feedback is a response to activities or processes. It is important for informing players about their current status within the framework of a game or gamified system. This information lets them know where they are in terms of their progression towards the goals promised by a player journey. This is where rewards (like more points) and punishments (like loss of points) come into play. Whether it is through a character, a dialogue window or an object found in an environment, feedback is critical for providing directions and guidance. Responsive and on-going communication with a player lets him know if his activities and strategies are working, and how he might modify them if they are not.

To facilitate aesthetic experiences at different stages of the player journey, consider the way that feedback satisfies different needs of players on their path to mastery. Beginners need to be intrigued, interested and sense the promise of personal and social growth. Feedback for this group should emphasize guidance, constraints and encouragement so that they can easily develop clarity of purpose. Players who have become proficient need to be surprised. Feedback, in this case, should focus on provoking exploration and risk-taking. Gamified systems can utilize rewards and progressively challenging obstacles and new opportunities for teamwork. The most learned and loyal group are those that have mastered the skill and knowledge to reach the highest level. This group wants to be convinced that their on-going participation is essential for the system's success. They need

Figure 6.4 Stages of achievement along a player journey (an adaptation and variation of the player journey map created by Amy Jo Kim).

Table 6.1 Aesthetic experiences and stages in the player journey

Aesthetic Experience	Novice > Get them interested	Proficient > Surprise them	Master > Make them feel special
Exploration	Give users a small taste of the world. Guides, characters and mentors can help give a sense of parameters and rules. The space should feel appealing and accessible, and rife with possibilities. Trial and error should occur in small doses.	Offer lots of surprises and in particular valued and hidden spaces. These can be rewards as well as safe bases to return to during the game to reflect on achievements. Smaller challenges work best.	Let them feel they know the world and their special place within it. Character development should imply privileged access. Supporting novices through character development should increase these privileges.
Empowerment	Let them achieve successes early.	Trial and error occurs in larger doses here. Let them begin to develop unique skills or abilities.	Offer special privileges. Communicate privilege, status and power privately (rewards and benefits) and publicly (display recognitions).
Fellowship	Friends invite them into the world. Masters provide mentorship, learning and advice. Guides make players feel included and welcomed.	Provide new opportunities to support novices and prove their value to masters. Encourage recruitment and outreach as a means of enhancing social bonding.	Give opportunities for sustained leadership and mentorship.
Expression	Offer the freedom to create one's character, shape one's environment or build one's avatar.	Put forward new opportunities for customization and display. More options to contribute to community.	Give this group more sophisticated functionality for self-expression and character, persona and item customization. This may include redefining the space or creating new roles for other players. There can also be reserved and special roles or unique possibilities for personal showcases and collective display.
Heroics	Make them feel like their contribution matters. Thank them for participating and let them know why the role they play is important in the overall scheme of the system.	Show them how their contribution matters. Let them have a memorable win, overcoming a real challenge or obstacle. Let them contribute something unique and important to the community.	Let them make strategic decisions and provide leadership in big wins.
Invention and nurturing	Give them something small to start or build. Let them finish it or see it experience growth early.	Show them the fruits of their labor. Something new should emerge and surprise. Allow for combinations of different game elements.	Offer possibilities for review, control, management and invention in relation to the gamified system. Other opportunities include participating in design decision-making, setting values or changing the way resources are allocated.

to feel unique and special, requiring feedback that reminds them that they are extremely valuable and appreciated.

Table 6.1 maps aesthetic experiences discussed in this chapter to the stages in the player journey, highlighting different feedback goals that a GS design should achieve.

REWARDS AND MOTIVATIONS

There is a significant amount of evidence that external motivation techniques like grades or points are at odds with the more important goal of building internal interest in a subject or task. Certainly, over-reliance on simple points systems to generate momentum is a mark of poor design. Rewards can be given to players to help them achieve specific goals. They can also support an overarching narrative, and they can enhance social influence. Feedback mechanisms like points and badges have proven over time to be effective methods for capturing attention and driving initial behavior. While there are many game concepts that we explore later in this chapter, understanding why these attention-grabbing reward structures are used by some gamified systems is an important place to start.

Points

Points provide immediate and rapid feedback, letting users know that their actions and input matter. They are also an accessible method for creating a sense of achievement and progression along a path. Finally, aside from commercial measurements like money, they tend to be something that is missing in everyday life. A few different point systems to consider:

- **Experience points (XP)**: Introduced by the creators of the table-top dice game *Dungeons & Dragons*, and used in many role-playing videogames, XP are a cumulative point system that indicates at all times and over time how a player is doing. They are notably distinct from the accumulation of treasure and items. Experience points can be awarded for a variety of behaviors including completing tasks and overcoming challenges. These points can drive character progression like the ability to level up and gain more abilities. GS designers can use XP to tie together different activities and targeted behaviors, giving users a big-picture perspective that makes sense of their individual interactions.
- **Skill points**: Used in a variety of forms in role-playing games, skill points relate to the development of specific skills and tasks. Not only do skill points encourage a player's sense of mastery, and generate a sense of autonomy by encouraging players to pursue their own interests, but they also can create a sense of relatedness or greater meaning. Rich collaboration is derived when individuals with different expertise can utilize their own unique approaches to accomplish tasks that are connected. Skill points allow for an inter-dependent team of people to experience social flow while reducing the potential for groupthink.

- **Redeemable points**: Redeemable points enable players to use their points to purchase virtual or real-world items. Frequent-flyer miles and virtual currency in social network games are examples of redeemable point systems. Although this approach is inherently attractive, it is a complex method that requires balancing along with a legal and logistics infrastructure that many projects may not be able to support.
- **Reputation points**: Reputation points are tied to the participation of the community online. These points usually correspond to votes or ratings that a user, member or organization gets for their interactions with others in the community. Reputation points can also represent the perception that other users and/or the project owner or sponsor have about the value of participation of different members in the community. Reputation points can be tied to access and privileges.
- **Victory points**: Commonly found in contemporary table-top games, victory points are points that players work for to win a game. In many cases, victory points are not publicly known by all players until the end of a game, when they are counted up to determine the winner. For finite competitive play and competitive team-play this obscured approach to scoring is an excellent alternative to leaderboards.
- **Obscured/hidden points**: Some audiences do not want to participate in a game experience, but would benefit from the structure that a gamified system provides. In certain situations there will be the need to utilize game elements and concepts but mask that a system has been gamified. Hidden

Table 6.2 Points and when to use them

Points	When to use
Experience points	To tie together multiple activities and create a bigger overall picture of an experience. To build on-going participation and personal investment.
Skill points	To provide freedom of choice and build autonomy. Asymmetrical skills create interdependency amongst players leading to social flow.
Redeemable points	When creating a virtual economy, a loyalty or consumer-based initiative. To incentivize user behavior.
Reputation points	When an individual's or member's participation and interactions with others in the community is critical to the success of the system. Can be used to constrain or enable access and privileges.
Victory points	For goal-oriented or finite contests. In some cases, scores and player statistics may benefit from being kept hidden until the end.
Obscured/hidden points	When your audience does not want to feel like they are playing a game. Or, when certain points, ranking or scores need to be kept as private information. At times, this is data only used by the system itself.

points are not used overtly to drive behavior. Though reward systems, rankings and user activities may be overt and public, the values and points assigned to these activities are not.

Show me your badge

Figure 6.5 Crane badge, 19th century China.

Nineteenth-century Qing Dynasty civil officials wore bird badges on their coats. The crane designated the highest of nine ranks. In the image, the crane is flying close to a red sun, which represents the emperor, and his proximity to the high-ranking official.

For most of us, badges carry a variety of meanings and associations. For instance, the badge worn by a police officer indicates that she is a representative of the law and therefore has a certain level of authority that civilians do not. The police officer's badge is a unique credential that defines her specific role in civil society. On the other hand, merit badges, worn on the sashes of Boy Scouts across the world since the turn of the 20th century, represent a certain level of proficiency at a skill. These skills range from leatherwork to cooking, and they can respond to historical changes. Now there is a badge for computers and game design, and no longer one for taxidermy (discontinued in 1952). Rather than signifying an official role like the police badge, the set of over 131 badges instead providea a public testament of achievement and growth over time. They encourage and validate exploration and the pursuit of knowledge and skill in a diversity of interests. As scouts perform more skills proficiently, they collect more badges. While doing this is a part of a larger system of growth, moving up the ranks to become Eagle Scout, collecting badges also provides a more diverse set of goals and a refined sense of progression. This creates social opportunities and activity-oriented synergies with the rest of the system, thus imbuing the rank badges and

Figure 6.6 Boy Scout merit badges acquired over many years. Courtesy of the Boy Scouts of America.

the individual merit badge collections with even greater meaning associated with particular memories and experiences.

In the digital world, badges provide users with on-going feedback. Because of the potential for visual permutations and variety, digital badges can recognize specializations at a granular level and the images on them serve as symbolic rewards of them. For example, the *Git Real* badges (shown in Figure 6.7), which are a part of Code School's online course offerings, represent the accomplishment of the six progressively challenging levels of *Git Real*, a gamified system designed to teach programmers the basics of the Git Source Code Management (SCM) system. Each of the courses offered by the company are designed to imbue a

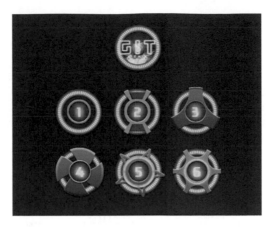

Figure 6.7 *Git Real* badges represent accomplishment and professional skills and capabilities. © Code School. Courtesy of Justin Mezzell.

unique experience that sets it apart from the others. The combination of the topic and theme utilized throughout a specific course creates distinction and variation. For instance, the level 4 badge indicates that a user has not only worked through thirty-two challenges leading to the badge, but also provides a symbol to employees looking for a developer with the specific skills required to simultaneously collaborate with other developers in the Git framework. This variety can encourage exploration of multiple pathways or solutions to accomplishing goals, creating greater opportunities for reflection and emergence. Badges indicate progression, which can unlock rewards, items and ultimately the opportunity for greater challenges and experience in the system. They also engender social capital, and can translate into special access, unique powers and privileged authority. Over the past few years, there has been a concerted effort to make badges synonymous with certification. The Mozilla Open Badges project enables individuals who have mastered skills in a program like Code School's *Git Real* to post their badges on their own website. The purpose of the project is to let individuals quickly inform potential employers of their capabilities.

Synergies of collecting

Recognizing, searching for, acquiring and valuing an item as part of a larger set, gives it new and greater meaning. If these items are limited in nature or very hard to come by, their public display increases their value even more. Collectors are driven by a variety of desires, including:

- The accumulation of items based on one interest.
- The need to complete a set.
- To acquire representative items from different sets.
- Collecting items for the purpose of trading or selling.
- The scarcity or rarity of specific items.

Contextualized collecting motivates progress towards bigger goals

Collecting badges in *Pokémon* is more than a sign of progress. The collection of badges is meaningfully integrated into the process. Collecting all the badges is not the end of the game. Instead the collection initiates the final and most difficult obstacles, which a player needs to overcome in order to receive the title of champion.

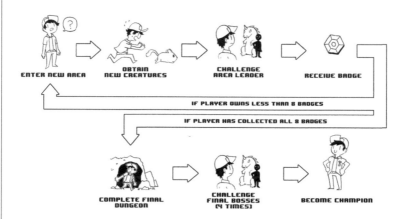

Figure 6.8 *Pokémon* contextualizes badge collection. Drawing by Alex Waskelo.

Whether it is baseball cards, badges or *Pokémon*, the desire to complete an unfinished set is a natural tendency. By promoting the act of collecting, games and gamified systems encourage players to create a meaningful archive that re-tells their story of accomplishments.

Leaderboards

Leaderboards are public displays of player scores, ranking players in relation to each other. Harkening from the days of the high score of arcade game screens like *Asteroids* and *Centipede*, and competitive sports before that, leaderboards are a method for making solo game-play feel social, giving individual players the feeling they are playing with and against others. Because the wide world of the Internet is significantly more anonymous and diffuse than a local arcade, most game platforms let players see their position through multiple data sets. In addition to showing a player his standing relative to everyone playing, leaderboards often provide views contextualized and localized according to a player's social networks, ranking him next to the people that he knows.

Two different approaches to leaderboards are shown in Figure 6.9. The first, created by Bunchball, prominently features the profile picture and sales figures

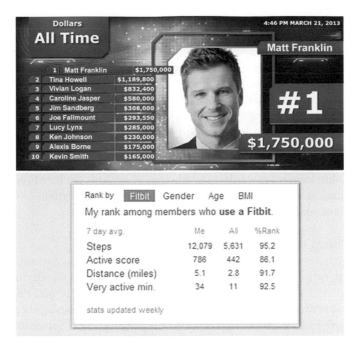

Figure 6.9 *Bunchball* and *Fitbit* use two different approaches to leveraging leaderboards for motivation. Top photo courtesy of Bunchball, Inc. Bottom photo *Fitbit*. Courtesy of Olson, an ICF International Company.

> ### Be sensitive about sharing user data
>
> If you are posting up information about players, be very careful about the information you are sharing publicly. For example, statistics related to purchases, finance or even dieting is information that should be kept private. If your target audience is under the age of thirteen you are legally obligated to adhere to COPPA, the Children's Online Protection Privacy Act. The federal law protects children from having their personal data shared with third parties like advertisers.

generated by the top sales person in an organization, followed by the names and numbers associated with the rest of the sales people who made it to the top ten. The second appears on the Fitbit dashboard, and is meant only to be a personal motivator, showing individuals how they compare to all other Fitbit users.

Reward schedules

In Chapter 3 we introduced the topic of rewards and how the pursuit of these kick-started the brain's release of dopamine. The uncertainty about when a reward would be given, the feeling of "maybe," has the greatest effect on an individual in terms of dopamine release. Reward schedules derive from practices introduced nearly a hundred years ago by behavioral psychologists. These showed how animals and humans behave and respond when rewards are distributed according either to time or to a specific activity.

Time-based rewards fall into two categories:

1. **Fixed interval rewards**—A reward is given at a certain amount of time. For instance, every twenty minutes a user stays logged on she receives 5,000 points.
2. **Variable interval rewards**—Distribution of rewards are based on time, but the time is not fixed. In some cases points will be distributed within two minutes, and some cases it will be ten minutes.

Rewards based upon behaviors are broken into:

1. **Fixed ratio rewards**—A reward is provided based on an individual's behavior. For instance, when a user invites three friends, he gets a new badge.
2. **Variable ratio rewards**—Rewards are based on performance, but when they are given varies and is not known to the player or user. Sometimes you get a mushroom; sometimes you don't.

Use variable reward schedules

Though fixed rewards are easier to design, they are far less impactful than their variable counterparts. The unpredictability of variable ratio schedules is one way of encouraging the motivation of a player to continue interacting with a system.

APPLYING LESSONS FROM GAME GENRES

Like the language of film, the language of games utilizes the notion of genre for definition. For games, genres like role-playing games or puzzle games are a means of distinguishing and understanding the interactive experience. For instance, a turn-based strategy game like *Civilization V* requires the analysis of many varied data points, including management of land, armies, citizens and resources. With so many options to consider, the player has the benefit of time to make her critical decisions. On the other hand, a first-person shooter (FPS) like *Halo*, in which a soldier is confronted by a stream of different kinds of opponents and different needs in terms of weapons, is marked by rapid decision-making necessitating a much narrower set of choices. Different genres rely on different methods of interaction for the player. These commonly recurring aspects are called game patterns, and will be discussed in more detail as we explore individual genres.

Looking at the ways in which genres and patterns can facilitate targeted activities and behaviors is an excellent way to invent and imagine new directions in GS design. Although this is not an exhaustive list, the genres presented in this chapter should provide a good place for the GS designer to start. Game genres explored in this chapter include:

- Action-adventure.
- Role-playing and massively multiplayer role-playing games (MMORPGs).
- Social media.
- Alternate reality games (ARGs).
- Table-top.
- Construction.
- Survival horror.

Action-adventure games facilitate exploration

Action-adventure games combine the exploration and problem-solving associated with adventure games, with time-based challenges that require precision, risk-taking and quick decision-making. This hybrid genre covers a wide swath from early text adventures like Zork to contemporary shooters like Call of Duty. What is important for our purposes are the ways in which action-adventure games promote exploration. Leveraging virtual and physical environments, and placing obstacles, information and challenges within them, creates significant opportunities for emergence, reflection and social expansion. Additionally, creating a sense of urgency in a space can be added through time pressures, limited resources, player vs. player or team-based competition, surprising twists and, of course, boss battles, which are enemy challenges marking the completion of a series of obstacles.

Leveraging location

To encourage users to seek and discover, gamified systems can leverage both physical and virtual locations. Location can hold a variety of values or meanings. For instance, a user may find special information like a clue about the location of a sought-after item in one space that links it to another in the game. Using puzzles as a means of overcoming obstacles or information discovery is another way to make the most of space or spatial references, causing players to linger in that location. Special locations also reveal elements of stories. For instance, fictional characters may leave journal entries, video feeds or audio messages. Opportunities to interact with objects and collect special items for use, like weapons or power-ups, generally have a precise virtual location. Defined areas might also be utilized as points where individuals can make risk–reward decisions, such as participating in combat or trading or selling items, goods or resources. In all of these cases, GPS-driven games can associate virtual locations with real locations, adding further dimensions. For example, the augmented-reality multiplayer game *Ingress* depends on GPS locations so that two opposing factions can compete over contested "portals" at real-world locations.

Some location-centric patterns that GS designers utilize include:

- **Levels**—A level is usually one specific area where activities take place until a specific goal is met, at which point another level is instantiated. Levels provide an overall sense of progression, but also a feeling that this progression is manageable. Activities and goals within and between different levels may vary. Each level usually distinguishes itself by being marked by particular resources, puzzles or "bosses," powerful characters usually associated with the achievement of completing the level. They are most appropriate for finite games that have defined end goals, and as such they delimit the game world. Levels can also form a portion of a game space that remains accessible for free play and perhaps higher-level activities once certain conditions have been

---

Apply lessons from level design

Designing a level involves several tasks. If you are using a real location or creating a virtual space, your tasks will include:

1. Mapping a space.
2. Defining the player's path of progression.
3. Placing and identifying obstacles.
4. Identifying skills required by a player to overcome obstacles.
5. Knowing when, where and how feedback will be delivered to the player.
6. Understanding the relationships between different levels and how they work together to move a player towards progressively harder tasks.

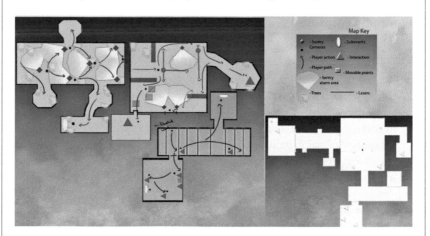

Figure 6.10 Image by level designer Qwenn Parker.

met. From a design perspective, each level usually incorporates its own clearly articulated rules, goals and theme.

- **Secret or hidden areas**—Secret or hidden areas can contain privileged information, unique items, limited resources, rewards, clues, secret paths, pick-ups and power-ups, and surprise elements like Easter eggs. Often these are used for bonuses or for jokes that generate a feeling of insider knowledge. These also can provide alternative options to the standard rules, goals and theme of the level.
- **Strategic locations**—These are locations that might have special value or status to access or control. Strategic locations offer opportunities for reflection and long-term planning. These locations can be used for pick-ups and power-ups, resource collection or production, confrontations and battles, trades and negotiations.

Puzzles

Puzzles are often used as gating elements to extend a player challenge before they can move forward along a path. Puzzles require the player to identify patterns and understand the steps required to derive a solution. They get individuals to slow down and reflect on their experience and the knowledge they have gained up to that point. They can also enable group interaction and collective problem-solving.

Puzzles feed progress paths

Puzzles can create the forward thrust required to keep players intrigued. Reflection and collaboration can emerge through the desire for a solution.

Because they require creativity, innovation and perseverance, when the solution to a puzzle is discovered individuals are likely to become much more invested in continuing forward.

- **Object-based puzzles**—Puzzles that require players to utilize objects or spaces to overcome an obstacle may include: a lock & key puzzle, finding an object and bringing it to a specific location, combining two objects or converting an object into a usable key.
- **Alignment/Sequence**—Some puzzles require players to move certain elements in a certain sequence or get them organized according to a certain pattern. Often times these challenges are time based and must be completed before the time runs out.
- **Information**—Some puzzles can supply necessary information that can only be gained by solving them. These can include riddles, cryptograms, codes and logic puzzles. In addition, conversations with certain characters or individuals may provide solutions as well.

Solving puzzles through "hacking" enemy drones is an essential part of the game *BioShock*. The alignment puzzles require players to guide glowing turquoise liquid from one side of the screen to another by moving elements of unused pipes from other squares and orienting them in particular directions. There is more than one way to solve the puzzle, but the time pressure of the flowing liquid means that decisions have to be made relatively quickly.

Figure 6.11 An alignment puzzle from the game *BioShock*. *BioShock* screenshot. Courtesy of Irrational Games, Inc., 2K Games, Inc., and Take-Two Interactive Software, Inc. All Rights Reserved. No part of this work may be reproduced in any form or by any means—graphic, electronic or mechanical, including photocopying, recording, online distribution or information storage and retrieval systems—without the written permission of the publisher or the designated rightsholder, as applicable.

Use puzzles to:

- Create a sense of urgency.
- Build personal investment.
- Make people feel smart.
- Promote collective problem-solving.
- Create obstacles.
- Reveal information.

- **Kid-friendly**—Simpler approaches to puzzles usually involve exposing an image or message through a simple set of instructions. Some ideas include: dot-to-dot, paint by numbers, fold and reveal, or using a rebus, where letters, words and pictures combine to create a message.

Role-playing games and MMORPGs develop character

Role-playing games like the *Elder Scrolls V: Skyrim* and massively multiplayer online role-playing games like *World of Warcraft* are meant to facilitate heroic journeys. Although exploration and adventure are essential ingredients, these always serve to progress and grow a player's character. By pursuing different challenges players can build up their character in the ways that they affect the world, and in the ways that they can support other people. Designers of gamified systems can give users a greater sense of individuality and purpose in an environment by considering:

- **Character creation & customization**—Character creation gives individuals an opportunity to role-play. Functions that let players define themselves in a variety of ways can generate a greater sense of agency and commitment. Some aspects a player might be able to create and customize are:
  - Character name or nickname.
  - Appearance, including using player-provided images.
  - Starting abilities/race/class, often related to particular kinds of gameplay.

Figure 6.12 Character customization functions like those offered in the MMORPG *Guild Wars 2* encourage a deeper sense of identification between a player and the character she is controlling. © 2010–2014 ArenaNet, LLC. All rights reserved.

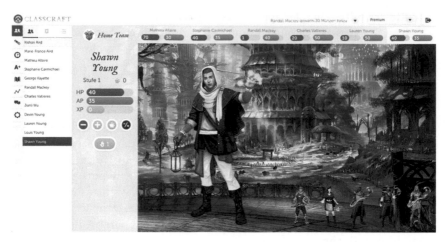

Figure 6.13 *Classcraft* is an educational multiplayer role-playing game designed to encourage positive performance and behavior amongst students. Letting students build and develop a character during the school year encourages a deeper sense of identification with the world of the gamified system. Courtesy of Classcraft Studios Inc.

- **Character progression**—Character progression is the bread and butter of role-playing games. Being able to choose how a character will develop over time provides autonomy and personal control. Though gamified systems may be lower in opportunities for pure fantasy, there is still plenty to be garnered from the ways an individual can grow his game-world persona, including:
  - Leveling up.
  - Gaining abilities and experience.
  - Attaining new and unique items.

By choosing to pursue a distinct set of characteristics and abilities, players create characters that can contribute in specific ways to support a group. The social bonding that ensues in turn provides the player and his character with greater opportunities for achievement and growth. When specialized roles and unique abilities are combined to accomplish a common goal powerful group dynamics ensue. Gamified systems can take advantage of these valuable asymmetric alliances. Jane McGonigal's *Superstruct* (described in Patrick Jagoda's interview in Chapter 1) is a perfect example of such collaboration through difference. At the onset of the game players constructed descriptions of their future selves including their imagined professions, skills, communities, experience and values. These identifiable distinctions helped players self-organize so that they could most constructively share ideas about possible solutions to urgent global issues on the horizon.

Self-organizing groups create synergy and collective strength to generate cooperation, reciprocity and the highest form of social flow—interdependency. At the same time, healthy competition as well as temporary and secret alliances can emerge between these different groups. Short term and long term groups

> ### Social bonding through asymmetry
>
> It is important to remember that each player or user is an individual with her own set of special abilities. Whereas one individual might be much more adept at physical challenges, another might be better at solving puzzles. Still others might be excellent at recruiting individuals or keeping people informed about events or challenges. Different people bring different skills to an environment. Your job is to make these distinctions relevant and useful.

form to accomplish a variety of tasks in MMOs. Some groups and motivations for working together include:

- **Party**—A party is an *ad-hoc* group that comes together under a temporary alliance as a team to complete a task. Players tend to be matched to balance their skills and abilities. They are instantiated for real-time live game-play where multiple people are needed to work together to overcome an obstacle.
- **Guilds**—Commitment and fellowship are the cornerstones of these groups. Guilds, which can be very large, are designed for long-term membership, and are organized according to the contributions and accomplishments made by each individual. Players get many special advantages through membership, and have a much more significant assurance of protection when facing new challenges.
- **Quests**—Quests require players to accomplish something of importance, such as fetching a prized item or killing a dragon. Quests tend to be associated more with adventures and journeys, and usually include battles, and the search for and discovery of some valuable object.

Social network games bring people in

Games like *Words with Friends* leverage social-networking technologies to support frequent asynchronous player interaction. As mentioned in Chapter 1, living on the edges of our online interactions means that they are always present in our lives. Because of their relatively low level of challenge and progression the contributions that these game have made are often overlooked within the larger industry. Gamified systems cannot dismiss the influence of these games because they are at the core of the concept of a game layer.

Some of the most salient aspects of social network games include:

- **Immediate access**—It takes as little as a tap of a screen to get to any social network game. Once in, we are directed immediately to the simplest of tasks. Quickly, we are rewarded and then given another simple task. Social media games remove the barrier of entry associated with most games. GS designs

Figure 6.14 *Words with Friends* is a social networking game that brings players together around the idea of playing the word game *Scrabble*. *Words with Friends* is a trademark of Zynga, Inc. and is used with its permission. Copyright © 2014 Zynga, Inc. All rights reserved.

can do the same by providing simple methods for getting in and quickly interacting.

- **Rapid feedback**—The continuous feedback associated with these games may seem repetitive, but they keep players on task, and make them aware of the different possibilities available to them at any moment. Most importantly, points, progress bars, gifts and rewards are all methods for giving players a continuous sense of progress. Feedback also provides players with timely information about their friends and acquaintances.

- **Gifts**—Social network games have masterfully incorporated one of the oldest practices in human history for building social solidarity: gift exchange. For centuries, expending wealth and effort to offer a gift has demonstrated a desire to strengthen a relationship. It has also been an important symbol of status and privilege. Social network games encourage players to give gifts to surprise, delight and show their friends online that they are thinking of them. In addition, they encourage gift recipients to reciprocate the kindness.

Reciprocity creates a circle of exchange, enabling virtual gifts to exist in their own economy, forming a potentially meaningful alternative to real currency. Not only do social network games encourage players to send gifts to each other within the game system, they have also managed to incorporate this age-old practice into the invitations that players extend to invite friends to join the game and play. Gift exchange in the virtual world has several values, which includes being a vehicle for viral marketing.

Cultures of gift giving

A *gift economy* or *gift culture* occurs when items of value are not sold, but instead given with no precise agreement or terms of future reciprocation.

In 1925 the French Anthropologist and Sociologist Marcel Mauss wrote *The Gift*, which studied gift exchange from around the world and showed that gift-giving pervades all aspects of society including politics, aesthetics, religion, law and morality. For Mauss, when a gift makes its way around society the gift-giver is responsible for changing the social fabric in some way. According to Mauss, though gift exchange is not constrained by contractual obligations bounded by time exchange value, there is always an unspoken and implied requirement of reciprocity in gift economies.

Figure 6.15 For Mauss gift-giving comes with three obligatory actions:
1. *Giving*—The first step towards building relationships.
2. *Receiving*—Accepting a gift affirms the social bond.
3. *Reciprocating*—Demonstrates integrity of the social structure.

- **Virtual goods and currency**—Virtual goods are digital items that have value within a specific virtual environment. Most of these items are decorative, and are used for display and creative self-expression. Others can be used to enhance performance or skills. Items are purchased with real money or virtual currency. Virtual currency can be accumulated through interaction with the game system, other players, participating companies and with friends in the player's social network. This insidiously addictive "earn-and-burn" feedback loop encourages players to keep playing to acquire currency and use them for goods.
- **Asynchronous interaction**—Because social network games are asynchronous, players have the opportunity to play together but to do so on their own time. Persistent and changing environments and interfaces, turn taking, and opportunities for messaging and gifting means that although players may not be interacting together in real-time they can still experience the joys of playing. Consequently, emergence and reflective story-telling become possible as well.
- **Minimal concentration but frequent interaction**—Marked by their very light interaction model, these games get players to participate by using a few core methods. As mentioned before, one of the most important methods to get players to return is through the invitations and gifts sent by friends playing. The use of what are called appointment dynamics is another practice. The idea here is that players will return at specific times during the day to maximize their benefits, and reduce the risk of negative punishment, such as the loss of resources.

Use with care

When using appointment dynamics to drive behavior it is important to recognize the potential for this method to create the experience of addiction or compulsion. If used, it should be used with care.

Alternate Reality Games change

Alternate Reality Games (ARGs), like Ken Eklund's *World Without Oil* (introduced in Chapter 2), create the experience of playing in a parallel world. This fiction manifests through a variety of forms found in both the physical and digital world. ARGs are usually played by large groups of highly devoted players who work together to solve challenges discovered through play. They are improvisational in nature, with a live team of designers, known as puppet masters, who are providing new mechanisms for play as a response to player input and activities. Because so many ARGs have been created to promote the release of entertainment and media properties, most are considered gamified systems. Although this genre is known for having a relatively high barrier to entry, it is a form that has started finding its way to wider audiences. For example, the game *Vanished* created by the MIT Education Arcade and the Smithsonian (covered in more detail in

Chapter 8) utilized the ARG form for middle-school students as a vehicle of engagement with natural science and the professional scientists in the field. The goals and the audience of the game meant that it had to be significantly more accessible. For this reason, the design team chose to be explicit about when the event was running, and to have one website as a constant source of information. ARGs distinguish themselves through:

*   **Pervasiveness**—The expansion into time, space, social networks and different media forms are what characterize and distinguish this form. It is important when considering design elements to think about the many different ways that these extensions into the real world can be used to create a sense of surprise, the experience of variety, social bonding and continued and on-going interest. While many ARGs like *World Without Oil* or *I Love Bees* tend to use a website as a base for information dissemination, communication and archival recording, one of the key characteristics of this genre is the way that it extends into multiple forms within a player's world. Pre-recorded phone calls, phone messages, e-mails, snail mail, newspaper advertisements, poster

Though not an ARG, the pervasive game *Humans Vs. Zombies* is a popular game on college campuses around the world. During the event, student "humans" try to fend off growing hordes of students who have turned into "zombies." Usually occurring over the course of an academic week, players are protected from attack in classrooms and academic buildings, but parking lots, dining halls and dormitories are all considered within the zone of play until the end of the event.

Figure 6.16 *Humans Vs. Zombies* pervades college campus life. Courtesy of Jonathan Springs.

boarding, live actors and of course web sites are all a part of the arsenal of tools that can be leveraged from this form.

- **Parallel fiction**—ARGs build interest by delivering an unfolding narrative. Through online and real-world exploration, seeking and discovering fragments and solving challenges alone and as a group, players put the story together while playing the game. This process of discovery often takes place in the form of a mystery that players need to solve. For example, Audi's *Art of the Heist* introduced the new A3 by creating an ARG based around the story of the stolen car. Players were encouraged to search the entire country for clues about the whereabouts and identity of the thieves.

- **This is not a game**—ARGs don't admit to being a game. By eroding the idea of the relegated magic circle, players and the people in their lives don't really know when they are playing and are not playing. This fuzzy state of existence encourages reimagining the regular world as one filled with infinite potential for surprise and intrigue.

- **Collective intelligence**—

> What is collective intelligence? It is a form of universally distributed intelligence, constantly enhanced, coordinated in real time, and resulting in the effective mobilization of skills.
> . . . No one knows everything, everyone knows something.
> —Pierre Levy, *L'intelligence collective: pour une anthropologie du cyberspace* (*Collective Intelligence: Mankind's Emerging World in Cyberspace*)

Collective intelligence as defined by the French philosopher and media theorist Pierre Levy is an essential aspect of Alternate Reality Gaming. Many puzzles and challenges can only be solved through the collective efforts of multiple players. The distribution of clues around the globe and the Internet makes working together as a community a necessity for finishing the game.

Since the inception of the ARG form, self-organizing groups have been essential. In fact, the first ARG, designed in 2001 as a part of the promotion of the Steven Spielberg film *A.I.*, and named "the Beast" by the player community, gave birth to just such a group. The game, which was set in the future fifty years after the film, subtly (and almost secretly) invited players to help solve the mystery of a fictional character's death. With no announcement of any *A.I.*-related game, in an effort to make sense of the hidden messages found in trailers and promotional posters, a group called the "cloud makers" formed. By the end of the game the group boasted over 7,000 players.

- **Puppet Masters**—These game designers support the game and move it forward when it is in play. They are the people who "pull the strings," releasing information, running events and making modifications to the game world based on players' activities and actions. Puppet masters must be highly improvisational, keeping the player community on their collective toes, and responding in the most creative ways to emerging player demands and ideas about how the system should play out.

A few more mentions

A GS designer can learn something from every game genre and should get in the habit of thinking broadly about the concept of a game.

Paper-based table-top games

Paper-based table-top games like board games and cards games create tactile game spaces that remove us from our increasing dependence on screens. When we play them, we are forced to interact face-to-face with other people in the very same room. This creates a much more intimate experience, providing many opportunities to get to know other people in the high fidelity of the real world. Most table-top games are turn based, a form that allows for players to reverse roles often, moving between strategic planning and enactment. Without the benefits of computer code, a table-top game requires players to facilitate, understand and translate rules and procedures, and make their own meaning of the experience. Like a good piece of literature, table-top games like *Dungeons & Dragons* or *Settlers of Catan* require their players to enrich and expand the space of imagination.

Construction and simulation games

Construction and simulation games as well as interactive toys provide endless opportunities for creativity and self-expression. Games like *Minecraft* or *SimCity* facilitate autonomy and personal control by encouraging the player to set his own goals and create his own strategies for accomplishing them. In addition to building and testing out the hypothesis and parameters of a system, some simulation games including virtual pets, virtual gardens and the widely popular *Sims* games, encourage nurturing tendencies. Players are expected not only to see that these virtual beings grow, but also that they are cared for over a long period of time. Although these forms are difficult to produce and are resource intensive, they are excellent mechanisms for building long-term, invested relationships with a player base.

Survival horror

Survival horror games succeed by building an atmosphere of tension. Though players know they are playing a game, the sense of imminent death lurking within indistinguishable dimly lit spaces is what makes games like the popular *Slender: The Eight Pages* so terrifying and iconic. In the game, the player must navigate a dark forest armed only with a flashlight that is quickly losing battery power. And, although the flashlight provides some light it also alerts and attracts the Slender Man to the player's whereabouts. The limitation (and in some cases total unavailability) of items or weapons for self-defense increases the sense of urgency. At the same time the lack of visual clarity heightens the players other senses. The immersive running game and audio-adventure *Zombies, Run!* leverages these ideas from the survival horror genre to get players running with purpose. The point of the game is to motivate a player to exercise, a kind of unpredictable interval training for runners. In the game, players complete a series of missions, such

Figure 6.17 *Zombies, Run!* is a gamified system that leverages aspects of the survival horror genre. Courtesy of Six to Start and Naomi Alderman.

as picking up collections of supplies like medicine and ammunition, all while running to the sounds of audio narrations and hordes of zombies. The game even includes a zombie chase where the player has to run faster than her normal speed to avoid being caught by zombies and losing supplies or failing her mission.

PUTTING IT ALL TOGETHER

As you explore different game concepts, it is a good idea to begin organizing these into meaningful categories. In some cases, your gamified system will contain **dramatic elements** related to a narrative underlying the player journey. These are likely to include a premise and characters, each with a back-story, and a motivation that unfolds over time. Dramatic elements, if your design includes these, are likely to inform all of the other game components known as formal elements.

Formal elements are features that are common to all games. They include: players, objectives, outcomes, resources, procedures, rules and boundaries. Players are understood by the role or character they play as. Their relationships to each other and to the system are referred to as player interaction patterns. Examples of player interaction patterns include players competing against each other, in teams, or as a group against a system. You might decide that one of the essential aesthetics of your game is social bonding, and thus might choose to utilize team play or collective play against a system.

Objectives, or goals that motivate a player towards a path of progression, need to be articulated. If you have defined dramatic elements, objectives will likely be

Dramatic elements

Dramatic elements make up the narrative components of any game or gamified system. These are informed by the aesthetic intention of your design and the goals of your project. These in turn affect and are affected by formal elements.

Formal elements

Formal elements make up the parameters and features required for a system to be considered to be a game or a gamified system. They include: players, objectives, outcomes, resources, procedures, rules and boundaries.

Goals → dramatic elements → formal elements

Use goals to define dramatic elements. These will in turn inform the formal elements you choose. The interaction with these elements should generate data, which can be used to support goals.

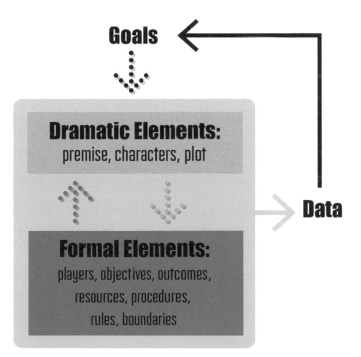

Figure 6.18

contextualized within this narrative. With your objectives, you can begin to identify where you will include conflicts like obstacles and challenges. These are going to initiate feedback-driven outcomes, such as rewards and punishments, and winners and losers.

Rules, which may be entirely transparent to a player because they are coded or programmed into a system, determine what a player is permitted to do and restricted from doing. Procedures, which are derived from rules, determine the order of events and activities, for example, what a player does on a turn. Procedures provide a structure for progression, informing the player what to do when.

If you are planning on having resources like points or virtual items, you should define what these are and how these will be distributed. You will need to decide how these will be collected, gained, managed, traded or lost. Finally, understand what boundaries of your game components exist in the system. Ask yourself when and where the game components start and end in time and space. This formal element is a bit different with gamified systems, because they do not respect the traditional border of the magic circle or sacred space. The boundary is likely to be roughed out at the beginning along with the player journey, and then refined as you go through the design process.

As you develop your dramatic and formal elements, it is important to make sure that your choices support your project goals in some ways. Try to articulate the ways that these ideas are generating data or promoting intended target behaviors and activities. Because you are designing a complex system, each choice may not directly do this, but should in some way support other elements that are helping you directly achieve your initiatives.

KEY TAKEAWAYS

- The MDA (Mechanics-Dynamics-Aesthetics) framework is a method for understanding how the functional elements of games match the emotional and emergent responses intended by the designer.
- Some aesthetic experiences that gamified systems strive to stimulate include: exploration, empowerment, fellowship, expression, heroics, nurturing and invention.
- Different stages in the player journey should be crafted to sustain and build upon the aesthetic experience. Beginners need to be interested and intrigued, whereas those who are competent need to be surprised and increasingly rewarded for exploration and continued engagement. Finally, the most experienced and consistent should feel special and important.
- Badges are a good way to reward individual achievements and proficiencies. They are also an excellent way to promote collection. To get the most out of them, consider how they can be meaningfully integrated into a larger context that supports progression.
- There are a variety of point structures that you can choose from for your system including: experience points (XP), skill points, redeemable points, reputation points, victory points and hidden or obscured points.

- According to the long history of behavioral psychology, reward schedules can influence action. Variable rewards, when recipients cannot anticipate exactly when they will be rewarded, are considered to be the most effective approach for continued engagement.
- GS designers can apply lessons from a range of game genres. Action-adventure games, multiplayer and single-player RPGs, social networking games, Alternate Reality Games (ARGs) and paper-based games are just some of these that provide methods for encouraging exploration, building character identity and facilitating asynchronous and real-time play.
- Use dramatic elements and formal elements to classify and organize your game components. Make sure these are driven by goals and can generate or support the creation of data.

EXERCISES

As you continue your work for the client you chose in Chapter 5 (the zoo, supermarket or record label), you should now be further developing your initial ideas and designing your game components. Using the information from this chapter along with the material already provided in the book and the supplementary website you should perform the following tasks:

6.1 Define the aesthetic experience

Identify the feelings and aesthetics you want your players to experience. Consider certain themes or narratives that will influence this.

6.2 Understand the dramatic elements

If you are planning on including narrative elements like characters, a back-story and a story that reveals itself over time, you should define these.

6.3 Map out a player journey

Illustrate, storyboard or diagram your player journey from beginning to end. How will you build interest, introduce surprise and reward loyalty? How will you satisfy different requirements of players at different stages on their journeys?

6.4 Imagine dynamics

Think about the types of dynamics you wish your players to have. What sorts of actions, verbs or moment-to-moment experiences do you envision? Know how these can translate into your game mechanics.

6.5 Apply genre research

Know how you will apply lessons from different game genres. How will you encourage exploration, build player identity and encourage relationships through collaboration, gift-giving and competition?

6.6 Identify core mechanics and target behaviors

Using the concepts generated in the previous tasks, you should begin to identify the actions or behaviors that you want to encourage.

6.7 Determine rewards and points

Knowing the behaviors you want to encourage means that you can identify the vehicles you will use to reward these activities. You should articulate if, when and how you can utilize badges, collections or points to build player engagement.

6.8 Map to goals

Review your concepts and identify the ways that these can best support your goals. Distinguish which of your ideas will directly or indirectly influence the generation of data or activity you want to collect, measure or drive (you should have defined your desired data in Chapter 5).

RECOMMENDED READINGS AND RESOURCES

- *Game Design Workshop: A Playcentric Approach to Creating Innovative Games*, Third Edition, by Tracy Fullerton, 2014.
  Tracy Fullerton is the Chair of the top-ranking game design program at University of Southern California. The book provides essential knowledge along with practical hands-on activities for those interested in designing and building games.

- *The Art of Game Design: A Book of Lenses* by Jesse Schell, 2008.
  The Art of Game Design is structured around 100 different lenses, each enabling multiple paths to help designers hone their practice at perceiving opportunities and overcoming challenges to create great designs.

- *MDA Framework, A Formal Approach to Game Design and Game Research* by Robin Hunicke, Marc LeBlanc and Robert Zubeck, 2001.
  This important academic conference paper introduced a formal approach for understanding games structures through Mechanics-Dynamics-Aesthetics.

- *Patterns in Game Design* by Staffan Björk and Jussi Holopainen, 2005.
  This book details different patterns that designers can leverage to create the most effective game-play.

- *www.gamasutra.com* is a respected web resource that includes regularly updated articles, essays, blogs and post-mortems about game design and the game industry.

INSIDER INSIGHT

DESIGN LESSONS FROM 2K'S JOSH ATKINS

Interview granted with permission by Josh Atkins.

Josh Atkins is the Vice President of Creative Development at 2K, where he is responsible for the editorial process, internal research and business development for its family of game titles, including the *Bioshock* series, Sid Meier's *Civilization* series and *Borderlands* 2. Prior to his role at 2K he was the Director of Game Design at Microsoft, where he managed the company's first-party portfolio for the Xbox and the Xbox 360. During his ten years at Microsoft he also held the position of Senior Design Director at Lionhead Studios overseeing the design of *Fable I, II* and *III*.

Figure 6.19
Josh Atkins.

What do you think are the most common mistakes game designers make?

It is probably easiest for me to answer this from the point of view of what are the common design mistakes I have made. Early in my career, I believed that I had to know all the answers to questions from my teammates. If I didn't know the answer or hadn't considered the question, I felt as if I had failed. I often answered questions too quickly or was afraid to say "I don't know" or "I am not sure," which was frequently the truth. This was at a time in the game business when designers were put on pedestals and the industry was less collaborative than it is now. Today, it is not only encouraged, but also necessary, to involve an entire team or group to solve some of the most challenging design questions. I think the biggest mistake can be losing sight of what's really important to a product. With the rise of indie development and small team projects we have entered a time where a game can really be a form of personal expression and with that comes a responsibility to create something true to yourself and your team—even if that thing is not following the latest trends or conventional wisdom. That is easier in the indie space but much harder when developing a bigger-budget title that generally has greater risks associated with it. However, in both cases, it is critical to ensure your design is true to yourself and your team, and not following the ideas of others.

How do you identify the strengths and weaknesses of a title?

Evaluating or assessing someone else's creative work is tricky because it is fundamentally subjective. Therefore, a lot of evaluation is our subjective opinion combined with objective customer information in the form of either telemetry data (data analytics) or market research. I always tend to trust our own instincts the most; however, we often learn things from customers we never would have thought of or considered.

Can you tell me about Xbox achievements and how these influenced your design practices? What were some of the big surprises you learned after it launched? How did it help support the mission of your division and company?

While I did not play a role in the creation of achievements, I was one of the first people to learn of the system and was part of the group that had to figure out how to use them in a meaningful way. Initially, I do not think anyone knew the power the system would have and how impactful it still is to the Xbox community. In the early days, many people often misused the system and held too many achievement points back and only gave them out for extremely difficult accomplishments. However, very quickly, we learned that giving achievement points out on a regular basis actually motivated players to continue playing, which is obvious now but at the time was far less clear. Now, many developers understand that they should hand out a good percentage of the achievements throughout the game and hold back a smaller percentage for the truly outstanding accomplishments.

You have worked with a variety of emerging tools and technologies. Can you tell me about any that do a good job of merging the real world and the game world?

Microsoft's Kinect literally merged the real world and the game world. In a lot of cases, I think that Kinect is the best example here; however, I think we also have to call out the iPhone as well. The iPhone has turned your life into a game, and the iPhone combined with Facebook and Twitter has turned everything we do into some kind of game. Sharing photos, communicating, sharing information are all aspects of playing a game that does not have clear rules yet.

How do you think gamified systems are or might impact the future of game design?

A gamified system is just another way of immersing users into a rule set, and therefore I think the impact has already happened and will continue. Traditional game designers will learn things from gamified systems, such as how best to motivate players to share information or how best to encourage players to feel like they are part of a greater community. However, those who specialize in gamified system design will continue to learn how best to encourage involvement by creating systems that take the best from the cooperative and competitive games and bring those elements into their products.

NOTES

Adams, Ernest and Andrew Rollings. *On Game Design*. Indianapolis: New Riders, 2003.

Björk, Staffan and Jussi Holopainen. *Patterns in Game Design*. Boston: Charles River Media, 2005.

Blair, Lucas. "The Cake is Not a Lie: How to Design Effective Achievements." *Gamasutra*, April 27, 2011, http://www.gamasutra.com/view/feature/6360/the_cake_is_not_a_lie_how_to_.php.

Brathwaite, Brenda and Ian Schreiber. *Challenges for Game Designers: Non-digital Exercises for Video Game Designers*. Boston: Cengage, 2009.

Campbell, Joseph. *The Hero with a Thousand Faces*. Second Edition. Princeton: Princeton University Press, 1968.

Co, Phil. *Level Design for Games: Creating Compelling Game Experiences*. Indianapolis: New Riders, 2006.

Feil, John and Marc Scattergood. *Beginning Game Level Design*. Boston: Premier Press, 2009.

Fullerton, Tracy. *Game Design Workshop: A Playcentric Approach to Creating Innovative Games*. Third Edition. Boca Raton: CRC Press, 2014.

Fullerton, Tracy, Steven Hoffman and Chris Swain. *Game Design Workshop: Designing, Prototyping, and Playtesting Games*. San Francisco: CMP Books, 2004.

Gosney, John W. *Beyond Reality: A Guide to Alternate Reality Gaming*. Boston: Thompson, 2005.

Hunicke, Robin, Marc LeBlanc and Robert Zubeck. "MDA: A Formal Approach to Game Design and Game Research." Developed and taught at the Game Developers Conference, San Jose, CA, 2001–2004.

Kim, Amy Jo. "MetaGame Design: Reward Systems that Drive Engagement." Presentation posted on Slideshare, March 10, 2010, http://www.slideshare.net/amyjokim/metagame-design-3383058.

Kim, Amy Jo. "5-Step Design Framework for Long Term Engagement." Presentation posted on Slideshare, October 19, 2013, http://www.slideshare.net/amyjokim/players-journey-5step-design-framework-for-longterm-engagement?related=1.

Kim, Amy Jo. "The Player's Journey: Drive Sustained Engagement with Onboarding, Habit-Building and Mastery." Presentation posted on Slideshare, June 9, 2014, http://www.slideshare.net/amyjokim/the-players-journey-drive-sustained-engagement-with-onboarding-habitbuilding-and-mastery.

LeBlanc, Marc. "Mechanics, Dynamics, Aesthetics: A Formal Approach to Game Design." Presentation at NYU, April, 2004, http://8kindsoffun.com/.

Lévy, Pierre. *L'Intelligence collective: pour une anthropologie du cyberspace* (*Collective Intelligence: Mankind's Emerging World in Cyberspace*). New York: Basic Books, 1999.

Marczewski, Andrzej. "Game Mechanics and Gamification." *Gamasutra*, March 6, 2013, http://www.gamasutra.com/blogs/AndrzejMarczewski/20130306/187906/Game_Mechanics_and_Gamification.php.

Mauss, Marcel. "The Gift: Forms and Functions of Exchange in Archaic Societies." Abingdon: Routledge, 2004. [Note: The original version of this essay was titled "Essai sur le don. Forme et raison de l'échange dans les sociétés archaïques" and was published in 1925 in *L'Année sociologique*. It was translated into English in 1954 and 1990.]

Montola, Markus, Jaako Stenros and Annika Waern. *Pervasive Games: Theory and Design*. London: Taylor & Francis, 2009.

Salen, Katie and Eric Zimmerman. *Rules of Play: Game Design Fundamentals*. Cambridge: MIT Press, 2004.

Schell, Jesse. *The Art of Game Design: A Book of Lenses*. Burlington: Morgan Kaufmann, 2008.

Zichermann, Gabe and Christopher Cunningham. *Gamification by Design: Implementing Game Mechanics in Web and Mobile Apps*. Sebastopol: O'Reilly Media, 2011.

7 VISUALIZING INTERACTION AND INFORMATION

CHAPTER QUESTIONS

At the end of this chapter, you should be able to answer these questions:

- How do project goals and user goals determine your design choices?
- What is emotional design? How does this idea translate into user goals?
- How does context of use shape the form and functions of a gamified system?
- What methods can gamified systems use to onboard new players?
- What devices work best for different implementations?
- In what ways can gamified system (GS) designs build social presence?
- How do management tools and data dashboards provide value for the different audiences they serve?

INTRODUCTION

Identifying how game components will deliver goals is one key part of the design and ideation process. Determining the best way to implement these ideas and, at the same time, identifying other essential functions to create a coherent and usable system is the other essential piece. This is where interactive and information design have important roles to play. Because gamified systems are meant to satisfy external goals as well as goals of engagement, the GS designer has the responsibility of detailing different user experiences for two distinct audiences: the players of the system and the project owners responsible for running, monitoring and overseeing the system once it is up and running. The first group needs to be motivated to play over time and share the experience with friends. The second group is most interested in collecting data and optimizing the system for improvements based on this information. During the design phase, the interactive components must be conceptualized at the same time as the game components are defined. This is not a sequential process, but one in which all aspects of the intended system must be considered at the same time. This chapter will show how to approach these design challenges.

GOAL-DRIVEN DESIGN

Although many gamified system projects share similarities in their approach or implementation, no two are identical. Your job as the GS designer is to identify the unique nuances of each project so you can deliver optimal experiences enhanced by game-based thinking. The articulated goals and Key Performance Indicators (KPIs) defined at the beginning of the project will not only help you measure success once your project has been deployed, but will also act as a roadmap during the design process. Goals help the project team narrow down the many options for implementations, including the type of interaction activities available to a player, and the devices that they will be delivered on. They will also shape important design choices including the functionality and visual design of your interfaces. Last but certainly not least, goals will drive data collection, as well as the visualization and display of this information for the purposes of assessing KPIs.

User goals

> Beauty and brains, pleasure and usability—they should go hand in hand.
>
> —Donald Norman, *Emotional Design: Why We Love (or Hate) Everyday Things*

Although the designers and project owners have project goals, players also have their own set of goals. Cognitive psychologist and human factors (the study of design for human use) luminary Donald Norman advocates addressing these goals with what he calls "emotional design." For Norman, good designs satisfy cognitive and emotional needs in three ways: viscerally, behaviorally and through reflection. **Visceral** processing occurs as a result of visual and sensory cues, and helps us make quick decisions about how we want to interact and react to a situation. Interaction design has traditionally emphasized human behavior because it can be easily perceived and evaluated. **Behavior** remains important because users have goals to accomplish and expectations for a system's ability to enable these. **Reflection** involves memory and experience as well as the articulation of that experience. For Norman, reflection is about mirroring and

Norman believes emotional design is processed:

- **Viscerally**—This happens through visual and sensory cues.
- **Behaviorally**—Occurs through the functions of a system as they relate to the completion of a task.
- **Reflectively**—Corresponding to the way that the use of a system or object affirms a person's sense of self.

the ego. By getting on-going feedback from your target audience about your system you should be able to regularly test out the user's initial impressions of the look and feel, if it behaves in the way he expects, and how he felt about the experience after using it.

Aesthetically pleasing interfaces are perceived to be more usable

Research has shown that users when confronted with attractive interfaces perceive greater ease of use. Because of this, they are more likely to make the investment of time required to learn the system. Behavioral processing is influenced by the visceral response a user has to a system. It also feeds reflective processing. The better it looks, and the more it delivers on initial perceptions, the more it will reflect the positive attributes that a player wishes to associate with.

An effective way to translate ideas about emotional and cognitive processing into design is to think about them in terms of the conscious goals of a user or player when interacting with your system. User goals tend to break down into three categories as well. **Experience goals** describe how someone wants to feel when using or playing a system. Some examples include: feeling happy, being challenged, focused, relaxed or energetic. **End goals** correspond to tasks and task completion like getting to the next level, completing a to-do list or finishing a quiz. Finally, **life goals** are about the image of the self that a person wishes to construct. Life goals include long-term drives, such as attaining a college degree, as well as the more immediate desire to be perceived positively by others.

The player brings her own goals

- **Experience goals**—What she wants to feel during and after play.
- **End goals**—What she wants to accomplish by using your system.
- **Life goals**—How it supports her ideas about her identity and her long-term goals.

CONTEXT IS EVERYTHING

Before you can begin your design it is important to have a very clear idea of where and how an individual will be interacting with your system. Will your players be moving around outdoors? Will they be sitting at a desk? Will they be on a bus or in a factory? Are they going to be working, or shopping or perhaps exercising? Will they be around other people using the system at the same time?

> **Context of use**
>
> Context of use characterizes the situation that any user is in when she experiences an interactive system.

Or, will they be surrounded by other people focused on accomplishing their own sets of tasks? **Context of use** characterizes the situation that any user is in when he experiences an interactive system. Knowing how the surroundings of an individual will influence tasks and performance is essential for making appropriate design decisions.

Physical characteristics

When thinking about the context of use of your future players it is important to consider characteristics associated with the physical environment. You will need to have an idea about the location or locations of your player. This might include salient information about architectural structures and elements of a building like hallways, pathways and landmarks. The physical conditions of a location like the amount of noise, light or space will also influence the types of tasks a person can be expected to perform. For instance, using audio messages or indicators for use in a public space may not work if the intended locations are consistently noisy. You will also need to have a sense of the infrastructure around the player, and whether he will have access to things like computers and Internet access.

Human factors

Human factors, the psychological, social and physical characteristics of a player, account for other contextual data points. Will she be using your system while she is running outside or eating at a restaurant? Or, will she be trying to learn a new time-intensive and intellectually demanding skill as a part of her work? Once you have a sense of the task, it is important to try to anticipate what the emotional state of the player will be while using your system. How does she feel about the task or tasks associated with the experience? Will she feel excited from the beginning, or will she feel scared and anxious? Finally, you will need to consider the player's social environment. You will need to know if there are going to be other people around her and, if so, how they might be interacting with her to interrupt, impede or support her interactions.

Understanding the context of use cannot be overstated. It will shape most of your choices in design, from where your system fits on the GS spectrum to the devices that you choose for implementation. Because our surroundings are always changing, it is important to understand that context is never a fixed state. Your challenge is to design a system that is sensitive to these dynamics. Fortunately, context-sensitive applications can accommodate for change.

The *SCAD Day* game was a project concept developed with Savannah College of Art and Design (SCAD) students for an Admissions Day gamified system. During Admission Day tours, prospective students do not get to see what the university experience is actually like because classrooms are empty, dark and quiet on the weekend of the tours. The goal of the project was to create a real sense of the intellectual and creative activity that happens in the building. We decided to utilize the architecture of the building to map out placement of QR codes (abbreviated from Quick Response code): barcodes that can store data including links to individual URLs or websites. These codes would be scanned with a cell phone, which would in turn display content and information about what it was like to be a student at SCAD. We were able to take advantage of the relative calm, mapping QR codes to display time-lapse videos of actual courses and projects that happened in the room where the prospective student was standing.

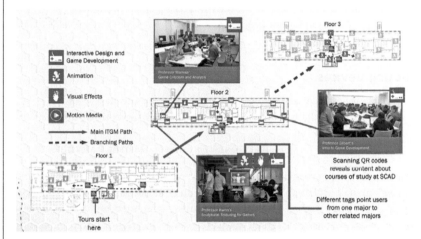

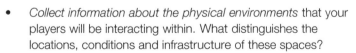

Figure 7.1 A location-based GS design to promote a deeper connection to the college amongst prospective students.

Understand context of use

- *Collect information about the physical environments* that your players will be interacting within. What distinguishes the locations, conditions and infrastructure of these spaces?
- *Identify the role of human factors* in your system. What tasks will be performed? What are the physical requirements that the player is expected to perform? What emotions or affect will the player likely experience during use? What social dynamics must the system maximize or negotiate?

Context-sensitive applications change their interactive capabilities and information display according to the changing environment of an individual. Often referred to as proactive or adaptive applications, these systems try to anticipate need. An example of this can be found in car-based navigation systems, where the system might use a sixty-second trigger that when reached submits the current location of a car to a remote server so that it can provide directions for the next leg of a trip based upon this new data. Mobile devices, because they can track locations and people on the move, are excellent devices for adaptation.

GS designs should be context aware

When designing interactive capacities, you can leverage context of use, including time, location and activity, to support players with relevant information throughout their daily activity:

- Provide different options or opportunities for a player.
- Execute commands automatically based on different triggers.
- Tag information for retrieval later.

Choosing devices

> Societies have always been shaped more by the nature of the media by which men communicate than by the content of the communication.
>
> —Marshall McLuhan

Before the days of personal computers, game consoles and mobile devices, media theorist Marshall McLuhan made the world think about the ways that technology shapes and changes us. His prophetic phrase "the medium is the message" captures what we now recognize about the ways that the different technologies in our lives fundamentally influence our perceptions and interpretations of the world around us. They also dictate the way we communicate with others.

The devices you select for your system will shape some of the most important aspects of your project. They will influence the amount of time players interact, your content strategy, the features you make available, and the kinds of social interactions that will occur as a result. For example, systems focused on supporting the acquisition of a new task or skill frequently are designed to work on a desktop computer. Gamified systems like Adobe's *LevelUp* (mentioned in Chapter 2), where achievement is based on skill acquisition, requiring individuals to focus their attention for long periods of time, are referred to as **sovereign** applications. Such applications require maximum real estate and access to the mouse and keyboard, and assume that a user will be sitting at a desk.

While sovereign applications demand screen real estate and lengthier commitments of time, transient applications come and go, enabling quick performance of a single task. Gamified systems like the *SCAD Day* game, which rewards players

Sovereign or transient?

Sovereign applications usually require a series of tasks, lengthy sessions and larger screen real estate. They tend to be designed for computer desktops fixed in one permanent location.

Designed to be "on-the-go," **transient** applications are used in short bursts. Mobile platforms and wearable devices are most appropriate for these implementations.

for exploring the school and learning about the academic opportunities, make themselves known and available to a player only when needed. The simplicity in design and structure enables players to quickly engage, disengage and re-engage. For this reason, when GS systems need to be **transient**, mobile devices are preferred.

Many gamified systems include both sovereign and transient modes to be used on different devices within different contexts. The fitness system *Zombies, Run!* (introduced in Chapter 6) delivers the audio-based game component on a mobile device so that players can focus on running while being immersed in the sounds of zombie hordes chasing them. The management portion of the system, which lets runners plan their routes and see their relevant statistics like the average time for a run for a given time period, requires focused attention and screen real estate. Consequently, this sovereign module is designed for a larger screen on a desktop computer.

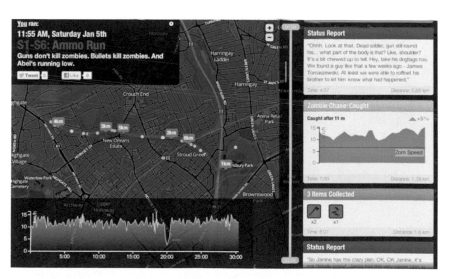

Figure 7.2 The *Zombies, Run!* web-based dashboard is meant to be used as a sovereign application when participants are monitoring their data and planning their runs. Source: Six to Start and Naomi Alderman.

DESIGNING GS INTERFACES AND INTERACTIVITY

Interactivity is made possible through the interface. The interface is the point of contact for player engagement. It generates the diverse and dynamic conversations happening between the system and the people interacting with it. Because there are so many different types of implementations, it is not possible to identify one specific type of GS interface. The design choices you make about your interface are most likely to be determined by the following:

- The articulated goals of your project.
- Discovery about your target audience and the competitive product landscape.
- Where your idea fits structurally on the GS spectrum.
- The context of use including human factors and environmental influences.
- If the system is meant to be a sovereign or transient experience, or if it warrants both experiences to support different tasks.
- The devices you have selected for implementation.

These basic elements should help you create a set of design guidelines for making decisions about both the overall style and particular elements of your interface.

Visual layout

The visual layout of your system conveys its capabilities and its priorities. The layout of your screens will be influenced primarily by the tasks that users are

Sovereign   **Transient**

Figure 7.3 Sovereign applications like Adobe's *LevelUp* emphasize activity within the interface. Transient applications like the GS design for prospective students touring the Savannah College of Art and Design are designed for a continuous cycle of disengagement and re-engagement. © 2014 Adobe Systems Incorporated. All rights reserved. Adobe and Photoshop is/are either [a] registered trademark[s] or a trademark[s] of Adobe Systems Incorporated in the United States and/or other countries.

expected to perform. For example, if you are creating a sovereign system where the primary goal is to teach a skill, then the majority of the space will be dedicated to that purpose. Adobe's *LevelUp* is an example of this. The focus of the mission system is to promote the use of Photoshop tools by expanding the set of tasks a user can perform within the program. For this reason, the application and tool sets are always given priority, whereas the game components are used much more for the purpose of framing and supporting the activity. On the other hand, mobile-based systems must make the best use of limited screen real estate. They do this by emphasizing game components and their relationship to new information coming from the player, the community or the environment.

Highlight accomplishments

The motivational role of rewards and accomplishments is maximized by giving these functions priority real estate. The display of points, badges, levels and accomplishments are often persistent, maintaining a continuous spot on the interface, appearing in most if not all of the system's screens. Because they are the mostly frequently updated, and can grow to very long character strings, points tend to have the largest amount of space reserved for their display.

Point displays are often accompanied by abbreviated information about badges. Emphasizing badges gained and badges in progress is a powerful interface feedback mechanism meant to keep players focused on immediate and longer-term goals. Selecting the badge area often accesses more information about rewards in the system. Usually, this information is connected to the player profile.

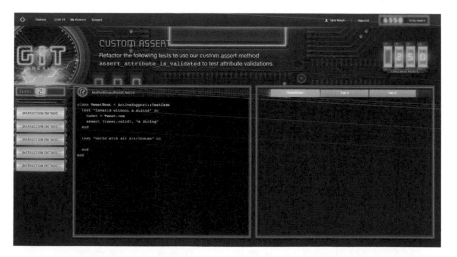

Figure 7.4 *Git Real*'s interface uses the upper right-hand side of the screen to highlight the display of points. © Code School. Courtesy of Justin Mezzell.

Celebrate wins

> Celebrate what you want to see more of.
> —Tom Peters, co-author
> *In Search of Excellence*

Players want to be acknowledged and praised when they do something well. The awarding of an achievement or badge should be treated as a celebration. You can use a variety of approaches to take a moment to let the player feel special and appreciated. For example, Nike's *Nike+ FuelBand* mobile app plays a reward sequence of a simple 3D animated character dancing or cheering the player on when he meets a specific goal. You might consider something as simple as darkening the screen and displaying a new window that presents the badge to the player for the first time. If your system is connected to social networking platforms, let players post their recent success to their social networking profiles. Once a player has received a badge, this information should be updated on the interface as well as in the player's profile. If the profile is public, other players will be able to see the achievements and collections of rewards and items.

Figure 7.5
Drawing by
Alex Waskelo.

Profiles foster identity

Player character profiles were originally introduced in table-top role-playing games. Character sheets provided information about the statistics and abilities of a character as well as any pertinent history or back-story that would affect performance or behavior. Player or user profiles are a variation of the character sheet, providing a visual display of information about the player and her accomplishments. The profile is one of the primary tools that users or players can access to

Figure 7.6 Player profiles enable self-expression. Drawing by Alex Waskelo.

Encourage identity formation and self-expression

- Give users or players *a unique identification* (ID) that means something to them. Allowing the use of an e-mail address is the most common approach to this.
- Let players define a *public nickname*. If they already have a unique ID in the system, they can choose whatever label they find fitting.
- Let players choose an *avatar or image* to represents themselves. They should be *able to change or replace this visual representation* whenever they feel like it.
- Provide mechanisms for *customization or decoration* of their profiles and avatars.
- Encourage players to define *attributes* about themselves and/or their player character. This will help them find other players and participants that they can play with or against.
- Give players *control over public and private display of information*. Let players decide the type of personal information they would like to let other people see.

express themselves and foster an identity for that specific system. The more options an individual has to define attributes about himself, the more he can feel a personal sense of ownership.

Facilitating a sense of presence

Games and gamified systems that are asynchronous must find creative ways to make individuals feel that they are always playing with others. Using interface elements to visualize player and community participation fosters the feeling of continuous presence. An excellent example of this is the way that social networking games use the interface and environment to give players the sense that their friends are playing even when they are not online. For example, the popular Facebook-enabled game *Chefville* is one of several restaurant games that let players experience some of the joys of cooking for friends by virtually feeding their friends' characters when their friends aren't really online. One way that Facebook games have perfected the art of asynchronous play is through visual design. By incorporating profile pictures and achievement status of friends on the interface, a player is meant to imagine that the activities that she is performing alone in a specific instance matter at that very moment to a much larger community. These kinds of implementations create what is referred to as **ambient intimacy**, the feeling of being a part of something social even when you are acting entirely alone. People who work by themselves on their computers in a packed Starbucks can identify with this concept. Though you may be entirely alone with your cappuccino and computer, the buzz of other conversations combined with the

> ## Ambient intimacy
>
>
>
> Ambient intimacy exploits interfaces to make individuals feel like they are surrounded by friends and family even when they are playing alone.
>
>
>
> **Figure 7.7** An interface with pictures of friends and family creates ambient intimacy, making a player feel less alone.

possibility that friends or acquaintances may walk through the door at any time are all means for perpetuating the feeling of being connected. Creating ambient intimacy is an important goal of any gamified system that relies on asynchronous play and interaction.

> ## Encourage social presence
>
> • *Display status and availability*. Showing when others are online can spark unintended interaction. Facebook and Skype both do this, making it easy for friends and colleagues to share a quick or unplanned conversation at any time. Location-based systems like *Foursquare* utilize the map and locations of others to spark interactions in the real world.
> • *Provide relevant updates and notifications*. Letting players know when others have participated re-engages players and encourages them to do the same. Leaderboards and public recognitions are excellent means for this.
> • *Archive and curate histories*. Timelines of activities can act as a curated archive of socially valuable content. Storing and organizing social media, and making it available to and from other social networking platforms, is an important way of building long-term investment in a system.

Get them socializing

Interesting conversations, fun activities and food are the essentials of any good party. Although the food may not be an option for your system, you must satisfy the other two criteria if you want people to participate and bring their friends. Game and play components should provide the fun; social media functions will facilitate the conversations. As you design your system it is important to note that there is no way to determine entirely what the content or direction of the conversations will be. Your goal is to deliver the tools to let your players feel like they are building the community and determining its direction. Your system needs to provide a venue for participation and mechanisms to support player recruitment and promotion.

Generative design

Generative design occurs when participants have the means, tools and support to generate their own experience.

Get them socializing

Provide functions for:

- Posting and sharing content.
- Collecting, saving, marking and tagging.
- The display of comments, voting, rankings and reviews.
- Quick emotive displays of approval or disapproval.
- Sending gifts and items.
- Inviting others.

Design for onboarding

> Our first impressions are generated by our experiences and our environment, which means that we can change our first impressions . . . by changing the experiences that comprise those impressions.
>
> —Malcom Gladwell, Blink: The Power
> of Thinking Without Thinking

Along the lines of a first date, the first impression your system makes with the player will determine whether or not he will continue to pursue the relationship you have worked so hard to build. Even if a player has been invited or referred to you by a respected source, it is your job in the first few minutes and even seconds of contact to make them personally value what your system is offering. You will need to accomplish many short-term goals during these initial precious moments, including:

- Making them feel welcomed and valued.
- Showing the benefits of the system.
- Acclimating them to the environment.

- Building a sense of confidence.
- Continuing the cycle of engagement.

The process of onboarding is an act of handholding. You will need to accommodate their desire to quickly understand the value proposition and welcome them at the same time. The social networking site Pinterest does this first by showcasing a hypothetical user's "board" and visually connecting these blurred images to the one displayed in the foreground, a small window that hosts a very clear **call to action** button to sign up with Facebook or e-mail. Once a user goes through the quick sign-up process, Pinterest responds by welcoming her by name.

Call to action

Call to action—elements that are meant to instantiate action by a user. Good examples are "sign-up" and "buy" buttons.

Once welcomed, a user needs to understand how to utilize your system. The best approach is to quickly get him performing a task. Sometimes the task is combined or immediately following a quick tour. Pinterest and the fitness system Fitbit both combine tutorials with tasks. The task should be absolutely achievable

Funneling

Gamified systems need to onboard players by funneling tasks and information. Rather than trying to explain the benefits of your system, get players interacting immediately by performing quick and achievable tasks. Done correctly, this will reduce the potential for negative judgments.

Be aware that people thin-slice

Thin-slicing is the process of making an evaluative judgment based on very short exposure to something. Studies have shown that within five minutes or less people develop predictions and judgments about products, including how they are to be used and whether they will be effective at accomplishing a task.

Cognitive efficiency helps us survive, requiring quick categorizations and judgments. A good onboarding process reduces all distractions while focusing attention. By decreasing task demands in the initial stages gamified systems can build trust while demonstrating their usefulness.

with no possibility of failure. For example, the new *Foursquare* asks you to click "ok" to letting the application access the current location of your device. Once complete, quickly acknowledge success to build up confidence and reduce fear of potential failure. Pinterest does this with a small pop-up window that reads "Yay. You've officially pinned your first pin." After such quick success, your user should be encouraged to take another simple action from a wider but still very small set of choices. Funneling in this way provides the illusion of control while promoting engagement and confidence over time.

INTERFACES THAT WORK BEHIND THE SCENES

While the GS designer must create usable and compelling interfaces for the player, she must also deliver tools that help another set of individuals run, manage and improve these experiences. Knowing how to design interfaces to collect and track data for those who administrate and manage the system is a fundamental skill that every GS designer needs to feel comfortable with. Behind the scenes interface designs fall into two categories: management tools and data dashboards. Management tools enable specific individuals to access functions to moderate and maintain the player experience while the system is "in play." Data dashboards provide project owners with access to information about player performance and engagement. This information almost always aligns with the KPIs identified during the goal-setting phase of the project.

Management tools

Management tools help individuals monitor and modify the player experience. In some cases they let certain system users identify themselves as leaders, who have access to special options to set up the parameters for play for other individuals within a group. For instance, the location-based platform SCVNGR gives registered users capabilities required to run a scavenger hunt style game. They can create challenges and set up rewards to get players visiting different physical locations. The building tool lets users identify locations using Google Maps, create tasks for players to do when they reach these locations, and assign points and rewards to be granted when a player has completed a task. Essentially, the dashboard contains a game-design tool to create scavenger hunts. Likewise, Project Noah, a non-profit organization that encourages citizen scientists of all ages to get outside and explore the natural world, gives teachers controls to run projects for their classrooms. They can create missions for their students, and then monitor their progress, participation and collections of photographs as they collect images of the species they identify while outdoors. In both cases, the dashboard is itself a simple gamified system design tool.

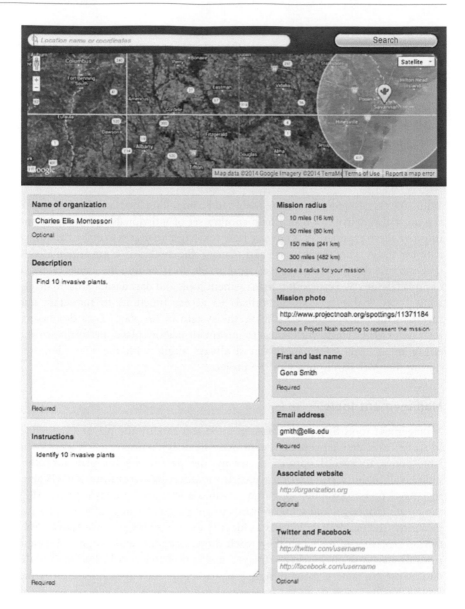

Figure 7.8 Project Noah's management tools let teachers and group leaders create location-based missions. Credit: Project Noah, www.projectnoah.org.

Figure 7.9 Bunchball's *Nitro* platform includes a comprehensive interface for creating, managing and fine-tuning a gamified experience. Courtesy of Bunchball, Inc.

Data dashboards

Data dashboards provide a picture of how a gamified system is actually working once it is up and running. These interfaces have the critical job of communicating key statistics, and visualizing how these have changed over time. When designing dashboards it is important to keep in mind that different audiences require different information. This means that there will need to be different views for these different audiences. For example, a CEO or division head might only need to access key information about how a gamified system is helping the company generate revenue or expand into new markets. Whereas, project managers or marketing managers responsible for fine-tuning and optimizing the system need to be able to see how the more granular aspects are interacting to affect the larger project goals.

The design of the data dashboard should come relatively early in the project, and should be considered at a level of importance equal to the player experience. Data dashboards need to provide an accessible overview of how the system is delivering on its KPIs. The more they can help users quickly grasp change, variations and relationships, the better those users can focus on improving and enhancing the player experience. While user stories are being created for players, they should also be defined for the people responsible for maintaining and enhancing the system.

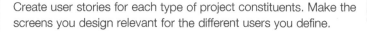

User stories and personas aren't just for players

Create user stories for each type of project constituents. Make the screens you design relevant for the different users you define.

Figures 7.10 and 7.11 The fitness device *Fitbit* (top) and the gamified system that accompanies it includes a comprehensive data dashboard for users to track their activities. In addition to a comprehensive set of management tools for creating the play experience *Nitro* (bottom) also provides a data dashboard so project owners can quickly evaluate performance. © Fitbit. Courtesy of Olson, an ICF International Company, www.olson.com (top) and © Bunchball Nitro Studio Dashboard (bottom).

Good data dashboards are designed for situation awareness

Situation awareness is a term that comes from the field of aviation. It accounts for how individuals in high-stress and often life-threatening situations perceive and comprehend change and variability of information display to forecast and plan. Though your clients and users may not be interacting with your system in life or death situations, the data you provide them is nevertheless important for efficiently evaluating and measuring their success. The best way to support their needs is to make sure that your interfaces convey information without requiring any cognitive load, that is, to overload an individual's capacity to access his stored memory and to utilize his working memory. In sum, the users of data dashboards do not have the patience or time to figure out the meaning of your designs.

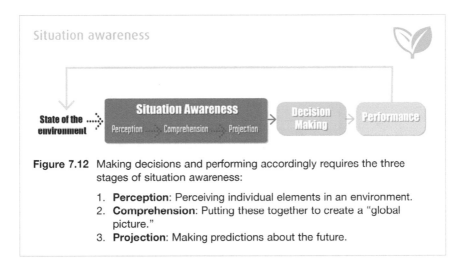

Figure 7.12 Making decisions and performing accordingly requires the three stages of situation awareness:

1. **Perception**: Perceiving individual elements in an environment.
2. **Comprehension**: Putting these together to create a "global picture."
3. **Projection**: Making predictions about the future.

Using graphs to shape data

Most designers don't consider the creation or use of graphs as an essential part of their job description. As managing and displaying data becomes increasingly important, designers must embrace this method of quick data visualization. Graphs communicate a message by shaping data to reveal relationships of different values.

- *Use a number and secondary statistic to quickly display one metric.* Displaying a secondary number that shows change allows the user to make a quick assessment about the value of the information. This approach is useful for your high-level KPIs, such as knowing how much revenue you have generated on a certain day.
- *Pie charts should be used when you are comparing parts of a whole.* Pie charts do not show change over time. If you are looking to get a sense of the different activities

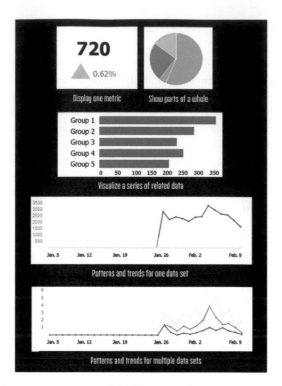

Figure 7.13 Different graphs accomplish different goals.

your users are performing within your entire system, a pie chart could be helpful.

- *Bar charts compare related data.* Bar charts make comparisons instantly clear. Looking at the bar chart shown in Figure 7.13 it is very easy to see which group is performing the highest and which is performing the lowest. It is also easy to decipher how all of the groups are performing against each other.

- *Sparklines show patterns and trends.* Sparklines are great for showing change over time, like the number of log ins, updates or length of time spent playing in a week. Charts with multiple sparklines are good for visualizing trends and patterns of different data sets. With multiple sparklines, rather than just looking at the one point of data like the number of logins during a time period, you can look at other activities at the same time. So, while there may be fewer users logging in, perhaps these users are generating more income for the company. By showing these comparisons, you are providing opportunities for users to see parallels and relationships that might have easily been missed.

Make data accessible and meaningful

Dashboard design is a challenging endeavor. Your designs must quickly communicate the most important data points for each audience. They should also provide functionality to reveal more granular data when needed.

Some guidelines to follow:

- *Avoid screen clutter*—Reduce your data to the most important information.
- *Personalize*—Make sure to provide the right data for the right audience.
- *Prioritize*—The most important information should be given the most valuable screen real estate. Keep branding, logos and anything supportive to a visual minimum.
- *Round your numbers*—Round numbers so that they can be quickly digested. For example, $1.7M is easier to read than $1,654,436.25.
- *Show comparative values*—Dashboard users want to see change. Make sure you make changes of key performance metrics obvious.
- *Do the calculations*—Don't force users to do math. Your interface should show the variations, while letting users drill down to the specifics.
- *Make critical cues salient*—Use obvious indicators, such as flashes, animation or red flags, to notify users about anomalies or pending emergencies.

RICH USABILITY

Whether you are designing a desktop dashboard or a mobile interface, you must always follow the principles for usable design. Usability focuses on human expectations and abilities with the goals of creating products that are enjoyable, accessible, easy to learn and effective at supporting task completion. Quality GS interfaces must follow the fundamental design principles of user-centered design, including consistency, visibility and appropriate feedback. Though the field may be new, the design goals are not.

Keep it juicy

> Juicy Feedback gives your users moment-to-moment joyful feelings when they engage with your design.
> —Robin Hunicke, game designer

In 2009 Robin Hunicke, one of the co-authors of the MDA framework, introduced the idea of a fourth vector to complement MDA-juiciness. Juicy feedback creates a sense of life and joy in the present moment. It is about moment-to-moment engagement with the various designed and emergent experiences of interactivity. Fidelity, responsiveness and the suggestion of intelligence all work to create the feeling of a great conversation between friends. According to Hunicke, some of the core characteristics of juicy feedback include being inviting, tactile and in real-time. You can see examples of juicy feedback with the way certain games like *Wii Tennis* or *Just Dance* leverage input from the Wii remote to respond and reward players for simple and subtle motions in real-time. Fighting games like the *SoulCalibur* series known for their responsive controls showcase the idea of juicy feedback. With its growing response to gestures and motion, each new generation of the iPhone and the successful apps that are released for the phone continue to push the boundaries of juicy feedback. Your job as a designer is to add this dimension so that players feel like they are being taken care of and are pleasantly surprised by the efforts you take to do this.

Figure 7.14 A road speed radar is a simple and juicy approach for providing real-time data to drivers about their driving speed.

Follow these best practices to make your gamified system enjoyable, accessible and effective:

- *Be consistent*—Use the same design choices throughout. Utilize common standards, patterns and practices wherever you can.
- *Make options visible*—Do not force players to have to recall how to perform tasks. Use images, sounds and consistent placement to encourage recognition.

- *Be familiar* — Use familiar language, metaphors, symbols and images.
- *Employ obvious affordances* — Provide interface elements that imply usage. For example, offer dimensional buttons for elements that should be clicked.
- *Provide on-going feedback* — Make sure to provide feedback, such as the updating of points when a player interacts with your system. Also, provide appropriate cues when the system is running a process or waiting for user input.
- *Keep data safe* — Make sure to save and update player data.
- *Be considerate* — Understand the context of use and always try to reduce unnecessary burdens.

KEY TAKEAWAYS

- Define your goals to narrow down implementation options, such as interaction activities, device choices, functionality, visual designs and data visualizations.
- According to Donald Norman, the three levels of emotional design (visceral, behavioral and reflective) are essential for effective design. These translate into player or user goals, which can be understood as experience, end and life goals.
- Context of use corresponds to the various characteristics of a physical environment and the human factors that will play a role in your player experience. Information from the type of location to the type of activity that a player will find herself in should all drive your implementation choices.
- People thin-slice information, giving new systems very little attention. Because of this, your system needs to onboard players by getting them quickly interacting and experiencing the benefits of the system.
- Creating social presence can be accomplished by providing functions that enable opportunities for self-expression, sharing, collaboration and ambient intimacy.
- Management tools and data dashboards support individuals who are responsible for monitoring and maintaining the play experience of others.
- Data dashboards are meant to provide a quick overview of KPIs. They should be designed to satisfy the requirements of the different audiences who will rely on data to measure the success and failure of the project.

EXERCISES

As you continue working on your client-based projects that you began in Chapter 5, you should use these exercises to scope out, detail and visualize the functions and interfaces that will support your ideas. Use this time to perform the following tasks:

7.1 Define primary and secondary tasks

Revisit the user stories you began as a part of the exercises you conducted in Chapter 5 to determine and prioritize the tasks that you want your audience to enact.

7.2 Identify your user's goals

Return to your personas and market research that you collected in the first part of this project (Chapter 5) and ask yourself the following about the goals of your user as they relate to your project:

* *Experience goals*—How does she want to feel during and after play?
* *End goals*—What does she want to accomplish by using your system?
* *Life goals*—How will your system support her ideas about how she wants to be perceived and what she works towards as her long-term goals?

7.3 Understand use of context > physical environment

Define your physical environments. What locations will you be expecting your players to be experiencing? What will the conditions be (light, sound, temperature, etc.)? What type of infrastructure (technology, furniture) will they have access to?

7.4 Understand use of context > human factors

Identify the role of human factors in your system. What tasks will be performed? What are the physical requirements of players? What emotional state do you imagine the player be in prior to and during interaction? What social dynamics will the player likely experience during play?

7.5 Identify devices and materials of use

Here you should clarify the devices and media you will be leveraging for deployment. Will you be using mobile devices and web browsers on desktops? Which features or functions will be available through different media?

7.6 Visualize the play experience

Define your visuals for the core play experience through sketches and flowcharts (these practices are covered in Chapter 5). This should include your visual layout, your interface components, and your functions or features that will support game concepts.

7.7 Illustrate your social components

Develop sketches of your social components. What interface elements will you utilize to increase self-expression, sharing, collaboration and ambient intimacy?

7.8 Map out first-time experience

Create flowcharts or storyboards to illustrate the first-time experience of a player. Know how you will direct players, show them benefits, reward them quickly and move them into more complex interactions including sharing it with friends.

7.9 Define management tools and data dashboards

Use your KPIs, your goals and your user stories to sketch out your management tools and dashboards. Identify the data you want to show and the audiences you want to show it to. Select charts and other elements for the most appropriate data display.

For additional support for sketching, flowcharting and prototyping please refer to the website www.gamifiedsystems.com.

RECOMMENDED READINGS

- *About Face: The Essentials of Interaction Design* by Alan Cooper, Robert Reimann and David Cronin, 2014 (Fourth Edition). *About Face* is a go-to book for many in the field of user experience (UX) design. It details the principles and practices behind interaction design.
- *Designing Social Interfaces* by Christian Crumlish and Erin Malone, 2009. Written by the creators of Yahoo's design pattern library, this book establishes best practices and principles along with a large set of applicable patterns for designers to create interfaces and artifacts to enhance social interaction.
- *Don't Make Me Think: A Common Sense Approach to Web Usability* by Steve Krug, 2000. Written by the usability expert Steve Krug, this book is a concise visual guide to user experience design.
- *Information Dashboard Design: Displaying Data for At-a-Glance Monitoring*, Stephen Few, 2013. This book is a practical guide to help designers create graphs, tables and data dashboards that quickly and efficiently communicate important information.
- *The Design of Everyday Things: Revised and Expanded Edition* by Don Norman, 2013. The seminal text established Norman as the leader of the human factors and usability movement. The book explores how the design of everyday objects utilizes different affordances to help (or hinder) people to use them most effectively.

SEBASTIAN DETERDING ON MEANINGFUL PLAY AND THE CONVERGENCE OF USER EXPERIENCE AND GAME DESIGN

Interview granted with permission by Sebastian Deterding.

Sebastian Deterding is a researcher and designer working on game-based experiences. As an independent designer and associate of the international design studio Hubbub, he has created gamified systems for clients including the BBC, BMW, Deutsche Telekom and Greenpeace. He is a sought-after speaker who has been invited to present and keynote at venues like Interaction, GDC Online, Games Learning Society, Google, IDEO and Microsoft Research. He is currently a visiting assistant professor at the RIT Laboratory for Media, Arts, Games, Interaction and Creativity (MAGIC) at the Rochester Institute of Technology. He is the organizer of the Gamification Research Network, and co-editor of *The Gameful World* from MIT Press.

Figure 7.15
Sebastian Deterding.

One of the things you are known for is talking about meaningful play. How do you define meaningful play, and how does it relate to gamified systems?

I used "meaningful play" as shorthand for what I found missing in current gamification, and I'm not strongly wedded to that term: few things become meaningless more easily than the word *meaningful*. It's like *true*, *real*, *hardcore* or *authentic*: usually signifying little more than some aesthetic contempt and distancing towards whatever is on the receiving "meaningless" end, with all the endless debates you find in subcultures about what *real* is.

That being said, with *meaningful play*, I tried to tease out five aspects crucial to the enjoyable qualities of game-play, but largely amiss in contemporary gamification: relevance, play, context, systemic emergence and design.

Relevance: Current gamified applications predominantly use virtual rewards, status indicators and competition to drive user behaviors that the system owner is interested in. However, human–computer interaction, user experience design and, more recently, product development and contemporary marketing all tell us that the only way to a sustainable (let alone ethical) business is identifying and satisfying customer needs. Game design elements that do not connect to the users' core needs with regard to your system might create a short-term novelty effect boost, but nothing more—as evidenced by the fact that many early adopters of gamification like *Foursquare* are currently removing gamification from their systems.

Rewards, status and competition only motivate users if they are relevant to them and the communities they identify with. As a board game aficionado, getting kudos from others on boardgamegeek.com is an achievement requiring skill and expressing real appreciation by the community, which I value, so it might motivate me—not so a badge for having rated fifty movies on a random movie review site.

Third, we know from a rich body of research that rewards are not what makes games enjoyable to begin with. Playing games is the prototype of intrinsically motivated activity—done for its own sake. It is enjoyable chiefly because it satisfies certain basic psychological needs: Just as we need food and water to survive and thrive, we need to feel *competent*, *autonomous* and in close *relation* with others. Well-designed games deliver on all these three needs, specifically competence, the sense of affecting change in the world and growing one's capacity to do so. In study after study, satisfaction of these intrinsic needs has been shown to predict sustained engagement and behavior change, whereas extrinsic motivators—like rewards or social pressure—have been shown 1) to undermine intrinsic need satisfaction and thus overall motivation and 2) to be effective in the short term, but not in the long term.

Play: One of these tricky terms. My definition is: the autotelic recombining of objects, actions and meanings. In *Les Jeux et les hommes* (Man, Play and Games), Roger Caillois suggests that human play phenomena span a spectrum between *paidia*—free-form, exploratory play—and *ludus*—rule-based, goal-oriented strife. If you look at gamification today, you will agree that it exclusively focuses on the ludic—adding goals, rules, structure, strife. That is fine and well if all we want is to tap into the motivational affordances characteristic for rule-based games. But if we want to foster curiosity, exploration or creativity, then paidic or playful design is the fitting approach: creating a risk-free safe space; fostering benign mischief; providing underspecified but highly emergent materials to tinker with. Such playfulness is largely amiss in the current gamification practice.

Context: Playing is a frame—a certain socially shared type of situation that organizes our experience and our action. Importantly, it is not determined by the object in front of us how we use or frame it: We can play with many things beyond games and toys, and we can engage with games and toys in many ways that are not play. Playing is a specific shared and jointly upheld agreement between the people present in the situation that *this is play*. This agreement comes with specific norms and understandings—lack of consequence, fair play, voluntary participation, to name but a few. If any of these are not upheld, people might not perceive what they do as *playing* any more, and the activity may lose some of its motivational appeal.

In my PhD research, I found that people engaging with games professionally—videogame journalists, e-sport players—often feel like they're not doing so voluntarily: there's a deadline to meet, a prize to win, a reputation to maintain. And this perceived lack of autonomy is both demotivating (in tune with the fact that autonomy is a basic psychological need), and leads them to experience the activity as *work*, not *play*. Arguably, the same happens with a lot of gamified applications: Because they are deployed in contexts like work or formal schooling, where participation in the system is mandatory and comes with high stakes, the gamified system can easily be perceived as a demotivating form of micro-management and control. This suggests that designers ought to take into account the social context of the system they create as much as the system itself.

Systemic emergence: Most of today's gamification subscribes to a kind of Mary Poppins "spoonful of sugar" idea of experience: If an activity is boring, just add some inherently enjoyable game elements, and *voilà*: fun ensues. However, we know from user experience research and game design that things are not so simple: Fun, enjoyment and other experiential qualities emerge from the interaction between a user and a total system. If you add time pressure to a game like chess, it doesn't become chess, only more fun, or more *chessy*. It will become speed chess, a very different game with very different strategies, behaviors and game-play experiences. Game design has formalized this insight in the *Mechanics-Dynamics-Aesthetics* framework: The mechanics or rules of a game form a systemic whole that, in interaction with a user, give rise to game-play dynamics, which in turn give rise to experiential aesthetics. This means that you cannot "funnify" an experience or create a target experience just by adding a design element like a point score. You have to design the whole system. Which brings me to my last point.

Design: Current gamification practitioners frame gamification as "just add points," the mere addition of pre-specified, white-label design elements to a given system. As noted, this is bound to miss the systemic emergent quality of user experiences. So what to do instead? The answer game design gives us is rapid, iterative, experiential prototyping: Build a functional prototype of your system as fast and crummy as possible to playtest it and see what experiences actually emerge, to then revise and playtest your design again and again until you've approached your target experience.

So to summarize, designing for meaningful play means 1) understanding and satisfying the actual needs and goals and motivations that are relevant to your users, basic psychological needs like autonomy, competence and relatedness in specific; 2) making the social context of play as much a part of your design efforts as the technical system you build; 3) considering both paidic, playful, and ludic, gameful, forms of play (depending on your design goals); and 4) using methods like iterative experiential prototyping to capture and improve the emergent systemic whole of your design and the experiences it affords.

Where do you think the world of UX design and game design converge? What can GS design take from both of these practices?

As utility and usability become more and more commoditized in UX, the field is moving toward motivation and enjoyment as the next big differentiators—something that was always at the core of game design, which in turn is moving more and more toward creating "real-world impact." So the natural convergence point is *motivational design*: creating systems that afford intended motivating experiences—sometimes in service of instrumental task or behavior outcomes.

And I understand that to be the next logical step in the evolution of both game design and UX design.

User experience designers are very good in formative and evaluative user research for instrumental, task-oriented user goals, and game designers excellent in creating non-instrumental, hedonic experiences. They engage in iterative experiential prototyping to slowly move the experience emerging from a systemic whole towards a desired design goal, and they know many patterns and techniques to afford specific experiences and motivations (such as competence, curiosity, suspense) that user experience designers have rarely if ever focused on. What we are missing is 1) an extension of user research toward experiential goals (game user research is moving there), 2) an extension of game design to support instrumental tasks, and 3) a bridging from user research results into game design ideas.

You've spoken about the ethics of design. What ethical guidelines do you think designers of gamified systems have a responsibility to uphold?

The typical notion of design ethics in gamification or persuasive design is: avoid deceiving, coercing or harming your users—however those three things are then understood. To me, that's a very narrow framing. I would invite designers to ask themselves: What vision of a good life do you aspire to? And in contrast: What vision of a good life does your design materialize? For whatever object or space we put in the world makes certain ways of acting, thinking, living easier and others more difficult. At the same time, it is an implicit message that says: "This is how things are supposed to be." If you ever lived in a European pedestrian city and then experienced a car-centric city as in the United States, you will immediately know what I mean: Not only do the long distances and the lack of bike paths, sidewalks and traffic lights make it practically impossible to get around a city like LA by bike or foot, it also makes a statement better than any propaganda poster could: "This is normal."

NOTES

Cooper, Alan, David Cronin and Robert Reimann. *About Face: The Essentials of Interaction Design*. Fourth Edition. Indianapolis: Wiley, 2014.

Crumlish, Christian and Erin Malone. *Designing Social Interfaces*. Sebastopol: O'Reilly/Yahoo Press, 2009.

Few, Stephen. *Effectively Communicating Numbers: Selecting the Best Means and Manner of Display*. White paper for ProClarity Analytics, 2005.

Few, Stephen. *Common Pitfalls in Dashboard Design*. White paper for ProClarity Analytics, 2006.

Few, Stephen. *Dashboard Design for Real-Time Situation Awareness*. White paper for Inova Solutions, 2007.

Few, Stephen. *Information Dashboard Design: Displaying Data for At-a-Glance Monitoring*. Burlingame: Analytics Press, 2013.

Gladwell, Malcolm. *Blink: The Power of Thinking Without Thinking*. New York: Back Bay Books, 2005.

Hunicke, Robin. "Loving Your Player with Juicy Feedback." Presentation at dConstruct 2009, Brighton Dome, UK, September 5, 2009.

Kim, Amy Jo. "Smart Gamification: How to Build Sustainable Social Systems." Posted to Slideshare on August 1, 2011, http://www.slideshare.net/amyjokim/smart-gamification?related=2.

Kim, Amy Jo. "The Player's Journey: Drive Sustained Engagement with Onboarding, Habit-Building and Mastery." Posted on Slideshare, June 9, 2014, http://www.slideshare.net/amyjokim/the-players-journey-drive-sustained-engagement-with-onboarding-habit building-and-mastery.

Krug, Steve. *Don't Make Me Think: A Common Sense Approach to Web Usability*. Thousand Oaks: New Riders, 2000

McLuhan, Marshall. *Understanding Media: The Extensions of Man*. Cambridge: MIT Press, 1994. [Note: The original version of this book was printed in 1964.]

McLuhan, Marshall and Quentin Fiore. *The Medium is the Massage: An Inventory of Effects*. New York: Bantam, 1967.

Norman, Donald. "3 Ways Good Design Makes Us Happy." Presentation at TED, Monterey, CA, 2003, http://www.ted.com/talks/don_norman_on_design_and_emotion.

Norman, Donald. *Emotional Design: Why We Love (or Hate) Everyday Things*. New York: Basic Books, 2004.

Norman, Donald. *The Design of Everyday Things: Revised and Expanded Edition*. New York: Basic Books, 2013.

Peracchio, Laura A. and David Luna. "The Role of Thin-Slice Judgments in Consumer Psychology," *Journal of Consumer Psychology*, 16:1 (2006): 25–32.

Peters, Tom and Robert H. Waterman. *In Search of Excellence: Lessons from America's Best-Run Companies*. New York: HarperBusiness Essentials, 2004.

Preece, Jenny, Yvonne Rogers and Helen Sharp. *Interaction Design: Beyond Human-Computer Interaction*. Third Edition. Hoboken: Wiley, 2011.

Zichermann, Gabe and Christopher Cunningham. *Gamification by Design: Implementing Game Mechanics in Web and Mobile Apps*. Sebastopol: O'Reilly Media, 2011.

Note: For an excellent resource on usability see Jakob Nielsen's articles at http://usable web.com/.

III IN THE FIELD

8 DESIGNING GAMIFIED SYSTEMS FOR EDUCATION

CHAPTER QUESTIONS

At the end of this chapter, you should be able to answer these questions:

- How do you describe the different market segments using gamified systems (GS) for learning and instruction?
- How are GS designs serving the needs of formal education settings like schools?
- What is assessment, and how does it drive design?
- What are the opportunities in the consumer market for game-based learning?
- How are corporations leveraging GS design for training and professional development?
- How are gamified systems being utilized by the military to support the changing nature of war and conflict in the 21st century?
- The subject matter expert (SME) performs what role in the development of any learning-based project?

INTRODUCTION

Imagine that the number one mobile download was for learning algebra. In 2012, *DragonBox* was downloaded more than any other mobile application in Norway, even outperforming neighboring Finland's *Angry Birds*. Within two weeks of launching, 10 percent of all iPads in Norway had a copy. Why were so many people interested in learning the fundamentals of algebra? Jean-Baptiste Huynh, the math teacher who developed *DragonBox*, had seen firsthand the problem of teaching students algebra and felt that the problem was not the students but the way the subject was taught. To many students the introduction to abstract mathematics in junior high school is a seemingly overwhelming and insurmountable obstacle. It often marks the moment that a student decides that she is not good at math. How could a game solve this problem?

DragonBox explicitly focused on changing the social setting for teaching algebra, getting kids to discuss strategy and concepts on their own in order to reduce the feelings of isolation and failure often associated with mathematics learning. For Huynh, this did not simply mean creating a game, because, "Playability, engagement, learning can't be dissociated from how, when and where the game will be played." He was inspired by Sugata Mitra's "hole-in-the-wall" ideas about unsupervised learning, the results of an experiment using a computer placed in a wall of the slums of New Delhi. That basic design philosophy—tested in the case of *DragonBox* in a variety of social settings with different numbers of devices and different levels of supervision—in turn allowed for greater scalability. So when the Center for Game Science at Washington State University used the app with over 4,000 K-12 students for their four-day Algebra Challenge in the summer of 2013, they found that even elementary-school students could master linear equations in a matter of an hour and a half. The success rate across grade levels was 92.9 percent. As Center director Zoran Popovic said, "This is shockingly good, but we think we can do even better." What Huynh and Popovic had shown was not simply that kids could learn algebra through a game but that a well-designed application could help create new systems and social settings for learning.

Sugata Mitra's "hole-in-the-wall" experiment was conducted over a period of thirteen years. Setting up computers with compelling content (such as Internet access) and filming children's interactions with hidden cameras, he discovered that they were teaching themselves and each other to use the technology, the web and to learn English to accomplish these tasks. Mitra refers to this process, influenced by constructionist ideals (introduced in Chapter 4), as self-organized learning.

Learning complex math is just one of many, many applications of games in the field of learning, and K-12 students are only one segment of the diverse and growing market for gamified systems. The use of game elements for learning and instruction is expansive. Schools, corporations, government agencies, healthcare professionals, museum, non-profits and consumers young and old are playing to learn.

The goal of this chapter is to provide a glimpse of the opportunity space for the expanding field of learning and GS design. We will explore a variety of projects to get a better sense of the processes unique to learning-based gamified systems. We will also meet some of the people behind them to get a better perspective of how games and learning converge at school, at work, at home and within the cultural institutions we visit and interact with.

Figure 8.1 *DragonBox* changes the game for learning algebra. © WeWantToKnow.

IN THE CLASSROOM

> A game is the opportunity to informally engage with the ideas behind any subject matter, which will later be dealt with in a more structured way in the classroom.
>
> —Scott Osterweil, Creative Director,
> MIT's Education Arcade

Primary, secondary and increasingly post-secondary teachers incorporate gamified systems into their classrooms for a multitude of reasons. The positive benefits of game scaffolding, discussed earlier in Chapter 4, can help to not only simplify tasks, but also, as with the case of algebra, make them less confusing and difficult to approach. At the heart of the movement to gamify the classroom experience, however, remains the overwhelming receptivity to games in the classroom by students themselves. The response should come as no surprise given that an estimated 91 percent of children between the ages of two and seventeen are playing videogames. Moreover, a significant number of adults have now grown up playing games and are increasingly accustomed to game-based learning. The positive associations that students have with games and game technologies means that by using them as a part of the school experience students are more likely to be internally motivated to learn new information, develop competencies in course subject matter and participate more actively in the classroom.

Mapping learning to curriculum

Teachers, district administrators, state and government officials are responsible for meeting standards according to specific milestones in a student's academic journey. Every country has different sets of standards, and they often vary from a state-by-state or region-by-region basis. In the United States, there has been a move to bring more consistency of such standards, resulting in what is referred to as the "common core" curriculum embraced by forty-six of the fifty states in the nation. Educators are thus increasingly connected to broader learning systems, having to map their curriculum to learning outcomes and create a structure designed to provide plenty of opportunities for students to learn and apply their knowledge.

For GS designers, standards provide clear frameworks to guide the development of project initiatives and applications. New York's Quest to Learn, already introduced in Chapter 4 by founder Katie Salen, relies on game-based concepts like missions and quests as an overarching structure for mapping an entire academic year's curriculum to learning units and lesson plans. Teachers can use these detailed yet open guidelines to develop learning modules that meaningfully tie into the framework. Figure 8.2 shows how a curriculum is created through the use of missions. Missions map onto long-term learning goals generally associated with a semester. They are broken into smaller initiatives called quests, which provide the foundation for daily and weekly lesson plans. Figure 8.3 shows the design templates used by the teacher to plug content into an overall game-like architecture.

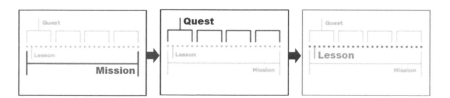

Figure 8.2 Quest to Learn's curriculum is designed around missions, which are then broken down into quests. These are divided again into individual lesson plans. © Institute of Play.

School-based GS designs vary significantly in terms of implementation, largely a result of the content that needs to be covered and the skills and competencies that need to be demonstrated as defined by the curriculum standards. For example, *Lure of the Labyrinth* was designed by MIT's Education Arcade to conform to the state of Maryland's middle-school math curriculum standards. The comprehensive educational program supports learning pre-algebra by engaging students in the subject matter through game-play and then extending this learning through classroom instruction. The program embeds nine math puzzles derived directly from the state curriculum into an overarching graphic-novel-infused storyline about finding a pet gone missing in a world of monsters. To incorporate the

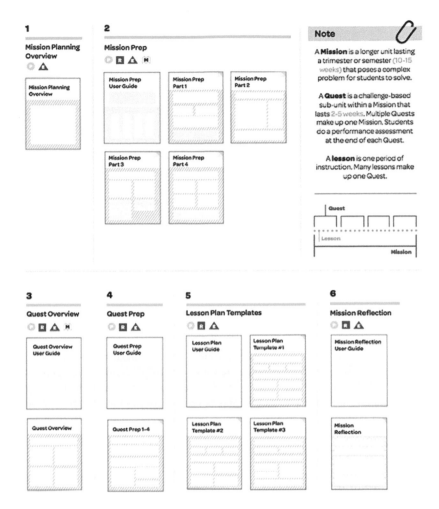

Figure 8.3 Examples of processes and documentation that Quest to Learn uses to design, implement and assess the school's game-like curriculum. © Institute of Play.

game into the classroom, teachers have access to extensive materials for creating lesson plans and for building these into their broader curriculum. For the students, the learning is intentionally sequenced to incorporate failure, continuous feedback and recursion. To enhance student motivation, every lesson plan in the program begins with game-play, often a puzzle related to that lesson. For example, the *Employee's Cafeteria* puzzle introduces equivalent ratios by requiring players to feed monsters by placing numerical portions of food on trays. By playing the game first students gain familiarity with the core concept.

Following the initial play session the teacher then covers his lesson plan that corresponds to the specific area of pre-algebra that was introduced (like ratios,

Figure 8.4 *Lure of the Labyrinth* by MIT's Education Arcade maps game-play to Maryland's pre-algebra curriculum. Used with permission. © Maryland Public Television.

fractions and proportions). Leveraging student motivation, the lesson plan directs and magnifies the important details, enabling students to return to the game with new knowledge and better strategies. Early experimentation becomes applied mathematics, emphasizing the usefulness of understanding more abstract methods of problem-solving. As learners advance along their path they are expected to solve harder problems, comprehend more abstract concepts and apply their learning to "real-world" situations.

Assessing learning

Because schools need to meet curriculum standards, GS learning must provide evidence that substantiates its effectiveness. Gamified systems have the capacity to generate valuable and multivariate data that can be used by educators to measure a range of different types of learning in the classroom. These metrics provide the requirements necessary for assessment, collecting and interpreting data about student performance from different sources. Traditionally, this inform-ation has been derived from test scores, written assignments and projects. Gamified systems allow automatic tracking of performance during play, enabling new and meaningful layers of measurement. Games can monitor a significant range of information about interaction, including moment-to-moment reactions to new and repeated challenges, and how these may change over time. They track performance based on curriculum standards like domain literacy and compre-hension, and they can also track students' abilities to problem-solve over time. This helps develop better decision-making among students more generally.

Assessment is a circular process utilizing data collected about student performance to modulate learning goals and educational experiences. The practice involves:

1. **Establishing learning goals and outcomes**—Goals are tied to outcomes, and the outcomes of the goals must be measureable.
2. **Defining learning opportunities**—This is the design and implementation process, where experiences are defined to provide sufficient opportunities for students to prove their abilities and achieve proposed outcomes.
3. **Collecting and analyzing**—Gathering, analyzing and interpreting data enables educators to determine if expectations are being achieved.
4. **Applying results**—With the goal of increasing student performance, data can be utilized to modify and fine-tune goals and experiences.

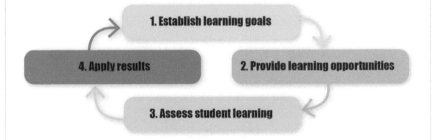

Figure 8.5 Diagram of the learning assessment process.

At the same time, teachers can access the information needed to provide individual students with additional scaffolding that they may need in-person to get them ahead. On a larger scale, school administrators, school and testing specialists and government officials can monitor and compare how students, classrooms, schools and regions are performing relative to each other. This information can then be utilized to refocus or reinforce future instruction.

Consider SimCityEdu, a modification of the popular computer game SimCity. Through "stealth assessment," the game unobtrusively collects data about individual student performance while students play. Players themselves take on the role of mayor, collecting research and documentation, interpreting data and making important decisions about the environmental, economic and social impacts of their choices. As students play the simulation, the game measures and evaluates their capacity for high-level problem-solving skills, such as interpreting diagrams and explaining relationships of complex systems. Students, teachers and administrators can then access this information through a dashboard and utilize it to refine the learning and assessment process. Building such a fine-tuned system took a significant amount of expertise, including the educational game design

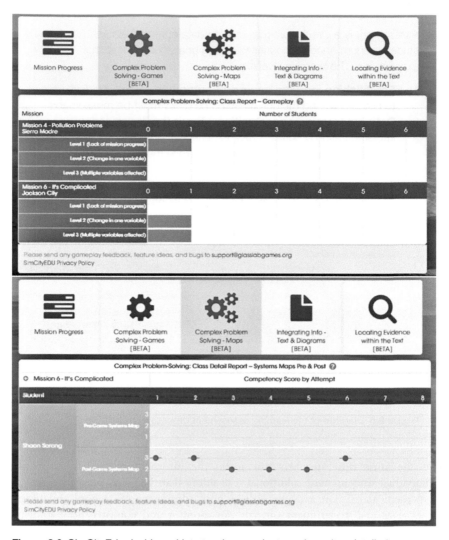

Figure 8.6 *SimCityEdu* dashboard lets teachers evaluate and monitor detailed information about individual student progress towards learning objectives. © Institute of Play.

team at GlassLab along with testing experts at ETS (Educational Testing Service) and Pearson, known for educational materials and assessment.

Encouraging self-discipline in the classroom

In order for teachers to effectively teach their subject matter, students need to be motivated to learn. Gamified systems in the classroom can be used to support and direct in-class behavior and participation. For example, *Classcraft* is an

educational multiplayer role-playing game designed to support positive performance and behavior amongst students. Shawn Young, an eleventh-grade physics
teacher, designed and built the system to encourage students to participate in the
classroom and contribute to the greater classroom community. Played in the
classroom, students work in teams of five, taking on roles of three different character classes (mage, healer, warrior), gaining experience points for positive actions
and taking damage for inappropriate, hurtful or harmful actions. As students gain
experience points, they level up to unlock rewards like extra time on test
extensions or assignment due dates.

Figure 8.7 *Classcraft* is a multiplayer role-playing game for encouraging positive
behavior and learning in the classroom. Courtesy of Classcraft Studios Inc.

INSIDER INSIGHT

MEET SHAWN YOUNG, THE TEACHER WHO CREATED CLASSCRAFT

Interview granted with permission by Shawn Young.

Shawn Young is the creator, designer and developer of *Classcraft*. He teaches high-school physics
and has an advanced degree in education. He
leverages his diverse skill set to innovate new
approaches to learning including project-based
learning and game-based learning projects.

**How did you come up with the idea for
Classcraft?**

The idea of applying role-playing mechanics to
the classroom had been sitting at the back of my

Figure 8.8 Shawn Young.

mind since I started teaching. It materialized when I jokingly told a student he should get experience points for his behavior. The students said, "That would be awesome," so I built it. The goal was to increase student engagement, have more fun in the classroom, foster collaboration and foster proper classroom behavior. I wanted an engaging, level-building type of game. RPGs fit that, and I have always found them a lot of fun as a gamer.

Were there any target behaviors you were trying to evoke?

I really wanted to foster collaboration, students helping each other out to succeed in the course. The game is built around that, with the students working in teams, the characters being complementary, cooperative powers being explicitly rewarded and students facing penalties as a team.

What game concepts do you think make Classcraft enjoyable for students?

Students embody a fully customizable avatar with powers and equipment, all of which is colorfully illustrated. Like most RPGs, the game includes leveling up, hit points, awarding experience points for progression, action points to use powers. Also, events add an aspect of randomness and thrill to the game. There is also a crucial dichotomy between incentives (acquiring powers) and punishments (for instance dying or getting detention) that make the game risky and enticing, and thus fun.

How has the game changed your interaction with the students?

All my interventions were passed through the filter of the game. Instead of saying to a student "don't do that" or "good job," I would attribute points in the game.

How have you changed or modified the game over time?

Based on the students' progression in the game, I adapted and refined the game over the course of two years, changing the powers, adding events, etc.

How are students bringing the game experience into the classroom?

Students are always aware of the game going on, of the pervasive aspect of the game. They behave differently in the sense that they are much more engaged, look forward to coming to class to level up their character and see what the random event might be. Some become leaders within their teams or develop crucial roles like being the best healer.

Are you seeing unexpected emergent behavior?

I was very surprised to see a lot of students forgoing interest in their grades. These became secondary to leveling up in the game.

GS DESIGN FOR PROFESSIONAL TRAINING

Schools are not the only organizations being retooled with games. In fact, corporate and government training is estimated to be a nearly $200 billion market worldwide. Within the next year it is expected that 25 percent of all redesigned business processes will include game elements. Companies of all sizes are finding that games are excellent mechanisms for a range of initiatives including new employee recruiting and onboarding, leadership training, professional development and on-the-job training. For example, Deloitte Consulting, the largest consulting firm in the world with over 200,000 employees providing services for auditing, tax preparation and financial advising, created a gamified system for producing consistency and depth in leadership training. The Deloitte Leadership Academy (DLA) uses missions that involve watching videos, taking quizzes to demonstrate knowledge, and then supporting and contributing to the community of other employees participating in the same program. The content comes from top-tier business schools like Harvard, Stanford and the Swiss International Institute for Management Development. Employees are rewarded with badges for completion of learning module missions and can also gain unexpected badges when multiple individuals from one department complete a mission at the same time. To encourage participation and even the playing field, DLA includes level-specific leaderboards, so players only compete against their own cohorts within the company. In addition, these boards re-set each week so that every employee has the chance to catch up even if they have taken time off to attend to other things.

Figure 8.9 Deloitte Consulting's DLA leadership academy. Source: James Sanders, Deloitte.

Figure 8.10 Code School's *Rails for Zombies* uses a zombie theme to teach web
developers Ruby on Rails. © Code School. Courtesy of Justin Mezzell.

Other examples of GS design for on-the-job training are *Git Real* and *Try
Objective-C* (covered in Chapters 6 and 4, respectively), both created by Code
School, a company dedicated to teaching working and aspiring web developers
and programmers the critical skills they need to do their jobs effectively. The
company's first project, a gamified system called *Rails for Zombies*, teaches Ruby on
Rails, an open-source web application framework designed to simplify the
creation of complex web applications. Combining instructional videos with
programming exercises and wrapping these in a zombie apocalypse aesthetic, the
company humorously warns users, "*Rails for Zombies* may leave you with a craving
for brains and entrails. The developers have no liability." Code School creates a
range of courses that covers deep learning paths through Ruby on Rails, JavaScript,
HTML, CSS and iOS application development.

INSIDER INSIGHT

MEET CODE SCHOOL'S DESIGNER
JUSTIN MEZZELL

Interview granted with permission by
Justin Mezzell.

Justin Mezzell is an art director and designer at
Code School. He works with subject matter experts
who specialize in teaching programming and web

Figure 8.11 Justin Mezzell.

development to deliver online courses for professional development. Justin has worked on fifteen courses for the company, and is currently championing user experience design across all of the company's projects.

Can you describe challenges of teaching hard concepts like programming?

There is a certain level of people we want to engage with. Many of them are at a very high level. As more people get in we need to help new people get up to speed. This makes the more robust stuff trickier. *Rails for Zombies* was at a very high level. We have seen more of an influx of people asking for more courses, and have recently set up discussion boards for each course. In this way, we can leverage the knowledge base of power users who really want to help other people learn. The community of people supporting others has been really organic.

What is your process?

We will have an original briefing with our content team. They figure out how to break down the information to the most basic components, and come to the table with something in mind. We review the information together, and when it starts making sense to me (I am not a coder), then we begin to craft a theme. With the theme from this meeting we come up with a story. I then work with illustrators to deliver imagery along with a narrative that covers different levels that will make up the project. Meanwhile, the content team is focused on the best way to present the information. Their job is to figure out how to make the content digestible.

After the initial discovery meeting, we usually do a weekly check in. A designer like myself will be on the course the entire time. We begin early with the branding, which matches the mood of the theme. We'll have the word mark and an illustration to go with it. We do in-house testing where we ask our developers to take the course. We then hold a public beta where we have local people come out and take the course while we are around. We can see when people get stuck and engage them in person.

What are some lessons you have learned about designing interfaces for learning and engagement?

The hardest design challenge is carrying consistency across the multiple languages we are teaching. We are just getting to the point where we want to create one user experience to be consistent. With the changing needs of the different courses there are so many moving parts. It is a difficult task to get functionality right. Some courses have multiple choices, different windows, as well as slides and video. That is what we are building right now. We want each course to be unique, but there has to be consistency. For example, users need to know exactly where to click, and where to expect dialogue windows to appear. You shouldn't have to have a tutorial for every course to relearn how to use an interface.

What should a designer know when trying to design play systems for teaching?

I want to encourage users. I want them to learn the material, but I don't want them to learn at the expense of them not feeling good about themselves. The system needs to ask itself, "Where is this user? How far along are they?" The way we respond to someone who gets close to a solution should be different than someone who is entirely off base. Our job is to respond positively and provide opportunities for wayfinding. There is nothing more annoying than hearing "wrong." I don't want people to have to think or scour our interface to have to get help to move on. We should celebrate just the idea that someone wants to learn a skill. I want a positive experience to be at the forefront. Maybe you didn't get it the first time. I would rather give the user the answer and then present him an opportunity later to evaluate his work. I want users to have a high level of confidence. I don't need to be harder on a user than he is on himself. I can celebrate with him and give him a new experience. This is hard stuff.

GAMIFIED SYSTEMS AND THE MILITARY

> Every Soldier will be a collector, consumer, producer and provider of information and intelligence.
> —Robert D. Steele, "Human Intelligence (HUMINT):
> All Humans, All Minds, All the Time"

The use of games by the military for recruiting, training and re-integrating soldiers into civilian life involves some of the most cutting-edge, technologically advanced and systemically extensive work in the field. Robotics, nanotechnology and biogenetics, all once considered too nascent and expensive for deployment, are now being increasingly utilized to support military initiatives around the world. Such devices generate an ever-increasing amount of real-time data. This is combined with data trolled from social networking platforms used by 1.7 billion people speaking more than thirty major languages, and hundreds of regional dialects. As information simultaneously becomes ever more disparate and important, the nature of war and the role of the military in the world drastically changes. Fighting is no longer between clear-cut geo-political enemies defined by specific borders. Mounting threats created by poverty, civil war, conflicting religious ideologies and natural resource shortages mean that the potential for conflict in the 21st century has become increasingly localized. Although military training once prioritized combat and following the rigid chain of command, today the emphasis is on preparing soldiers who can think for themselves, making informed and expeditious decisions to reduce or abate the chance of a potential conflict. Prioritizing stabilization means interacting with local populations, requiring cultural sensitivity and contextual understanding in real-time. With the heavy emphasis on developing skills in listening, leading, information sharing and negotiating unique and nuanced situations, training in the military is more important and more subtle than ever before.

Sponsored by the Department of Defense, the University of Southern California's Institute for Creative Technologies (ICT) brings social scientists and game industry professionals together to help members within the military improve critical skills like leadership, decision-making and cultural awareness. One example is BiLAT, an immersive training program designed to help soldiers conduct meetings and negotiations in unfamiliar cultural contexts. Acting as army officers, mission objectives given to players require them to conduct several meetings with local leaders. In one campaign, a player must determine why a marketplace built by the United States is not being utilized. These simulated interactions require relationship building, sound negotiation strategies and sensitivity and awareness of the cultural conventions of others. In-depth feedback includes run-time coaching and reviews after the fact.

> You have to think through the cause and effect of your decisions. Like chess, you have to look two or three turns down the road.
> —Colonel Todd Ebel, Director of the School for
> Command Preparation

UrbanSim, another ICT project, utilizes a game-based environment to simulate the complex requirements of stabilization and counterinsurgency operations. Players take on the role of army battalion commanders responsible for planning and executing operations under highly unpredictable and stressful scenarios. Encouraging situational awareness and adaptive strategies, UrbanSim works through a narrative layer that interjects real events experienced by commanders in the field. The system uses a "socio-cultural behavioral model" to focus player attention on cultural sensitivity. The game's characters function as autonomous agents reacting to the overall climate that emerges during play rather than to specific actions or choices made by the player. For example, members of a specific tribe may consider jobs their highest priority, but they may still join insurgents if they do not feel secure and safe. To reduce this type of negative outcome and build resident support, players must interact with civilians, patrol neighborhoods, meet with tribal elders and find ways to create economic opportunities. Through a scaffolding mechanism of intelligent and continuous guidance, players get the opportunity to safely learn and anticipate the chain of effects and consequences of their actions.

With similar goals to UrbanSim, Full Spectrum Command is a PC-based game from the Institute's Full Spectrum Video game series developed in conjunction with Pandemic Studios. It is meant to train soldiers in both the United States and Singapore in the cognitive dimensions of light infantry leadership under counter-insurgency operations. Light infantry has to be nimble, independent and often operate in stealth conditions, and these soldiers commonly perform with very limited knowledge of an environment. On top of this is the general experience of uncertainty and confusion on a battlefield, commonly referred to as the fog of war. For these soldiers and their commanders, situational awareness and rapid tactical decision-making are essential.

Players begin by choosing scenarios and missions that were created with subject matter experts from the US Army Infantry Center at Fort Benning, Georgia. Once a mission is selected, players receive an operational order, which may require interpretation and analysis while the game simulation is running. The next step involves customizing the composition and equipment of the company's platoons. The player then goes through the most critical part of planning the phases of execution. With planning complete, the game engine runs the execution phase, giving the player the perspective on the ground of the commander. Radio calls from company platoon leaders and real-time GPS locations of troops add situational awareness. During the execution phase, players can issue orders to adjust to the changing nature of the engagement. Full Spectrum Command takes these new orders and hands them off to the highly refined artificial intelligence (AI). The AI distributes directions to non-player soldiers, who also behave autonomously and respond to situations when direction is not clarified. After the mission has been executed, players have access to a comprehensive feature set for the after-action review, including an execution matrix and the reveal of the enemies' plan for the first time. Players can view key events by scrubbing a timeline of the recorded operation. By doing this, they can dig into the rationale behind the choices made by the system's AI. A player may find when looking at the decision

Figure 8.12 *UrbanSim* screenshot. Photographs used with permission of the University of Southern California Institute for Creative Technologies.

Figure 8.13 *Full Spectrum Command* screenshot. Photographs used with permission of the University of Southern California Institute for Creative Technologies.

logic used by a non-player soldier that when ordered to shoot he did not because of low levels of ammunition. Rather than simply listing a series of contingent possibilities that might emerge on a battlefield, players experience them before live fire simulations or actual combat.

With both UrbanSim and Full Spectrum Command gamified systems are interventions to help support the increasingly complex training required of today's military personnel. Soldiers at every rank of the organization must rapidly increase their skill set and capabilities so that they can adapt to the paradox of globalization— the manifestation of highly unpredictable localized tensions. The military has maximized the capacity of game design and game technologies proving that they are some of the most effective tools for preparing individuals for the constantly changing demands of the job.

THE CONSUMER MARKETPLACE

Games and learning go far beyond the formal and professional educational settings already explored. In fact, the consumer market for game-based learning generates respectable revenues of approximately $2 billion a year. Unlike some of the more recent comprehensive efforts, the consumer marketplace has a longer tradition of publishing individual and series titles. The computer game *Oregon Trail*, first released in 1974, let players take on the role of a 19th-century pioneer taking a wagon of settlers across the United States. It became very popular among middle-school teachers for classroom use. In the late 1980s, Davidson's *Math Blaster* provided an arcade-style approach to math drills, laying the groundwork for applications like *DragonBox*. Then in the early 1990s, Knowledge Adventure's *JumpStart*, a series that I developed, combined early learning curriculum with games, music, welcoming environments and animated characters, encouraging parents to treat the home computer as an early learning tool. Likewise Broderbund's *Where in the World is Carmen Sandiego* taught children geography following the criminal mastermind Carmen Sandiego around the world. It was so popular that it was spun off into its own public television series. Online and console games eclipsed this market for learning games for a number of years, stalling the convergence phenomenon, but higher-speed Internet services and personal devices from phones to tablets have resulted in a re-emergence of the market and increasing integration of such applications into schools and daily life.

The multi-platform MMO *School of Dragons* is a good example of the shift to mobile and educational from what in the past would have been console and entertainment. Based upon DreamWorks Animation's film and media franchise *How to Train Your Dragon*, the game currently hosts 500,000 daily active users (DAU). An experienced team of curriculum and game designers partnered with DreamWorks Animation to artfully map science education to game-play and tap into enthusiasm for STEM (science, technology, engineering and mathematics) learning. Quests, mini-games, puzzles and cut-scenes meaningfully leverage material tied to the *Next Generation Science Standards* for second through fifth grade, an evidence-based approach to science learning currently created by the National Academy of Sciences and embraced by fourteen states in the United States. The

Figure 8.14 *School of Dragons* contextualizes scientific experimentation through game-play. *How to Train Your Dragon* © 2014 DreamWorks Animation LLC. All Rights Reserved.

game mixes film footage from the original movie with newly recorded voiceover introducing material about earth, life and physical science. It begins with visuals from the original film of the main character Hiccup watching the young dragon Toothless trying to fly. An original scene rewritten for the game then has Hiccup explaining the steps of the scientific method, as he observes and then hypothesizes that Toothless cannot fly because he is missing part of his tail. With the expectations established, players are primed to experiment, observe and apply knowledge gained as they continue to develop their dragons. Later, in the science lab, players team up with the dragon Toothless to test how dragon fire will create combustion reactions with different rocks. Players get the opportunity to test and observe the reactions that different rocks create alone and in combination.

Though most developers do not have multi-million dollar franchises to help their educational games get off the ground, DreamWorks' choice of the educational game developer and publisher JumpStart as a partner is significant. Both companies know that parents will continue to make entertainment purchases with the hope that their children will benefit from the experience they provide. They are also looking at the popularity of newly published games like *Robot Turtles*, which build STEM concepts into the play. Published by Thinkfun, this board game introduces children to programming while parents take on the role of the computer, setting up the space and then moving a turtle to collect gems according to the instructions (code) defined by the child through the cards in the game.

Figure 8.15 *Robot Turtles* is a board game designed to help parents introduce their children to computer programming concepts. Text and graphic design © 2014 ThinkFun Inc. All rights reserved. Game by Dan Shapiro. www.RobotTurtles.com. Copyright © 2014 Robot Turtles, LLC. All rights reserved. Robot Turtles and the Robot Turtles logo are among the trademarks of Robot Turtles, LLC.

The advantage of the board game in this case is that it leverages some of the social learning innovations that computer applications like *DragonBox* have tried to incorporate in their designs.

Although children are the audience we tend to conjure in our minds first when we think of the consumer marketplace for educational games, adults are also increasingly interested in using games to learn new skills, develop or enhance cognitive capabilities, and build new kinds of relationships in social networking environments. In cooperation with a team of neuroscientists, Lumosity has created a series of games for a much older population interested in training their memory and attention. Used by 60 million people (generally forty-five years and older) the service includes games designed to enhance problem-solving abilities that require processing speed, flexibility and attention. An example of this is *Familiar Faces*, which is one of the more than forty games designed to be played in fifteen-minute daily increments to boost brainpower. In it, players act as restaurant employees interacting with patrons. Working for the highest tip, players must remember faces, names, orders and other relevant information learned during previous encounters. Though research studies in the past few years have not proved that cognitive abilities can be trained and improved through games like this, studies will continue as the growing prosperous baby boomer generation continues to look for helpful and joyful ways to cope with the deficits that come with aging.

INSIDER INSIGHT

MEET SCHOOL OF DRAGONS' QUEST DESIGNER BRIAN YOON

Interview granted with permission by Brian Yoon.

Brian Yoon is the quest designer on JumpStart's *School of Dragons* educational MMO. He worked on the overall narrative and design of the initial game, and continues to produce new player quests regularly for the popular title. Before joining JumpStart he spent nearly a decade as an RPG designer and writer at the table-top game company Alderac Entertainment Group.

How did you work with the curriculum team in the initial design?

The first step was to develop the theme and overall story arc of the game's quests. Once we figured out which direction we wanted to move, I got together with the curriculum team to hammer out the details of our approach. We used the Next Generation Science Standards to create a list of subjects we wanted to teach. Then we designed quests to best highlight those subjects.

Figure 8.16
Brian Yoon.

Next, we wanted a sandbox of interactivity and fun that would be tightly woven with the quest system. There, the players could fiddle around with substances from the real world, play with their dragons, and learn when the components reacted. We wanted all the items to react in the way that they would in the real world, no matter what you did within the lab. As you imagine, this was a very difficult process. Our game designer Matt Ekins worked closely with the curriculum team for months to fine tune the laboratory. Now, it's one of the core mechanics of the game.

How do you work with them to develop quests? Can you describe the process?

It's a constant collaborative process between us. We meet frequently and design each educational quest from the ground up. The curriculum team will propose certain standards they would like to cover, and we brainstorm game mechanics that would be fun to play and teach the subject. Once the framework is set, I create the dialogue, decide the flow of the quest (when the game mechanics are used and which connective elements will get the player to the mechanics) and implement it within the game.

How is DreamWorks involved in the design process?

DreamWorks has been a wonderful partner in quest design. They become involved from the get-go of most of the educational quests, starting from the brainstorm process. Once the curriculum team and I have ideas on several possible education quests, we present them to DreamWorks and we figure out together which ones we should create. They get us assets from the movies and the TV shows, video clips for use within the game, and share their keen insight on how to present the world and the characters to remain true to the franchise. Their enthusiasm and belief in our educational model is palpable every time we meet. It has sincerely been a joy working with them.

What are the biggest challenges?

The biggest challenge is creating interesting quests that will compel the player to play through. I want players to want to complete these quests because they want to see what's going to happen next. These players will enjoy the game and learn along the way, even if they weren't intending to, because the quest is interesting. This is not easy, but thankfully I have a lot of support to help get the quests polished to that state.

How is this work different from working at a purely entertainment-based game company?

When I first started working on School of Dragons, I had a very traditional mindset to content creation. I would create quests with story and fun in mind, then think, "Ok, how do I fit education into this quest?" I quickly realized that was the wrong way to go. Now, I'll work with the curriculum team to find a science standard we want to teach then design the quest around the education. The fun is equally important, but it comes in at a slightly later stage than in a non-educational game company.

CULTURAL AND CIVIC ENGAGEMENT

Public institutions like monuments, state parks and museums have the challenging task of bringing in visitors, generating interest during visits and driving on-going revenue through ticket sales and memberships. Back in Chapter 1, we took a look at the Junior Ranger Program offered at the National Parks throughout the United States. Organizations like the National Parks utilize game concepts to reach new audiences and re-engage existing ones. Not only do gamified systems like badge collecting motivate people to visit, but they also facilitate experiences that connect visitors to each other and to the objects of interest within an environment or exhibition. The voluntary nature of learning that takes place at such sites creates expectations, and public institutions want to ensure that visitors feel like their visit has deep meaning and carryover, as if they have joined a special community of individuals sharing in discovery. Parents and their children, teachers and their students, as well as groups of friends all come to these informal learning spaces to expand their worlds together.

As intriguing as the collections, archives and changing exhibits awaiting visitors at museums and cultural institutions may seem at first, walking in to these unfamiliar and dense spaces can often feel overwhelming. What should I do here? Where should I start? What are the most important lessons in this exhibit? What will satisfy the different interests of the people in my group? These types of questions are so common that many institutions rely on docents and volunteers to provide direction. Unfortunately, not every institution can always provide these guides and not every visitor wants to experience such a group-centric and pre-planned tour. This is exactly where games, game concepts and game-like structures can provide guidance and feedback to visitors so that they can construct their own experience. For example, the children's area of the National Museum of the American Indian in Washington, DC provides empty play passports at the entry, encouraging children along with their guardians to visit and interact with each installation within the exhibit while subtly reminding them that the category American Indian is composed of many nations. As they learn about the different aspects of Native American life through history their passports get stamped. This basic game-like approach to anthropological and historic learning aims at basic coverage, an effective approach to getting children (and grown-ups) to think about the range and diversity of topics addressed by a museum's exhibitions and to map their progress.

While progress paths like badges, passports and scavenger hunts provide the overarching structure to get visitors on their way, propelling visitors forward requires sparking interest through individual moments of interaction. Since the

1970s, science museums like San Francisco's Exploratorium have created social spaces for bringing generations together through interactive exhibits. Buttons, circuits, switches, pendulums, microscopes and magnets each accompanied by a "do this" label give instructions to visitors about how they should interact, all while experiencing the science behind the interaction. Learning, experimentation and play become synonymous—a cognitive and behavioral goal beyond the simple conveying of content. Over the past few decades, museum visitors have also been re-conceptualized as not mere recipients of information but as participants and contributors to the museum itself, and game systems have an important role to play in this process.

The exhibition spaces in the re-designed California Academy of Sciences meaningfully integrate games within the artifacts, collections, animals, insects and marine life. In the Islands of Evolution exhibit, the Collecting Bugs game uses a Wii-like hand device to let players take on the role of an etymologist collecting bugs to learn about the large variety of insects and arachnids on the island of Madagascar. Once the player has completed her search, the specimens are separated and shown in a display case, marking the end of game. Surrounded by children waiting for their turn to play, the game was designed with such popularity in mind. Each play session is marked by a timer, which begins after a few minutes of play. This reminds players and the other visitors waiting that the museum game is not like other games they play. It must provide a fulfilling experience for as many visitors as possible, while getting players finishing the game excited to continue exploring the rest of the exhibit. The Connect the Continents game in the Earthquake exhibit lets five different players work together to recreate the ancient continent of Gondwana. Sitting in a circle in front of mounted iPads around a large screen, players use their hands to rotate and move the continents of South America, Antarctica, Australia, Africa and India. Players must strategically work together to get the separate pieces to click into place. As a result, conversations abound between strangers playing and watching the game, and trying to complete the puzzle. Participatory museum design like the installations at the Academy of Sciences focuses on taking the individual experience of an object or environment and facilitating collective engagement. The goal is to generate a communal experience, one that is much bigger in terms of the connection to time and community than the singular experience of one individual. Gamified systems at cultural institutions provide guidance, pique interest, start conversations and then motivate deeper and more connected learning.

By letting visitors and the community contribute to and participate in an exhibition, gamified systems can transform a singular experience into one that is connected beyond the moment and the room.

Figure 8.17 The California Academy of Sciences emphasizes learning and collaboration through game-play with games like *Collecting Bugs* (top) and *Connect the Continents* (bottom). Courtesy of Exploratorium, the California Academy of Sciences.

Informal education institutions of every size must find creative approaches to stay present in the minds of its public, rethinking how to foster an ongoing relationship beyond the irregular visit. The Smithsonian, the world's largest museum complex with over nineteen museums and nine research centers, has recently defined a strategic plan for the 21st-century to instantiate its vision of "shaping the future by preserving our heritage, discovering new knowledge, and sharing our resources with the world." As a part of this commitment to helping generations solve critical issues facing the world, the Smithsonian approached

MIT's Education Arcade about making a game to introduce teens and pre-teens to the scientists working at the venerable institution. Out of this came the National Science Foundation-funded game *Vanished*, a science-fiction-themed Alternate Reality Game that brought thousands of teens together for eight weeks of play. During the game, players acted as science detectives, trying to solve an environmental mystery as they discovered a range of scientific fields. To advance

When we first met with the Smithsonian, they knew they wanted to create an educational game that was more than your usual museum scavenger hunt. In the first meeting between our group at MIT and the Smithsonian scientists, there was a conversation about some of the issues with contemporary science education in the schools, particularly that most learning is done in isolation, and that students weren't encouraged enough to experiment, get creative and problem solve together. There was a consensus that we wanted the experience that we created to be collaborative, potentially messy and open ended. Our [the MIT Education Arcade's] Creative Director Scot Osterweil and designer Jason Haas came up with the idea of using an Alternate Reality Game to create that kind of experience.

—Caitlin Feeley, game designer and project manager,
MIT's Education Arcade

Figure 8.18 *Vanished* was an Alternate Reality Game created by MIT's Education Arcade and the Smithsonian.

the story, players had to work together while communicating with different Smithsonian scientists, including a paleo-climatologist, a bee expert, a paleontologist and a volcanologist, each providing specialized information and guidance during the event. The game design team that ran the event created a situated learning experience with the scaffolding required for players to understand the science required to solve the mystery. Most importantly, the game facilitated connecting players to diverse subject matter experts, a key goal in many learning systems.

The role of subject matter experts

Gamified systems like the ones mentioned in this chapter enable and benefit from the participation of experts in a particular field, like mathematics and math education. Although a number of distance learning strategies aim at broadcasting content to large audiences, games allow for far more flexibility in terms of delivery, scaffolding for ensuring basic skills, more precision in terms of interaction with experts at key learning moments, greater depth for advanced users, and building conceptual and cognitive aspects of the subject matter directly into the game. Standards alone are therefore not enough for the process of creating a gamified curriculum. Team members with subject matter expertise or subject matter experts (SMEs) are an essential part of any project that will be used for measuring learning against curriculum standards. SMEs ensure that standards are met, working with the design teams to identify and validate the creative approaches for doing this. These experts are most often academics or researchers,

Figure 8.19 Selden Map game design workshop. Courtesy of Robert Batchelor.

Figure 8.20 *Fujian Trader*, a strategy board game based upon the Selden Map.
Courtesy of Robert Batchelor.

who have spent the majority of their time working on one problem related to their field.

The board game *Fujian Trader* provides an example of how designers can leverage the value of an SME. The game, intended for students learning East Asian and global history in middle schools, is based on a 17th-century Chinese navigational merchant map, which was found after sitting unexamined for nearly 300 years in the archives of Oxford University's Bodleian Library. Dr Robert Batchelor, the historian who rediscovered the map, participated as a core member of the game design team. To begin the project, we ran several workshops to teach the history during the design and testing phases of the project. By having a content expert within the game design team, the group gained valuable insights that filtered through every aspect of design from the aesthetics to the mechanics. Once the game was complete, we were then able to work with teachers, educators and Dr Batchelor to assemble lesson plans that aligned the game with core curriculum standards.

MEET THE SUBJECT MATTER EXPERT, HISTORIAN DR ROBERT BATCHELOR

Interview granted with permission by Robert Batchelor.

Dr Robert Batchelor is a historian whose work focuses on the history of East Asia and its influence on 17th-century China. He is known for his discovery of the Selden Map of China, a treasure of Oxford University's Bodleian Library. He is the author of *London: The Selden Map and the Making of a Global City, 1549–1689* (Chicago: University of Chicago Press, 2014). An associate professor of history at Georgia Southern University, he is a co-designer of the board game *Fujian Trader*.

Figure 8.21
Robert Batchelor.

What is so important about the Selden Map?

It is the earliest Chinese maritime merchant map we have, and it shows how trade routes across East Asia were plotted out. Uniquely, it tells us about how Chinese merchants were thinking about systems and navigational mathematics in the 17th century.

Why were you interested in making a game around it?

I wanted people to experience the map rather than simply look at it, and ultimately I wanted them to think like a 17th-century Chinese merchant. The map lends itself to being a game. It was a strategic map for merchants to see where they might trade and the relationship of these trading locations with the Ming Empire. But the map is in classical Chinese, making it very difficult to read even for modern Mandarin speakers let alone those who don't know Chinese characters at all. Making the map readable and playable allowed players to go deeper into understanding it both as a map and as an expression of the early history of globalization. The game in particular used movement and cards to show trading relationships between places and how the Ming Empire related to the world outside its boundaries.

What were your goals for the project?

I hoped the game could overturn common assumptions about Chinese history, and open people to understanding that history in more complex ways. There is a basic cliché about China associated with the Great Wall that suggests isolation and stasis. But games are about interaction and movement, and so are the routes shown on the Selden Map. I also wanted to understand the map better myself, which happened as I worked to articulate the different mechanics it implied with teams of game designers.

How do you think the game is supporting your learning goals?

By letting players take on the role of 17th-century Chinese merchants managing overseas trade, the game creates a window onto important aspects of Chinese and indeed global economics during this period. This was a time when the Ming Empire and its successor the Qing drove much of the world economy because of their demand for silver and production of manufactured goods. Historians usually show this with a map of trade routes. One of my goals was to encourage players to pay attention to the routes and the ports identified on the map by moving along them, facilitating a close reading. Controlling ports that fall within different regions of exchange means that players think about specific locations as well as the system as a whole, what goods were produced and valued in a region, its relationship to other ports, and its distance from the Ming Empire. To place the map within its time period, we structured a narrative layer using the Manchu invasion of 1644 as a key turning point of the game. The end-of-game mechanic related to that invasion builds tension associated with the impending doom of a collapsing empire, conveying important moments in history while providing significantly more texture to the player experience. Finally, with the curriculum, we introduced a series of activities— readings, analysis, research, game modifications—that could not only fulfill different educational standards and STEM learning goals but also make the game-play a richer experience that is fully integrated into broader classroom learning.

Given that there are so many history-based board games in existence, what do you think makes this game different?

Most importantly, the game teaches players how to read and understand the map, so that what initially was an inaccessible object becomes an object of conversation. The game engages with a real historic artifact, and this means that unlike a textbook there are always extra dimensions of historical depth. One aspect of this is the wide variety of relationships a game entails, so that different players experience different patterns of historical movement and they get to share these socially. This is also one of the things that the curriculum does, allowing the exploration of tangents and deeper research once all the players know the basic game. All of this keeps the game from falling into a sterile repetition of previous forms. In many games, history only serves as a kind of window dressing for abstract mechanics, and often there is one "back-story." In this game, the structures help to elucidate the complexity of history and its experience by many different kinds of people by making each player story unique. So one player might focus on a trading relation with Manila and the surrounding areas while another might have far-flung ports ranging from Nagasaki to Sumatra. Likewise, there were 17th-century merchants who pursued each of these strategies. Rather than the teacher telling one story, the students see different ones and can thus focus further exploration on the relationships they find most compelling in explaining the period.

As the content expert, what were the challenges of working with game designers? What was unique or positive about the process?

Game designers are primarily concerned with enjoyment, playability, mechanics and balancing. The first issue involved getting us together and thinking collectively about history and historical documents as something that opens up new possibilities for creativity rather than some didactic limiting factor. What happened next for me was a kind of media shock, in particular switching from a written narrative to a game format involving flexibility and multiple narratives. I had to think about what would normally go in a textbook that could not be included, like particular dates and causal relationships, and then think about what kinds of spatial and systems learning could now be included because the game allowed more of a focus on formal and systemic issues in history, such as how trade routes develop over time or what a crisis like the Manchu invasion does to a system as a whole.

KEY TAKEAWAYS

- The use of gamified systems is on the rise in formal and informal educational settings including schools, corporations, the military and the consumer marketplace.
- With growing evidence about increased motivation and enhanced learning, use of gamified systems is spreading in formal education settings.
- Mapping game-play to curriculum standards provides teachers with appropriate mechanisms to incorporate game-based learning into their classrooms.
- Gamified systems for learning require subject matter expertise. Content experts who are specialists in their fields are key members of every learning-based design project.
- Gamified systems must provide means for assessment and evaluation. Data collection about student performance is essential for success.

EXERCISES

By this stage in the design process you should have a very clear idea about what your system will behave and look like. Use the exercises in the last two chapters of the book to help you refine and improve your designs. Now is the time to get input and feedback from other people that can help you clarify unanswered questions and support your initiatives.

8.1 Find a subject matter expert

Although the projects in this book are not necessarily aligned with educational goals, each has the potential to benefit from the participation of a subject matter expert. Try to find an expert in an area who might help you craft and improve your designs. For example, if you are working on the super-market project, consider how you might include insights from a nutritionist or a gourmet chef.

8.2 Develop prototypes

Before you can begin testing your concepts on your intended audience, you will need to create a prototype. You may create a low-fidelity prototype by printing your screens on paper. If you have the time and resources you might also consider using a prototyping tool to build an interactive prototype. There are a large number of accessible and easy-to-use prototyping tools available for use. You may refer to this book's website www.gamifiedsystems.com for the most up-to-date recommendations.

8.3 Test your concepts on your audience

With your paper or interactive prototypes ready, it is now time to sit down with members of your perspective audience and get feedback. Usability testing is an entire discipline that is only briefly covered within this book. Please refer to www.gamifiedsystems.com for additional usability testing resources.

RECOMMENDED READINGS

- *Games, Learning and Society: Learning and Meaning in the Digital Age*, edited by Sasha Barab, Constance Steinkuehler and Kurt Squire, 2014.
  This reader contains a range of insightful essays written by leaders in the field of games and learning.

- *The Multi-player Classroom* by Lee Sheldon, 2011.
  Lee Sheldon's book explores and details how he and other teachers around the world have successfully incorporated game-like structures into their elementary, secondary and university classrooms.

- *Video Games and Learning: Teaching and Participatory Culture in the Digital Age* by Kurt Squire, 2011.
  A leader in the field of game-based learning, Kurt Squire writes an accessible and practical book showing how games can promote learning in and outside the classroom.

LUCIEN VATELL IS BUILDING AN EDUCATION ECOSYSTEM

Interview granted with permission by Lucien Vatell.

Lucien Vattel is the founder and CEO of GameDesk. Named one of Fast Company's Top 10 Most Innovative Companies in Education, GameDesk develops new models of education, changing the way students learn by embedding academic content and assessment into hands-on experience, digital games and simulations. Prior to founding GameDesk, Vattel helped design the master's and undergraduate Computer Science Program in Game Development at the University of Southern California, where he also served as the Associate Director for interactive research.

Figure 8.22
Lucien Vatell. "The thing that stays constant is our underlying approach—how we map out this terrain at being better at what we do. All of these are constants; what changes are the activities and projects."

Can you talk about your background and how it led you to GameDesk?

When I was at USC I ran a bunch of initiatives that focused on bringing departments together, particularly the Learning sciences and the Engineering school. I got interested in seeing what happens when you bring learning science to game mechanics and interactive entertainment. What I saw was that there needed to be a mapping between learning outcomes and affordances. What I mean by affordances are the interactions, software and narratives that create different types of learning experiences. I became interested in seeing what specific technology elicits in the mind of the learner and how this was connected to different types of learning.

Game-based learning is not effective enough at describing what we are doing. If I am trying to teach a particular procedure or process, the mechanisms that I use to do these may be very different. Maybe they are called games. Maybe they are simulations that show systems, like plate tectonics. Maybe it's the simulation and visualization and how you scaffold them that really gets at effective learning. Perhaps it is something that involves embodiment, perhaps moving the body to learn physics or about accretion. Perhaps being outside moving in a park may be more effective for learning these concepts as opposed to sitting in a digital sandbox and trying to learn these same ideas.

In the university there is a lot of the funding around different types of games and projects, but these are only funded for limited times to see if they work in school. Researchers will build a prototype, test it in a school, publish the data and have their name on a white paper. I wanted to start doing projects that were

Figure 8.23 *Tectonic Plates* utilizes Leap Motion technology to teach players about continental drift and plate tectonics through a multi-sensory experience. Courtesy of GameDesk/Lucien Vatell.

designed around engaging stakeholders, like students and teachers, in deeper and more complex ways. As opposed to dropping in and leaving, I wanted to see what would happen if we engaged the schools more directly. That was further solidified when a bunch of teachers told me that what is happening at the university was not translating into positive change in the schools.

We started by building stuff for at-risk kids. Then we started asking ourselves, "Which games do we want to do?" and we looked at grant opportunities for funding these. We mostly follow the passion and interest of people who work here. Some ideas come from seeing what is working well in a classroom. For instance, our most successful curricular module is a no-tech historical LARP, where students learn language, trade and law. The thing that stays constant is our underlying approach—how we map out this terrain at being better at what we do. All of these are constants; what changes are the activities and projects.

What does GameDesk do?

GameDesk brings academia, industry and schools together. We are a mission-directed organization, and want to perfect the process of interactive learning. We want to identify the best approach for a classroom experience and then to scale the work. GameDesk has started building experiences that translate into long-term impact, and have grown into a unique ecosystem. We have a research institute, a commercialization arm, and our own school where we incubate projects, and then share these with a national teacher community. Our mission was to build an ecosystem. On any given day, you will see an eclectic group. For instance on our Geoscience project *Aero* we had five folks from Caltech, a team of game designers, and a poet. Bill Nye the science guy was here narrating the

Figure 8.24 Funded by the Bill and Melinda Gates Foundation, GameDesk's PlayMaker school brings the work of the organization directly to teachers and students, where concepts can be evaluated, refined and perfected for distribution to other educational institutions. Courtesy of GameDesk/Lucien Vatell.

story of the science behind the project. At the same times assessment experts were in the room making sure we knew how to identify and create evidence that would show that the students of the project were in fact learning. Out of this National Science Foundation (NSF)-funded project we built five different games.

Can you describe Educade?

We realized that there was no place for teachers to access models or recipes for incorporating game-based learning into the classroom. Teachers don't want to be told how to teach. But they love great ideas and enough structure that makes them feel supported. We decided to create 600 to 1,000 lesson plans that would help teachers engage. Through Educade teachers can see how to facilitate projects and what their value is in relation to curriculum standards. In an effort to capture their enthusiasm, we have weekly featured teachers. All of the teachers are creating their own versions. Their examples will further the incorporation and adoption into the classroom. It is a cultural change agent. We are influencing the teaching culture and the teaching practice.

What advice do you have for aspiring GS designers interested in the field of game-based learning?

You can have the smartest people in the room coming up with ideas, but if the programmer doesn't program it right, and if the artists and designers don't get their jobs done correctly, it will likely result in a bad game. Making educational games is a translation exercise. Even if you have the best content you still need to create an experience of that knowledge. The teams bring varying degrees of different expertise. Games require instructional designers, programmers, producers and designers. You have to do a mind meld in thinking, which can then be translated into a meaningful and fun learning experience. Your production process needs to show that you can do this effectively. Many educational game developers don't hit the mark because the folks don't have the full process right.

NOTES

Barab, Sasha, Constance Steinkuehler and Kurt Squire. *Games, Learning and Society: Learning and Meaning in the Digital Age.* New York: Cambridge University Press, 2014.

Berget, Lori, David Jaloza, Sudhir Krishnaswamy, Justin Prate and Christopher Williams. "School of Dragons: Inside Look into an Evolving Game." *Gamasutra* (blog), April 14, 2007, http://gamasutra.com/blogs/ChristopherWilliams/20140414/215470/School_of_Dragons_Inside_Look_Into_An_Evolving_Game.php.

Bersin, Josh. "Spending on Corporate Training Soars: Employee Capabilities Now a Priority." *Forbes,* February 4, 2014, http://www.forbes.com/sites/joshbersin/2014/02/04/the-recovery-arrives-corporate-training-spend-skyrockets/.

Bolkan, Joshua. "Adaptive Game-Based Platform Helps Students Master Concepts in Algebra Challenge." *The Journal,* April 24, 2014, http://thejournal.com/articles/2014/04/24/adaptive-game-based-platform-helps-students-master-concepts-in-algebra-challenge.aspx.

Brousell, Lauren. "How Gamification Reshapes Corporate Training." *CIO,* February 5, 2013, http://www.cio.com/article/2388614/social-media/how-gamification-reshapes-corporate-training.html.

Lewis, Jordan Gaines. "Are Brain Training Games Worth It?" *Slate,* January 28, 2014, http://www.slate.com/blogs/future_tense/2014/01/28/lumosity_cognifit_cogmed_are_these_kinds_of_brain_training_games_worth_it.html.

McGonigal, Jane. "Gaming the Future of Museums." Presentation at the Center for the Future of Museums, Washington, DC, December 2, 2008, http://www.slideshare.net/avantgame/gaming-the-future-of-museums-a-lecture-by-jane-mcgonigal-presentation.

Mead, Corey. *War Play: Video Games and the Future of Armed Conflict.* Boston: Eamon Dolan/Houghton Mifflin Harcourt, 2013.

Meister, Jeanne C. "How Deloitte Made Learning a Game." *Harvard Business School Blog,* January 2, 2013, http://blogs.hbr.org/2013/01/how-deloitte-made-learning-a-g/.

Mitra, Sugata. "Kids Can Teach Themselves." Presentation at LIFT, Geneva, February 7–9, 2007, https://www.ted.com/talks/sugata_mitra_shows_how_kids_teach_themselves.

Mockenhaupt, Brian. "SimCity Baghdad." *The Atlantic,* January 1, 2010, http://www.theatlantic.com/magazine/archive/2010/01/simcity-baghdad/307830/.

Nicholson, Scott. "Strategies for Meaningful Gamification: Concepts Behind Transformative Play and Participatory Museums." Paper presented at Meaningful Play, Michigan State, East Lansing, MI, 2012.

Palmer, Doug, Steve Lunceford and Aaron J. Patton. "The Engagement Economy: How Gamification is Reshaping Businesses." *Deloitte Review,* 11 (2012): 55–57. http://www.deloitte.com/view/en_US/us/Insights/Browse-by-Content-Type/deloitte-review/c7cee86d96498310VgnVCM1000001956f00aRCRD.htm.

Salen, Katie, Robert Torres, Loretta Wolozin, Rebecca Rufo-Tepper and Arana Shapiro. *Quest to Learn: Developing the School for Digital Kids.* Cambridge: MIT Press, 2011. [Based on the design document originally written in 2008.]

Sheldon, Lee. *The Multi-player Classroom.* Boston: Cengage, 2011.

Shute, Valerie and Matthew Ventura. *Stealth Assessment: Measuring and Supporting Learning in Video Games.* Cambridge: MIT Press, 2013.

Simon, Nina. *The Participatory Museum.* Santa Cruz: Museum 2.0, 2010.

Squire, Kurt. *Video Games and Learning: Teaching and Participatory Culture in the Digital Age.* New York: Teachers College Press, 2011.

Steele, Robert D. "Human Intelligence: All Humans, All Minds, All the Time." Research report for the Strategic Studies Institute of the US Army War College, 2010.

Swain, Chris. "The Mechanic is the Message: How to Communicate Values in Games Through the Mechanics of User Action and System Response." *Ethics and Game Design: Teaching Values Through Play.* Edited by Karen Schrier and David Gibson. 217–235. Hershey: IGI Global, 2010.

The HR Specialist. "Game on! How HR Can Use 'Gamification' to Recruit, Train and Engage Employees." *Business Management Daily,* February 10, 2014, http://www.business managementdaily.com/37753/game-on-how-hr-can-use-gamification-to-recruit-train-and-engage-employees#_.

Notes:

- For information about *Full Spectrum Command, UrbanSim* and *BiLAT* see the USC Institute for Creative Technologies website: http://ict.usc.edu/.
- For more information about *Lure of the Labyrinth* see the game website: http://labyrinth.thinkport.org/www/.
- For game player data see the Entertainment Software Association website: http://www.theesa.com/facts/gameplayer.asp.

9 GS DESIGN FOR MARKETING AND ENTERTAINMENT

CHAPTER QUESTIONS

At the end of this chapter, you should be able to answer these questions:

- How does gamified system (GS) design satisfy the various goals of integrated marketing initiatives?
- What are some examples that showcase brand building and experiential marketing?
- How are gamified systems driving product sales and generating revenue?
- How are gamified systems being utilized to manage on-going interactions and relationships between companies and customers?
- How are GS designers supporting marketing efforts of media properties like films, television and videogames?

INTRODUCTION

No matter the sector or the size, every business requires the same basic structures to survive and thrive. Traditionally income and profits have been the measurement of a company's value and success. Over the past two decades, the Internet introduced the importance of a sizeable and growing user base as a key determination of value for an online business. Today, consumer-oriented companies face a significant challenge staying relevant and present in the minds of audiences with fickle and distributed attention spans. For this reason, corporations ranging from retail stores to videogame makers are looking to the benefits that gamified systems deliver to engage and build user bases. This chapter introduces readers to projects and people in the fields of consumer marketing and entertainment who are utilizing GS designs to achieve their most important goals—building brands, audiences and revenue.

THE MARKETING MIX

Marketing focuses on identifying, understanding, influencing and satisfying the needs of customers. To market a product or service successfully means addressing fundamental issues that will ultimately drive customer reception initially and over time. The essential **"seven Ps"** of this marketing mix address the primary concerns of:

1. **Products/services**—Describes the features that make a product or service valuable and differentiated to a customer.
2. **Place**—Identifies the physical and virtual points where customers and consumers can find the product or brand.
3. **Price**—Defines the cost to the consumer. It is the only part of the marketing mix that ties directly to revenue.
4. **Promotion**—Determines how the audience of current and potential customers will be reached. Branding falls under promotion.
5. **People**—Relates to customer service and support, detailing how people representing the product or service will support customers.
6. **Processes**—For service-oriented and Internet-based companies, processes correspond to all systems involved in providing a customer with the total experience of the service from beginning to end.
7. **Physical Evidence**—Corresponds to the credibility and reliability of the environment where a product or service is delivered. It is particularly relevant for companies leveraging the Internet, computers and mobile devices for sales and communication.

Figure 9.1 Gamified systems provide continuous feedback between customers and companies about the seven essential Ps.

What makes gamified systems so compelling for marketers are the touch points they create for the seven Ps of the marketing mix. GS designs allow companies to get critical and continuous feedback about the impressions and sentiments of customers to every part of the marketing mix, including product plans, customer service, pricing and promotional strategies. With valuable, timely input marketers can move quickly to satisfy customer requirements, and in turn leverage gamified systems to convey these modifications. Urban Outfitters' *Urban On* (described more in this chapter) is an excellent example of this. Designed to provide a point of affiliation and community between its young adult customers, its store locations and the products it sells, the application, which includes games, music and specialized and personalized rewards, leverages play as a fulcrum for meaningful conversations that provide the foundation for long-term loyalty and affiliation.

BRAND BUILDING

> The barrage of channels and devices has collapsed the concept of a marketing funnel to create consumer expectations that are always on. Today, the most loved brands aren't built one campaign at a time; they are built by winning the hearts and minds of consumers, one experience—or moment—at a time throughout the customer lifecycle.
>
> —Brian Powley, CEO, iCrossing

Branding, which falls under the "product" umbrella of the marketing mix, is the art of directing and convincing consumers to associate ideas, images and feelings with names, signs or symbols related to a product or service. All points of contact between a company and a prospective or current customer play into a web of complex conversations shaping perceptions of a product or media franchise and the company that is responsible for it. Logos, advertising, retail stores, celebrity endorsements, websites, apps and games all contribute to a brand's perceived value or equity. A **brand's equity** is based upon the positive or negative perceptions that consumers have of it. It is built through impressions and experiences with the brand, either personally, through word of mouth, advertising or through promotion. The proliferation of Internet-enabled devices like phones and touch pads has meant that companies and their customers can be in contact on a more frequent and regular basis. Consequently, branding has

Brand equity

Brand equity corresponds to the value of a company's brand. It is driven by the positive or negative perceptions that consumers have of it, and the way that translates into how the company is meeting its goals or objectives.

Figure 9.2 Branding involves a range of technical, creative and strategic practices.

become the driving force in consumer product marketing. It is the potential for building and enhancing relationships between a company, each customer and the different networks of relationships that she influences that accounts for the increasing interest in gamified systems for marketing.

Branding focuses on generating positive feelings, emotions and attitudes amongst consumers, and aligning these to properties, products and services. Apple, Nike, Disney and Coca-Cola are just a few companies whose successful branding strategies have created powerful associations that go far beyond the products they produce. Today, building and sustaining a brand's equity involves a complex web of practices including: strategy, experience and creative design, technical implementation, data analysis and collection. GS design is so intriguing because it integrates and connects all of these core initiatives.

Gamified systems facilitate brand integration

GS design is so intriguing because it integrates and connects all of the essential branding initiatives.

Building brand equity

Building brand value involves shaping how customers think, feel and relate from their initial introduction to the brand and the choice to continue the relationship and share the benefits with others. Dartmouth Marketing professor Kevin Keller's brand equity model identifies four important phases for building brand equity. It begins with identification or salience, which is the basic act of building awareness of a product or brand, answering the question "Who are you?" in the customer's mind. The second step relates to meaning and involves awareness about products or services, what they look like and how they function. This phase answers the question "What are you?" The third phase corresponds to the emotional response to the brand and its products and services. It is about how a customer judges a brand's merits and how she feels about it, answering the question "What about you makes you valuable?" Finally, the last stage is "resonance," and is ultimately about the relationship between a brand and customer answering the question "What about you and me?"

The always-on Internet has given companies the capacity to build relationships with consumers on a much more personalized basis, often letting each user define when and how she interacts with a brand. Social networking platforms and rich-Internet applications with data analytics have spurred the field of marketing to now include and anticipate unpredictable dimensions of exponentially growing and changing networks of individuals who are sharing, comparing, ranking, rating, repurposing and redistributing relevant information about a company. The unpredictable scale of connectivity means that marketing is no longer about controlling messages, but instead about curating them. Encouraging the positive direction of these conversations, and fostering relationships as a result, is exactly where gamified systems come in to play. Your job as the GS designer

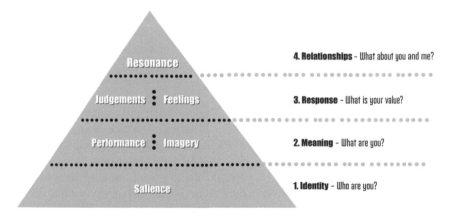

Figure 9.3 Keller's Brand Equity Model. Adapted from *Strategic Brand Management: Building, Measuring, and Managing Brand Equity* by Kevin Lane Keller. © Pearson Education Limited 2013.

of a brand-building project is to guide customers through a positive play experience that builds and reinforces a company's brand.

Branding with GS design

> Today consumers are much more empowered. You need to communicate with them. We have more than 33 million fans on the Coca-Cola Facebook page—the largest Facebook page of any single brand—and it wasn't even created by us. You still need great advertising, but that's just part of a dialogue.
> —Muhtar Kent, CEO Coca-Cola

Gamified systems designed for consumer marketing and brand building fundamentally embrace the Do-It-Yourself (DIY) and open-source philosophy of today's savvy customers. Not only can marketers provide the feeling and experience of freedom, but they can also do this while directing focus on specific content and messaging. With one of the most impressive and memorable brands in history, Coca-Cola is also at the leading edge of gamified design for consumer marketing. The company commits to constant innovation in the field as a means of enhancing its relationship with customers through a shared love for play.

Launched in 2006, and recently redesigned to incorporate social media more effectively, the *My Coke* rewards loyalty program has over 20 million members. The original version encouraged members to collect and redeem points by entering codes on bottle caps, resulting in 60 million codes entered and over 100 million points redeemed. Half a decade later, as a response to the growth of social media networking, the company redesigned the experience to emphasize individuals and their personal relationships. Today, users are rewarded for connecting Coke to their own social networks. Rather than making the conversation about the company or its products, they are encouraged to connect to each other through their own personal passions, such as the mutual affection for a particular college football team. These connections are meant to generate conversation on social networks like Twitter and Facebook. By encouraging interaction around subjects that members are already talking about, the marketing angle becomes much more subtle. As a result, Coke becomes the host of the party, while each user remains at the center.

Beyond its on-going efforts with *My Coke*, the company continues to cleverly engage customers with cutting-edge implementations. The *Chok campaign*, a complex and finely tuned program, created for the Hong Kong market, included a downloadable smart phone app that was used by television viewers in conjunction with a pre-scheduled Chinese Coca-Cola advertisement. As the advertisement played, Coca-Cola bottle caps flew in the direction of the screen. In response, players held up their smart phone to catch the virtual bottle caps flying from the screen. By successfully catching caps, players earned points that they could later redeem for rewards. Although ambitious, the program was extremely successful with nearly half a million downloads of the app in the first month alone.

Figure 9.4 The Coca-Cola bottle cap transforms into an object of play. Coca-Cola's Chok campaign let Hong Kong television viewers catch virtual bottle caps while watching an advertisement for Coke.

DRIVEN BY STRATEGY

No matter how experimental a marketing initiative is, it must nevertheless be driven by a clearly defined strategy. This is true whether you are working in a marketing department or practicing your craft at a creative agency. In every case, the gamified systems you pursue will always be driven by strategy articulated within a marketing plan. A marketing plan is a roadmap that a company uses to articulate the big vision of the company as well as the strategies and tactics that will be initiated to accomplish that plan. It involves four major steps: 1) setting goals, 2) analyzing the current state of the business and the business landscape, 3) defining a strategy and executable plans to achieve it, and 4) allocating resources and implementing plans defined in stage 3.

In marketing as with many other kinds of business strategy, the planning process begins with a mission statement. The mission statement concisely describes the goals that the company or project is trying to achieve. These visions are more often than not nuanced statements that combine organizational objectives with larger values or ideologies. The three examples of mission statements provided below do not mention money, projected user numbers or return on investment. Instead, they are examples of how mission statements should encapsulate and validate a company's direction. A mission statement conveys why the company exists and why people should care. It is a compass and point of reference for the strategy that follows it. Every design and experience created must support the mission.

Marketing plans drive GS designs

The four stages of the marketing planning process include:

1. *Setting goals*—A mission statement is created leading to a set of business objectives.
2. *Analysis of current state*—This stage focuses on taking an honest assessment of the business's strengths and weaknesses, particularly in relation to other players in the industry.
3. *Strategy*—The critical portion of the process occurs when the strategy along with the tactics for executing them are defined.
4. *Allocate resources and initiate programs*—The last phase of the process requires assigning resources, such as money and people, to begin and implement the activities defined in stage 3.

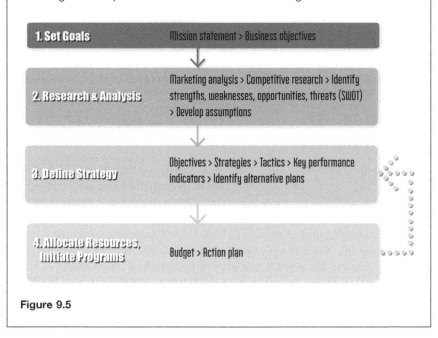

1. Set Goals   Mission statement > Business objectives

2. Research & Analysis   Marketing analysis > Competitive research > Identify strengths, weaknesses, opportunities, threats (SWOT) > Develop assumptions

3. Define Strategy   Objectives > Strategies > Tactics > Key performance indicators > Identify alternative plans

4. Allocate Resources, Initiate Programs   Budget > Action plan

Figure 9.5

Strategy turns the mission into executable initiatives. Usually this includes an integrated plan for combining traditional media like broadcast and print with a range of digital media initiatives. Gamified systems are becoming an important part of this mix for many reasons. In addition to greater and more frequent opportunities to influence the conversations happening between customers and their brands in a positive direction, gamified systems provide real-time data about these interactions. Marketing strategists can access data analytics to quickly measure effectiveness and to get a picture of how the system delivers on the Key Performance Indicators (KPIs) defined within the goals of the strategy.

What a mission statement looks like

Blizzard Entertainment:
> Dedicated to creating the most epic entertainment experiences . . . ever.

Fitbit:
> To empower and inspire you to live a healthier, more active life. We design products and experiences that fit seamlessly into your life so you can achieve your health and fitness goals, whatever they may be.

Khan Academy:
> Khan Academy is an organization on a mission. We're a not-for-profit with the goal of changing education for the better by providing a free world-class education for anyone anywhere.

INSIDER INSIGHT

CP+B'S HAROLD JONES ON GAMIFYING DOMINO'S PIZZA

Interview granted with permission by Harold Jones.

Harold Jones is the Creative Technical Director at the top-tier creative agency Crispin Porter + Bogusky (CP+B). He has a decade of experience helping lead digital strategy, creative direction, development and innovation for big-name brands including Domino's, Kraft Mac and Cheese, Jello and Triscuit, Coke Zero and Microsoft.

Can you describe the genesis of the Domino's project?

In 2009 the company along with CP+B conducted what they named "the pizza turnaround" (pizzaturnaround.com). We started conducting

Figure 9.6
Harold Jones.

consumer research and discovered through that process that consumers thought the product was not very good. The turnaround was about being super honest with the public. Domino's is about truth and transparency. They did a bunch of research on cheeses, improving the crust and the pizza sauce. The new recipe was the outcome of the turnaround. This was back before utilizing social media as a way of being honest and transparent about business was an accepted practice. Domino's decided to use it to apologize and get better.

Figure 9.7 Screenshot from Domino's *Pizza Hero*. DOMINO'S® is a registered trademark of Domino's IP Holder and used with permission. The Domino's Screenshots are the properties of Domino's IP Holder and used with permission.

How did you decide to develop the mobile game Pizza Hero? How did you determine the various components of the game?

Because Domino's was considered a pizza chain, the public associated its cooking of pizzas with an assembly line process. We wanted to emphasize that the pizza is hand made. We decided that a game was a fun and accurate vehicle for educating folks about Domino's pizza-making process. We wanted to make it as real as possible. We want to create a way for people to experience the act of making pizza in a way that is similar to the real store.

First we teach with pizza prep school. Players need to stretch the dough using a touch screen. Next, the same hand gestures are required to layer sauce. We wanted to make sure that the tips of the fingers were being used to spread cheese so we used multi-touch events because when you sprinkle cheese on a pizza you need to spread the cheese across. We could have reduced the touch requirements, but we wanted the game to emphasize the process of making a real pizza.

With a pizza made, players can place their order for delivery. Otherwise, the game leads to taking orders. At the expert level everything is timed and measured, including the quality of the dough, the way you lay the sauce and how you distribute the cheese. As the game gets more difficult the pizzas and orders get more complex. Ultimately, it is always playfully emphasizing how to become a better pizza maker.

After the app had launched, it was running in the top three most downloaded apps in iTunes. We saw the success and we wanted to leverage that buzz, so we

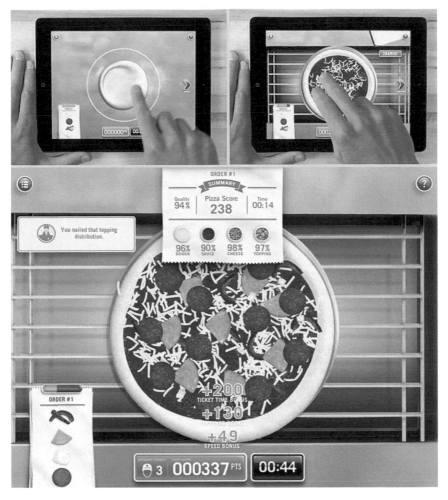

Figure 9.8 *Pizza Hero* lets players learn and practice the various steps involved in the process of making pizza. DOMINO'S® is a registered trademark of Domino's IP Holder and used with permission. The Domino's Screenshots are the properties of Domino's IP Holder and used with permission.

decided we wanted to create a physical component. We decided that we could use the game to change the way we recruited pizza makers. We thought that we wouldn't get a lot of people applying. We originally had a goal of hiring one pizza maker. We actually had twenty-five people apply, and five of those were hired. This all tied back to the marketing strategy. Domino's is focused on digital innovation, so it made sense that we decided to use the device to hire. That was something really interesting, and like the ordering of pizzas made in the game, it tied into the physical world.

Figure 9.9 Making pizza well enough translates into an invitation to apply to the company as a pizza chef. DOMINO'S® is a registered trademark of Domino's IP Holder and used with permission. The Domino's Screenshots are the properties of Domino's IP Holder and used with permission.

What advice can you give to designers interested in using games to carry out marketing initiatives?

When you are making a game think about the user experience and how a story is told. Even though I studied game design and interactive design at school, the one thing that I didn't understand was how a game can tie to the strategic value of a brand. It wasn't until we started making sure that the game reflected what the pizza-making process was like that it all made sense to me. The game has to reflect what the brand is. It needs to apply to the business and the core values of that brand. Designers need to ask themselves how the features, components and levels they are designing fit into what the brand is trying to do.

BUILDING REVENUE AND DRIVING PRODUCT SALES

Branding builds connections. For consumer-based product companies like Urban Outfitters, such connections should ultimately lead to sales. Affirming the Bohemian aesthetic of its target audience, hip urban women and men ranging between their late teens and mid-twenties, Urban Outfitters carries an eclectic mix of clothes, home furnishings and other objects. With its funky brand persona and technically savvy audience, the company sensibly made an early move into social media, and now accounts for nearly a million followers on Twitter and Tumblr. Yet, despite the devoted set of online followers from the target demographic, this affection was not translating into sales. In fact, in 2013, revenue fell hundreds of millions of dollars short of corporate and stockholder expectations. In an effort to turn the online community into online customers, the company launched Urban On in September of that year. Urban On is a mobile app designed to generate sales of products by enhancing and reaffirming its audience's ironic and hip lifestyles.

The mobile application includes games, free music downloads and a retail store check-in function that can offer location-based offers. Players can participate in challenges like posting to Instagram or Twitter to receive special items and early notices about sales. The reward system provides its most loyal customers with early access to deals, notifications of special discounts and invitations to sponsored music events that correspond to their music-related purchases. One of the most powerful aspects of Urban On is its personalized reward system. Leveraging data about user behavior within the app, as well as viewing and purchase history, the system translates this information into tailored and customized rewards. By putting such specificity into feedback mechanisms, rather than just driving one individual sale, the company continues the conversation and subtly directs the follow-on purchase. Since the launch of the system there has been a significant uptick in online sales conversions. In fact, just three months after the app was launched sales had increased by 7.5 percent.

Urban On is just one example of how gamified sales platforms can drive product purchases in a way that feels personal and affirming. While hipsters have their requirements for engagement, so too do gamers. Valve's gaming platform Steam uses Steam Trading Cards as a tightly conceived mechanism for indirectly encouraging the sales of games created by participating game developers. Though Steam boasts over 75 million registered users and supports millions of users online playing and shopping for games at any given time, it is constantly developing new methods to sustain the enthusiasm and the activity of the Steam community. Pricing strategies, special sales and now gamified systems are all mechanisms that help make this platform so dynamic and compelling for so many different audiences.

At the core of Steam's collecting system are visual assets from games being distributed and sold through the platform. Every game developer who chooses to participate in the program contributes artwork for individual cards and badges as well as background art for profile pages and emoticons, which can be used in conversational text with other Steam members. Players can begin collecting a set just by playing one of these games. Cards are dropped at different moments during a play session. For this reason, Steam Trading Cards can easily be perceived as added value that is cost-free to the Steam user. Yet, in order for a player to begin collecting a trading card set and the digital items they unlock he must first own the game. As a result, the system indirectly generates sales of games, benefiting game developers and Valve, with both parties collecting revenue from the sale of a game.

The system is designed to make the most of a player's social networks to generate more sales of and perpetuate ongoing interest in a participating game. Players cannot collect all of the cards in a set simply by playing a game, but must get them from other people who are also playing the game. Players can trade cards with friends who are playing the same game, or they can visit the trading card marketplace and purchase the card from another player. Once a player has

Figures 9.10 and 9.11 *Steam Trading Cards* from Valve © Valve Corporation.

collected his card set, he can then craft a badge, unlocking special content like background images and emoticons, which can be utilized within the social networking functions of the platform. Cards get put back into the system, and players can continue collecting to level up, crafting more badges and unlocking more content. This symbiotic approach to marketing and product sales has resulted in an increase in purchases of *Steam Trading Cards'* games. Some developers have claimed an increase of nearly 150 percent in sales of their game since joining the program. While this increase may be temporary the momentum gets extended as players encourage their friends and the community to share and trade their cards for the game.

THE ROLE OF BIG DATA

> With big data, a business can learn a lot about what to do, where you do it, when you do it, and what you like.
> —Rajat Paharia, *Loyalty 3.0: How to Revolutionize Customer and Employee Engagement with Big Data and Gamification*

While companies are building their brands and revving up product sales, they are also collecting marketing data that can be utilized to modulate and improve a system, while building and driving sales. For years, companies have collected information about their customers, including zip codes, phone numbers, e-mail addresses, gender, age and purchase patterns. Today, this data is only in some cases the starting place for a company to begin building its web of knowledge about a customer. Added to this are the changing data streams coming from GPS locations, shopping patterns, Internet usage patterns and social networking technologies. Massive in scope and variability, this "big data" is constantly in flux. Big data is information that is large, complex and dynamic. Although it can not be captured in one place, tracking various emerging and changing data streams is one important way that companies are identifying trends, predicting consumer demands, and delivering new products and services to meet these.

Although the field of marketing has always involved identifying and defining groups and segments within the areas of the market, today demographic data gets the addition of very granular information about purchasing patterns and online behavior. This micro-segmentation enables companies to create an experience that has been entirely built for the very, very smallest of segments—the individual. With such specific data, recommendation engines can compare and combine with even more data about the purchases made by others who share similar purchase choices and demographic profiles as a customer. Predictions can then be made about the most appropriate and relevant items to offer at that moment in time. Companies like Amazon and Urban Outfitters do this, letting each customer feel like her needs are being anticipated before she even considers them.

GS DESIGN FOR CUSTOMER RELATIONSHIP MANAGEMENT

Companies leverage this combination of precise data to drive awareness and sales in a variety of ways. Integration and systemization of data about current and prospective customers is known as customer relationship management (CRM). Any business that employs sales people to build and retain relationships with customers on an on-going basis benefits from tracking the different points of contact that a customer has made with a company. Whether it is support for software, devices, products or services, the companies that interact with you and each and every other customer benefit significantly from storing and tracking information about these individual interactions. By implementing CRM effectively across an organization, different departments and individuals within these departments can build customer confidence by focusing on the specific time-sensitive needs of a customer. Through this real-time coordination of information, a company is much more likely to expedite purchase decisions.

> Long-term benefits of documenting interaction with customers are clear; however, CRM systems traditionally provide few or no short term incentives for performing the menial tasks of recording activities such as calls, meetings, tasks, and notes.
>
> —Ray Stoeckicht, Co-Founder, Zurmo, inc.

Although it is clear that CRM systems increase visibility, encourage collaboration and shorten sales cycles, it has been estimated that nearly 2 billion dollars has been wasted on CRM software because they are not being utilized by the companies that purchased it. The biggest challenge that any company has is getting its employees to record information about customers and their interactions with them. In fact, it is estimated that there is a 40–50 percent failure rate of CRM implementations, primarily because employees see many of these big systems as a waste of time that does not reward them for the extra effort.

Figure 9.12 Screenshot of the CRM gamified system by *Zurmo*. © Zurmo

A primary role for gamified systems in CRM is to solve this data collection problem. Zurmo, a gamified CRM system, was built with the goal of increasing user adoption. The system uses points, levels, badges and collectible items as rewards to users for recording their activities like tracking phone calls and recording notes about meetings with customers and potential customers (or prospects). The software is being used by a variety of companies to drive CRM adoption. For example, the software screening company Tazworks has seen a 100 percent rate of user adoption since its implementation. Though entering data can easily be perceived as a menial task, adding game elements not only rewards and incentivizes users for conducting the task but it also highlights the significance and importance of it across an organization.

GAMIFYING ENTERTAINMENT

> By convergence, I mean the flow of content across multiple media platforms, the cooperation between multiple media industries, and the migratory behavior of media audiences who would go almost anywhere in search of the kinds of entertainment experiences they wanted.
>
> —Henry Jenkins, *Convergence Culture: Where Old and New Media Collide*

In the 1930s, millions of families and friends would gather together around the radio to spend evenings listening to popular syndicated radio shows like *The Lone Ranger* or news reports by the famous voice of Edward R. Murrow. At the time, there were only four radio networks. This small set of broadcasters and channels carried their dominance through the advent and proliferation of television. As late as the early 1980s there were still few enough channels available on our television set that we were willing to get up off the couch and turn the television knob to change the station. With hundreds of digital cable channels and millions of web-based content providers creating and posting by the millisecond, the media landscape has become an entirely different beast. Every entertainment company, no matter how well established, is now in a constant fight for mind share. For this reason, executives in film, television, music and the videogame industry are looking to various implementations of gamified systems to market and extend their properties. This is the age of convergence, where the line between producers and consumers is becoming increasingly fuzzy.

The game industry understood the nature of this new dynamic relationship between producers and consumers very early. Making its development tools available to anyone who purchased their game titles, companies like ID software (the creators of *Doom*) and Valve, the owners of Steam (and the creators of *Half-Life*, *Portal* and many more groundbreaking game titles) grew their player base and product line by letting game players become game makers. Through this open source-inspired marriage, whole worlds like the team-based first-person shooter *Counter-Strike* were born. This modification (mod) of the *Half-Life* engine, which ten years later boasts half a million players a day, and continues to sustain its own community of even more mods and mod creators, is just one affirmation of the new entertainment landscape. The desire for a personal sense of control over and ownership in the consumption of media goes far beyond games, creating a challenge for many entertainment companies, some of which are nearly a century old. Gamified systems are one way for these companies to loosen the reigns a bit, while still retaining a certain amount of control. With the right design, companies can protect their intellectual property and the conversations around them while still giving audiences increased access to their properties, brands and artists. With the right scenario, everybody wins.

> We've seen our fans go from enthusiastic to rabid online evangelists or self-described 'PSYCHOS', spreading the word for Psych offerings and encouraging others to participate.
>
> —Jesse Redniss, Senior Vice President
> of Digital, USA Network

Though not every organization has the resources, capacity or tools to let its audience turn their passion and fandom into sustainable game titles, media companies must find ways to give audiences a greater sense of ownership in their properties. The cable company USA Network leveraged its content to grow its committed fan base of the detective/comedy show *Psych* by creating *Club Psych*, a gamified system that rewarded fans with show-related digital and physical

Figure 9.13 Students from universities across the country competed to have their school logo appear on the television show *Psych*.

collectibles for watching videos, re-posting content, playing games, participating in online show-related conversations and for tuning in to the show when it was being broadcast. The program included a *Psych Vision* app that let players use their phones to enter keywords that appeared during the broadcast. The network's initiative successfully grew the online audience for the television show by 30 percent. It also grew the on-air viewership of its target demographic by 40 percent. The network was able to leverage this strong foundation to run more campaigns to perpetuate its growth. For example, *Campus Wars* had college students and alumni competing to get their school logo on an episode of the show. Over 11,000 college teams were formed to collectively recruit members and earn points to win this prized and original mark of status. The *Psych* project is just one example of the types of creative tactics that the entertainment industry is experimenting with to compete for the hearts, minds, ears and eyes of audiences.

INSIDER INSIGHT

ROBERT NASHAK TALKS ABOUT HOLLYWOOD'S GAME-CHANGING LANDSCAPE

Interview granted with permission by Robert Nashak.

Robert Nashak has spent over two decades in the field of interactive entertainment. He has held executive-level positions, overseeing product development and strategy at BBC Worldwide, Electronic Arts, Yahoo, Vivendi and Acclaim. Robert also teaches Business and Management of Games in the Interactive Media and Games Division at the School of Cinema and Television at the University of Southern California.

Figure 9.14
Robert Nashak.

Can you try to explain the current state of the entertainment industry?

It's hard to overstate the impact of the massive upheaval going on right now in the way media is financed, produced and distributed. The rise of crowd funding, the increase in cheap and available production resources, and the proliferation of digital distribution platforms are forever changing the way movies, television, music and videogames are produced and marketed. The explosion in indie content, the increasingly fragmented media landscape, and the expectation that media should be free or close to free are just some of the things keeping Hollywood executives up at night. Frankly, it's a mess out there. Movie attendance in North America and Europe is down, TV show ratings are a fraction of what they once were, and music labels are struggling to stay relevant. When it comes to mastering this new reality, no entertainment medium even comes close to what the games industry is currently achieving. In terms of sheer time spent, nothing drives engagement like games. Games and only games have figured out how to build audience acquisition strategies into their creative design. And of all entertainment categories, games are seeing the biggest revenues on social media, smart phones and tablets. Truth is, Hollywood has a lot more to learn from games than games do from Hollywood. But that's been true for quite a while.

How are gamified systems being leveraged by the film industry for marketing a film and for building a media franchise with merchandise and sequels?

The obvious demographic synergies between prime movie-going audiences and gamers has led to a feeding frenzy over the years for gamified marketing campaigns and videogame spin-offs. In my experience, movie studios and producers love games but it is a conditional kind of love based on achieving three goals: getting butts in seats, keeping audiences engaged with movie franchises in between theatrical releases, and driving ancillary revenues to fund more movies.

Using gamified systems for marketing movies is what fueled the growth and popularity of Alternate Reality Games (ARGs). The pioneer in this space was 2001's runaway success *The Beast*, which had 3 million players involved in an online/offline futuristic murder mystery game created to promote the film *A.I. Artificial Intelligence*. By far the most ambitious ARG of all time was around Warner Bros.' *The Dark Knight*. The game launched during 2007's Comic-Con where "Jokerized" $1 bills were distributed to attendees directing them to go to whysoserious.com, a recruitment site for Joker henchmen. What followed was a massive year-long multi-platform viral initiative that used puzzles and scavenger hunts to bridge the story gap between *Batman Returns* and the new release.

But let it be said, stand-alone video games based on movie licenses almost always underperform in terms of critical response, commercial expectations or both. The notorious 1983 burial in the Nevada desert of millions of unsold copies of the widely panned Atari 2600 video game *E.T. the Extra-Terrestrial* is a cautionary tale for movie executives who think of videogames as merchandise. Unlike toys, bed sheets and other merchandise, when games become a function of licensing efforts by movie studios they usually fail to deliver the goods. Faced with fixed timelines, limited access to film assets and creative approval nightmares, game developers are just not well adapted to delivering games timed with movie releases. The three exceptions to this rule are when film producers are highly engaged in the game development (*The Chronicles of Riddick*), when game creators are allowed to go beyond the limits of movie franchises (*Batman: Arkham Asylum*) and when multi-year long-term franchise relationships are forged between movie studios and game publishers. We got this right at Electronic Arts with *Harry Potter*. A development team was nurtured over many movie sequels and given unprecedented access to the production team and film studio, resulting in over $1 billion in games sales.

As game publishers have reduced their retail offerings to focus more on original intellectual property (IP), only blockbuster global movie franchises with proven legacies stand a chance at seeing expensive retail game offerings. When it comes to movies, the action has almost entirely moved to mobile. Fox, to take one example, had enormous success partnering with mobile games developer Rovio on *Angry Birds: Rio*, which included in-app scenes that bridged the story from *Rio 1* to *Rio 2*. It was an innovative (and risk-reducing) exercise in brand-mashing that also worked extremely well on console with the Lego movie-franchise games. It goes to show that when two strong global brands with tens of millions of fans come together in a creative way that makes sense to consumers, the sky's the limit. And when it comes to movies and games, it's worth noting that the flow of IP is increasingly going in both directions. The creative team at Naughty Dog, for example, is deeply involved in the movie adaptation of their hit game *The Last of Us*. And game publishers like EA and UbiSoft are now developing movie scripts in house in order to exert more creative control over their gaming IP.

Recently, in an effort to combat the decline in theatrical audiences, Disney gamified the movie-going experience with *The Little Mermaid Second Screen Live*, in which audience members were encouraged to play games on their tablets and smart phones during the movie. It was a cool idea, but it serves as an example of how the relationship between movies and games still remains more tactical than it is strategic.

Can you talk about television and the rise of the second screen?

Gamified systems have a more strategic role to play within the current television landscape where the marketplace dynamics are rapidly shifting and network executives are scrambling to find ways to attract viewers and to keep them watching. Platform fragmentation is one of the chief problems facing the TV industry at this time. Fully 10 percent of all TV content consumption has shifted to tablet or smart phone. For the first time ever people are spending more time online than watching TV. It's a phenomenon known as cord cutting and it's particularly impactful for younger viewers under twenty-five, 30 percent of whom get all of their TV online. And for those who are still subscribing to cable or satellite providers, 50 percent or more are simultaneously on another device while watching TV.

In the face of such rapid change, network execs and TV producers are increasingly turning to gamified systems to combat divided attention and drive tune-ins. A slew of generic check-in apps such as *tvtag* and *Beamly* brought tried and true gamified elements to TV watching by allowing people to check-in, get badges and participate in social chat around the shows they love. By using story world extensions, quizzes and chat, "show companion apps" (often synched live to television shows through audio watermarking) helped promote a wide variety of scripted dramas and reality shows such as *Top Chef*, *Breaking Bad*, *Psych* and *Game of Thrones*.

But it's the game show, the oldest TV genre and by nature the most interactive, that is currently paving the way to the future of television. It started with the rise of voting through mobile devices, which launched a number of worldwide franchises such as *American Idol* and *Dancing with the Stars*, and revolutionized the way people engage around TV watching. But thanks to smart phone and tablet proliferation, telephony voting is giving way to even deeper engagement and more participatory viewing. A UK company called Monterosa pioneered this in the UK with a show called *Million Pound Drop* in which contestants answered questions based on live polls of the studio audience and online viewers at home.

While earlier attempts at creating interactivity for television screens were plagued by issues surrounding user interface design, navigation and input devices, second screen apps have gotten around those issues and their impact is going way beyond traditional marketing. The revenues that TV producers are receiving from second screen applications such as *Deal or No Deal* far outpaced what the traditional game-licensing model ever delivered. The current recipe for success is still pretty rudimentary: Use simple forms of synchronous participation that mirror existing viewer interests and add elements of asynchronous participation to help bridge between episodes and series. Having said that, much greater things are on the horizon for second screens. Take a look at how Nickelodeon has reinvented Nick for iPad to get a taste of what TV of the future will look like.

What about the increasingly fragmented music industry? Can you describe how artists are leveraging GS design to connect with fans?

The impact of music piracy and the tremendous upheaval brought upon by the success of services such as iTunes, Pandora and Spotify have created whole new paradigms for how music is marketed and promoted. Since music sharing is an intrinsically motivated fan activity, music discovery services like Turntable. fm and Phantasy Tour sought to build upon and amplify existing fan behavior through game-play. And just as music artists have increasingly seized upon social media to build a direct connection with their communities of fans, they've used gamified systems to keep them engaged and to keep them buying albums and concert tickets. Nine Inch Nails, for example, launched a Webby-award winning ARG called *Year Zero*, a treasure hunt set in a dark, war-ravaged world, which used secret phone numbers and clues hidden on NIN T-shirts, the toilets of concert venues, and websites to drive fan engagement. Lady Gaga teamed up with Zynga's *Farmville* in a massively successful Facebook promotion that gave players special seeds that blossomed into fan-created expressions of Gaga herself. And to promote his book *Decoded*, Jay-Z signed a partnership with search engine Bing who funded an ARG treasure hunt where Internet users were invited to use Bing's 3D-photo-based maps to find pages in Jay-Z's memoir that were hidden in billboards and other real-world locations.

But even as artists seek to find new ways to build upon their relationship to their fans, they first and foremost seek to protect that relationship. I've taken meetings with the managers of many music artists including Beyoncé, the Jonas

Brothers and Lady Gaga, all of whom began and ended the conversation by emphasizing the importance of maintaining credibility and authenticity with their fans. Björk knows this better than anyone. Her innovative and abstract iPad app *Biophilia* was a perfect embodiment of her quirky personality and values. What's more the app uses a game mechanic to let players co-create her music, blurring the lines between listening and participation. In that sense, *Biophilia* took a lesson from *Guitar Hero* and *Rock Band*, which were utterly transformational in showing how, in a rapidly changing industry landscape, games can not only create new forms of music discovery, but also whole new forms of music entertainment as well.

What is the future of transmedia?

In an increasingly fragmented media landscape, games provide fresh new avenues for audience acquisition, engagement and revenues, so it's not surprising that transmedia is often touted as the next frontier for entertainment. You'll often hear Hollywood executives dismiss transmedia as too expensive and too complicated to be workable. But the fact is, developing cross-platform IP in a 360-degree fashion from the ground up is already showing promise. The most ambitious transmedia project to date is SyFy channel's hit show *Defiance*, the first concurrently developed TV show and videogame. Five years and $100 million in the making, *Defiance* teamed up online game developer Trion Worlds with SyFy to chronicle a post-apocalyptic clash between humans and aliens. Their experience is worth reading up on as a case study for how difficult and rewarding transmedia development can be.

Figure 9.15 *Defiance* is a massive online game from Trion Worlds and the SyFy channel. © Trion Worlds, Inc.

KEY TAKEAWAYS

- The "seven Ps" of marketing stand for products/services, place, price, promotion, people, processes, and physical evidence.
- Branding is the practice of directing consumers towards a positive emotional connection with products and services.
- A company's brand equity is considered one of it most valuable assets, commonly translating into a company's bottom line. Gamified systems are being utilized by consumer-oriented companies to increase and enhance their brand equity.
- GS design facilitates brand integration by connecting all of the essential branding initiatives including: strategy, experience and creative design, technical implementation, data analysis and collection.
- A marketing plan is the company roadmap that articulates the big vision of the company and the strategies and tactics (like gamified systems) that will be utilized to get there.
- Gamified systems like those implemented by Urban Outfitters and Valve's Steam are being used for customized and targeted product marketing, leading to increased sales and revenue.
- Big data is large, varied and dynamic data that cannot be stored or captured in one place. It is utilized by companies for spotting trends and making informed business decisions.
- Customer relationship management (CRM) is an infrastructure that centralizes all points of contact between a company and a customer. Despite the benefits, employees often resist the work that is required to input data about contacts. Consequently, game concepts are being utilized to increase adoption rates of CRM by employees.
- Entertainment companies across the media landscape are turning to games as a way of promoting, building and extending their artists, properties and franchises.

EXERCISES

By now, you should be at the point where you are refining your projects. Although this book does not cover technical implementation, what you should be developing as a part of these activities is a refined prototype that demonstrates your idea, and a presentation or pitch that supports it. Using content in this chapter as well as the supplementary materials at www.gamifiedsystems.com, you should:

9.1 Validate your project

Now is the time to begin evaluating your project, measuring it against marketing goals. Ask yourself the following questions. How is your design supporting or extending the brand experience? How is it supporting the mission and strategy of the organization? In what ways will your project build awareness, increase loyalty or generate revenue?

9.2 Craft your pitch

Now that you have evaluated your project against the goals, and received feedback from subject matter experts and members of your target audience, you will need to let others know about the merits of your work. Perhaps you want to raise funding for your project. If you are doing this project as a class assignment you are probably interested in getting the best grade possible. In either event, you will need to craft a presentation. Pitches and presentations can come in many forms, but should ultimately answer the question "Why is this valuable?" Though this book does not cover the art of pitching, the book's website (www.gamified systems.com) has resources and samples to help you accomplish this task.

RECOMMENDED READINGS

*   *Brand Thinking and Other Noble Pursuits* by Debbie Millman, 2013.
    Millman explores what branding means in the 21st century through a range of interviews with leaders in the field of design, marketing, anthropology and psychology.

*   *Convergence Culture: Where Old and New Media Collide* by Henry Jenkins, 2008.
    Media theorist Henry Jenkins details the cultural shift happening between producers and audiences as a result of media convergence.

*   *Loyalty 3.0: How to Revolutionize Customer and Employee Engagement with Big Data and Gamification* by Rajat Paharia, 2013.
    The CEO of Bunchball provides a concise and highly readable account about the fundamental role that big data plays in building loyalty through gamified systems.

INSIDER INSIGHT

ERIC ASCHE KEEPS THE TRUTH IN FRONT OF TEENS

Interview granted with permission by Eric Asche.

The American Legacy Foundation is a DC-based non-profit organization founded in 1999 with funds from a major settlement between the tobacco industry and forty-six states. The organization is best known for its groundbreaking Truth brand. Led by Chief Marketing Officer Eric Asche, Truth targets teenagers with bold and edgy messaging about

Figure 9.16 Eric Asche. "We must communicate with this audience through this vehicle [games] or we run the risk of being irrelevant."

tobacco products and the way they are manufactured and marketed, so that they can make informed decisions about their use. Over the past few years Asche and his team have started using games and game dynamics to reach their 12–17-year-old audience. These have included games like the mobile game *Flavor Monsters*, and the alternate reality game *Graffiti Collective*. I worked with Eric on a gamified system at the Savannah College of Art and Design's Collaborative Learning Center.

Do you see games as an essential part of your brand?

Our (Truth's) bull's eye target is teens between the ages of twelve and seventeen. This is the age when people are the most at risk for starting to smoke. Playing games is intrinsic to the lives of 12–17-year-olds. Ninety percent of boys and girls play games at least once per week. This is an overwhelming majority. We must communicate with this audience through this vehicle or we run the risk of being irrelevant.

We are in the business of creating an on-going dialog with our consumer. For us, to be relevant gaming has to be a part of that conversation. There are a lot of ways to use gaming as a platform to engage with the consumer. What is the appropriate mechanism? What do we hope to achieve? Depending on which way we decide to engage the consumer takes us down a different pathway. If our focus is on marketing primarily or instead on monetizing our product this facilitates different partners and platform choices. Because the primary goal for us is to have an impact on the way consumers think about tobacco this gives us some freedom in terms of the choices we make. Unlike companies solely in the business of making games for this audience, money isn't the primary reason that we are engaging the consumer. Our mission takes precedence over our desire to make money. It gives us focus. Through our gaming platforms we try to change their ideas about tobacco.

How exactly do you make a game with your message and make it fun?

If I am honest about our topic, tobacco is a no-interest category. There is zero momentum with the consumer. There is not a 12–17-year-old in the world who would think "My life would be complete with a game about smoking." People are not interested in us. We have to swim up stream against the momentum. We have to use entertainment as currency. Arguably, we have to use entertainment as social currency. Our audience—they are not waiting for a message, and they don't want to hear from us. I have to reward them for listening to us. That is where we have to be judicious and really wise and honest about the fact that if we are going to use entertainment we have to be willing to diversify. That gives us a certain amount of freedom to use things like humor. We definitely have a public health message, and have taken great attempts to create a brand. In the area of public health, there are so many mandates with the messages—wear a condom, go exercise, get the flu shot. We realized if we were to tell our audience what to do we would fail, and it would backfire. Essentially, it would be like jet fuel to get them to smoke. We made a critical strategy decision, adding things to our games that reflect our brand. It would not be entertaining if all we did is tell them not to smoke. We want to have a conversation with them, but they don't want to talk to us, so we have to use entertainment to reward them.

What do you think have been the major challenges of implementing games into your branding efforts?

Well, we don't have a lot of experience. As we started to get in the space we had a tremendous knowledge gap, because making games is not our core competency. Producing a game felt like we were jumping into the deep end. We didn't know if we should go after the console market or go after the social platforms. Analyzing where the opportunities lay, and making intelligent informed decisions about where to place our energy was difficult. There were a lot of trials and errors getting comfortable with our gaming strategy. Also, it has been very hard for us to find partners we can trust that are willing to work with us where money is not the primary objective. It is a challenge. Early on when we were trying to find a partner, we were exposed on both ends. We didn't have the capacity in house to identify or validate the right partner. Early on we made a lot of mistakes. We went through multiple partners, either because of disagreements or because companies went out of business. We had a really hard time finding the right partner to execute the vision. There were a lot of delays and stops and starts. We had blind spots because this was not our core competency. Trying to build out this knowledge base takes time. We've started hiring people on who are gamers. These aren't game designers. They play a lot of games and go to tournaments. They speak the language to help deal with partners. Once we have a product the marketing is easy, because that is our sweet spot.

So, you are looking for people with game knowledge?

Yes. We want to find people who have affinity for the lifestyle we invest in. We spend a lot of time investing in those categories. I have to have people around me that have their finger on the culture.

How has marketing to teens changed because of games?

When I was a kid playing games was an activity that was done for a fixed moment of time at arcades. Then, it lived on your TV console. It was appointment based. Without stating the obvious, the world is nothing like what it was when I was a teen. It was all encompassing in a specific moment in time. The way games permeate every activity all throughout the day is so deeply infiltrated in a teen's life. As marketers we are behind in terms of embracing the new model. It is such a broader platform. It is frustrating and challenging for a marketer when you think about how to put games into a silo when games cross so many silos. Now, in order to keep our audience engaged we must get them to share the assets we have produced, reward them for doing this and for building buzz, all of these things are happening at the same time with such hyperactivity.

**In what ways do you think the world of marketing as a whole has
changed as a result of games?**

The terminology that marketing uses doesn't do justice to what needs to be
done now. The old-school model was more like carving out swimming lanes.
We created a marketing calendar and planned separate activities to fill it. What
is challenging with the gaming bucket is that it is so expansive. It is social, it
creates PR, it is an asset that you can monetize, and it can generate activity. There
is real currency with games.

The real challenge for a marketer is around maximizing the opportunity. Games
bleed over into so much, creating an unbelievable opportunity that crosses over
so many touch points. Thinking in terms of games forces cross-pollination. In
terms of the management structure, working on games often disrupts the
traditional sense of hierarchy and ownership. We have learned that making games
creates so much complexity.

**We worked on a game project together with students from SCAD, some
of whom were game designers and many of whom were from other fields
like graphic design, sequential art and motion media. How did you find
the experience different than working with the game developers you
worked with in the past?**

Because you started by getting to know our brand, and you all did so much
research about us and our audience, the group you were running started with a
strategy, and the product was so much better as a result. It was something that
I could actually execute because it was based on real consumer insights. It wasn't
just about "We just had a great idea for a bad ass game. Let's get sponsors. Can
we shoot someone's logo and get it into the game?" I get this across my desk all
the time. This was a much more sophisticated and elegant approach to the
process. You started with what we were trying to accomplish and understood
the tenets of the brand. They didn't know what it was about the brand that we
were trying to accomplish, and how we should marry the brand with the
consumer in light of its identity. As a result, the final product was excellent. In
my world this would be the ultimate compliment. We had a hard time knowing
who was a game developer and who was not. The game designers on the team
were not developing in a silo. They were talking about strategy and consumer
insights and longer strategic insights. The deliverable took the form of the game.
That expanded view was not what I had expected going in.

**Do you think there is a place for game designers outside of the game
industry?**

I believe that there is a significantly untapped potential for somebody who
brings that lens to the table. The trap for someone like me is to put the game
designer into a silo. To just think, "This person develops games." That is a mistake.
I liken it to the way that the social strategy permeates everything we do. The
mistake for such tools is to think that the social strategy team member just manages

the Facebook page. Instead, this person is the voice of a brand. She or he is actively engaging our conversation with consumers, and will continue to play a more prominent role.

I think gaming is much more of a strategy than it is a deliverable. I have been conditioned to think of gaming as a separate silo. That is a mistake. I think gaming as platform is not tethered to a prescriptive set of deliverables. What does my handheld game look like? How do I replicate *Angry Birds*? That is part of it. Gaming needs to be thought of as a strategy. I think it is the ability to have a gaming strategy about how you gain a consumer. We should no longer expect game designers to play alone in their box. The tension is that gaming is becoming a part of everybody's corporate strategy.

The individual that brings the gaming lens has a lot on strategy. For someone who comes with a lot of experience in the marketing field, the best thing that I can do is to listen more and talk less. I am so prone to apply and engage and direct. That is what I do. As we get into this new space the roles are shifting quickly. To leverage the unique lens the designer is bringing to the table I have to talk less and listen more. Marketers that will succeed at this will have to be honest about what they don't know.

NOTES

Cukier, Kenneth and Viktor Mayer-Schönberger. *Big Data: A Revolution That Will Transform How We Live, Work, and Think*. London: Eamon Dolan/Mariner Books, 2014.

Eisenfeld, Beth, Esteban Kolsky and Thomas Topolinski. "Gartner Survey: 42 Percent of CRM Software Goes Unused." *Gartner.com*, February 28, 2003, https://www.gartner.com/doc/387369/gartner-survey–percent-crm.

Gosney, John W. *Beyond Reality: A Guide to Alternate Reality Gaming*. Boston: Thompson, 2005.

Hatfield, Tom. "How to Make Money with Steam Trading Cards." *PC Gamer*, July 14, 2013, http://www.pcgamer.com/2013/07/14/how-to-make-money-from-steam-trading-cards/.

Ignatius, Adi interview with Muhtar Kent. "Shaking Things up at Coca-Cola." *Harvard Business Review*, October, 2011, http://hbr.org/2011/10/shaking-things-up-at-coca-cola/ar/1.

Jenkins, Henry. *Convergence Culture: Where Old and New Media Collide*. New York: NYU Press, 2008.

Kanaracus, Chris. "Gartner: CRM Software Top Priority for IT Spending in 2013–14." *Infoworld*, March 6, 2013, http://www.infoworld.com/d/applications/gartner-crm-software-top-priority-it-spending-in-2013-14-213921.

Kapferer, Jean-Noël. *The New Strategic Brand Management: Creating and Sustaining Brand Equity Long Term*. Fourth Edition. London: Kogan Page, 2008.

Keller, Kevin Lane. *Strategic Brand Management: Building, Measuring, and Managing Brand Equity*. Fourth Edition. Upper Saddle River: Prentice Hall, 2012.

Kennedy, Dan S. *The Ultimate Marketing Plan: Target Your Audience! Get out Your Message! Build Your Brand!* Avon: Adams Media, 2011.

Kirby, Julia. "A Unique Approach to Marketing Coca-Cola in Hong Kong." *Harvard Business Review*, February 14, 2013, http://blogs.hbr.org/2013/02/a-unique-approach-to-marketing-coca-cola-in-hong-kong/.

Kuo, Ivan. "Chok! Coca-Cola's Most Successful Hong Kong Marketing Campaign in 35 Years." *Gamification.co*, February 21, 2013, http://www.gamification.co/2013/02/21/chok-coca-cola-marketing-campaign/.

McDonald, Malcolm. *Marketing Plans*. Sixth Edition. Oxford: Butterworth-Heinemann, 2007.

Madigan, Jamie. "The Psychology Behind Steam Trading Cards." *gameindustry.biz*, July 17, 2013, http://www.gamesindustry.biz/articles/2013-07-17-the-psychology-behind-steam-trading-cards.

Millman, Debbie. *Brand Thinking and Other Noble Pursuits*. New York: Allworth Press, 2013

Paharia, Rajat. *Loyalty 3.0: How to Revolutionize Customer and Employee Engagement with Big Data and Gamification*. New York: McGraw Hill, 2013.

Phillips, Spencer. "Revamping the Agency Model." *Digiday*, September 27, 2013, http://digiday.com/announcement/revving-up-for-the-digiday-agency-summit/.

Stock, Kyle. "Urban Outfitters' New App Strategy: Be Cool." *BloombergBusinessweek*, September 24, 2013, http://www.businessweek.com/articles/2013-09-24/urban-outfitters-new-app-strategy-be-cool.

CONCLUSION

Welcome to the finish line. Here's the takeaway—games are going to be everywhere and you now have the principles and tools to shape how that happens. Making us happier, smarter and more attentive, games and play are leaping from our consoles to our classrooms and boardrooms. While this book focused on business and education, gamified systems are being designed and utilized by an ever-growing number of institutions. By honing your skills in interaction and game design, and continuing to work on and learn about gamified system (GS) design, you are training yourself for a career filled with intellectual and creative challenges that can lead to real changes in people's lives.

The art of GS design requires a fine sense of balance between fun and the objectives that serve external purposes beyond play. Creating progress paths with meaningful choices, interactivity and feedback, and then generating data to support a project's goals, is challenging and demanding, a significant advance from the early gamification efforts of badges and points. Being able to evaluate gamified systems, developing a sensibility of how individuals learn and are motivated through play and combining these with a strong set of skills that include game design and interaction design are the cornerstones of GS design. Developing this knowledge base has been the mission of this book. By working through the material, you have already begun to develop new approaches to play that support goals that extend beyond any one play session.

Although you may not know precisely how you want to put your new proficiency to work at this moment, rest assured that a growing landscape of opportunities awaits individuals trained in the field. The technology will change in the years to come, but the principles will remain the same. Bring your new skills to organizations and help them to reimagine the world and the things they can do in it. Use your growing tool set and your own creative vision to design play experiences that will inspire, guide and support future audiences through our increasingly complex world.

APPENDIX: PRINCIPLES OF GAMIFIED SYSTEM DESIGN

The first section of this book introduced twenty-three principles for designing gamified systems. These have been aggregated in the list below:

1. Bigger meaning
Small systems can generate bigger engagements. With the right design choices, individual elements can lead to bigger meanings. Collecting badges or rewards can mean significantly more if they are part of a larger system.

2. Guided exploration
Gamified systems combine opportunities for structured play with real-world data, enabling individuals and communities to have the ability to explore and attend to the world around them.

3. Directed focus
Gamified systems can re-frame reality, directing attention and focus to create new meanings and attitudes about the world.

4. Permission to experiment socially
Gamified systems like improvisational theater games can provide a bridge for racial, economic and language barriers outside of the game context.

5. Long-term engagement
By providing a rich, measureable and on-going system of rewards and incentives for users, and a comprehensive picture of their progress, GS design enables long-term relationships promoting deep and varied engagement.

6. External goals drive design
GS designs distinguish themselves by being driven and shaped by non-game goals.

7. Game components as a point of translation
Game elements can create a conversation between the real world and the game world. Game elements should encourage targeted behavior, integrating and generating data to support project goals.

8. Data is fundamental
Gamified systems put data to work. The integration, collection and analysis of data are essential to GS design.

9. Reflection through emergence
Challenges, surprises and opportunities to play with and against others can generate emergent behaviors, making for memorable and repeatable tales about the experience.

10. Relevance through pervasiveness
Gamified systems expand into the real world temporally, spatially, socially and across different forms of media.

11. Accomplish insurmountable tasks
Gamified systems can encourage and support crowd-sourced activities, enabling and directing the completion of large-scale tasks.

12. Propel towards PERMA
Gamified systems can propel us towards the ingredients for short- and long-term happiness (PERMA): Positive emotion, Engagement, Relationships, Meaning and Achievement.

13. Intervention in the everyday
Through integration into the process of work and everyday life rather than simply "serious," "virtual" or "entertaining," gamified systems provide interventions that positively bridge us to the everyday.

14. Disrupt functional fixedness
Putting users in a positive state of mind, well-designed gamified systems jump-start, broaden and enhance creative problem solving.

15. Broaden and build
Gamified systems can generate positive emotions that have long-lasting effects beyond the momentary.

16. Agency for change
Gamified systems help bring personal agency to the real world. Individuals have unique opportunities to become agents of real change.

17. Reality over realism
Rather than relying on realism of virtual spaces, gamified systems connect to the real world.

18. Narrow complex relationships
Gamified systems provide navigable structures to manage the widening array and complex nuances of relationships.

19. Collaboration through difference
Gamified systems can maximize differences between people, leveraging their distinct skills and abilities.

20. Combat groupthink
Gamified systems can loosen the fear of upsetting pre-existing relationships. By providing clear goals and challenges, structured play can facilitate idea contribution and productive conflict amongst group members.

21. Meaningful contribution
Whereas games offer meaningful choices, gamified systems offer meaningful contributions. By playing and participating, we can add something positive to our own world.

22. Promote hard fun
Gamified systems generate hard fun by:

- Enabling what is not possible in the non-digital world.
- Tools that let players create knowledge.
- Freedom from imposed time limits.
- Maximum opportunities for experimentation.
- No punishment for failure.

23. Maximize continuous partial attention
Good gamified systems are often designed to support the needs to regularly change and re-focus attention. Visual and auditory clues orient us towards important elements, ideas or activities, enabling individuals to fixate and sustain their attention to solve a problem.

Index

T - #0273 - 071024 - C334 - 229/152/15 [17] - CB - 9780415725712 - Gloss Lamination